UNDERSTANDING FINANCIAL
STATEMENTS

GUS GORDON
STEPHEN F. AUSTIN STATE UNIVERSITY

COLLEGE DIVISION South

Cincinnati Ohio

Sponsoring Editor: Mark R. Hubble
Developmental Editor: Sara E. Bates
Production Editor: Sharon L. Smith
Production House: Shepherd, Inc.
Cover Designer: Bruce Design
Interior Designer: The Book Company
Marketing Manager: G. M. (Skip) Winstrup

AM67AA
Copyright © 1992

by South-Western Publishing Co.

Cincinnati, Ohio

1 2 3 4 5 6 7   D   6 5 4 3 2 1

Library of Congress Cataloging-in-Publication Data

Gordon, Gus
    Understanding financial statements / Gus Gordon.
       p. cm.
    Includes index.
    ISBN 0-538-81516-7
    1. Financial Statements   I. Title.
    HF5681.B2G667 1992
    657' .3—dc20   91-16133
                                       CIP

Printed in the United States of America

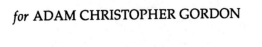

for ADAM CHRISTOPHER GORDON

Preface

This book is directed to readers who have little or no accounting background. First, investors and potential investors who lack formal training in accounting or finance should not contemplate investment without the knowledge and understanding of financial reporting that this book imparts. Second, this book might also be used as a survey of accounting text for M.B.A. students who do not have business degrees and as a text for a core course for schools that offer minors in business. Third, accounting professors can use this book as a supplemental text to enrich students' learning experience in intermediate accounting courses.

Understanding Financial Statements is written with the primary objective of dispelling the notion that financial statements are the result of a precise measurement and valuation process. Financial statements are the culmination of the accounting process, which is designed to record and to measure the economic consequences of transactions. Financial statement users often overlook the fact that judgment plays an important role in interpreting the economic consequences measured by the accounting process. The application of judgment can result in different interpretations of the same events. Therefore, while financial statements can *appear* to be the result of a precise measurement and valuation process, they are not.

Furthermore, in a classroom setting, students often become lost in the details of understanding rules for debits and credits without understanding the *implications* of debits and credits in financial reporting; the forest becomes obscured by the trees. Also, students can become preoccupied with the details of applying specific accounting principles, and can miss an understanding of the implications of acceptable alternative principles and an insight into *why* those alternative principles are acceptable. In short, focus on debits and credits can cause students to lose sight of the "big picture". Accordingly, debits and credits are not discussed in this book. This aids in preventing students from acquiring a bookkeeper mindset mired in debits and credits. The earlier students become aware of these implications, the deeper their understanding becomes. Therefore, this book assists professors in directing students to a broader focus.

The philosophy, or strategy, underlying this book's presentation is the development of a basic, but comprehensive, theoretical structure that includes a discussion of the influential and interactive processes that impact financial reporting. This approach is intended to deliver the reader from the constricting, but apparently prevailing, notion that financial statements are precise.

The primary objectives of this book are accomplished in two phases. Chapters 1 through 6 introduce the reader to accounting and financial statement analysis, with an emphasis on the notion that accounting is not a precise science.

This is accomplished by developing an understanding of the accounting model and the principles and conventions upon which the model is constructed. The accounting model attempts to capture to and reflect the economic consequences of transactions. Because of the uncertainties present in a business environment, the accounting model has inherent limitations that are not always obvious. Furthermore, because of the individual judgment used in applying the model, different reported results can evolve from similar circumstances. This is demonstrated through examples from current practice.

Once a realization exists that financial statements are not precise measurements, a natural question evolves: Do financial statements make a difference in the analytical process? That is, if the same fact situation can result in different reporting consequences, are financial statements a useful device for analytical purposes? To answer this question, related research (such as market and event studies) is discussed in nonsophisticated terms.

Chapters 7 through 10 address this broader question, as well as the issues of public policy and political influences on the standard-setting process. While these topics are rather esoteric, they are discussed in straightforward terms that should provide the reader with a broader focus for the potential consequences of accounting information. This provides a more comprehensive view of accounting that enables the reader to understand the implications of events on financial reporting, and it should provide a more interesting forum for addressing accounting issues.

The ultimate objective is to enable the reader to conduct an intelligent analysis of financial statements. Financial statement analysis requires an awareness of a broad set of factors that are not always obvious and that are not always limited to accounting numbers. No user of financial statements should conduct an analysis without this broader understanding.

ACKNOWLEDGMENTS

I hope this book assists the reader in understanding financial statements. My efforts toward that goal significantly benefited from the help of others, and I gratefully acknowledge their support.

A very special thanks is in order for those professors who conscientiously reviewed the manuscript:

Jack Ethridge
Stephen F. Austin State University

Stevan K. Olson
Southwest Missouri State University

Mark A. Turner
Stephen F. Austin State University

Also, special thanks is in order for the editorial support from Sara Bates of South-Western Publishing Co., who always communicated with a perfect blend of constructive criticism and encouragement; for Larry H. Powell, president of Fountain Capital Management, and Professor Gary Tidwell, College of Charleston, who both graciously contributed material to the text; and for Paula Cundiff and Stephanie Clark, who expertly typed the manuscript.

Comments from readers would be appreciated.

Gus Gordon
Stephen F. Austin State University

Contents

Chapter 7
POLITICS AND ITS EFFECT ON GAAP   155

Chapter 8
SELECTED ISSUES AND DECIDED QUESTIONS   181

Chapter 9
DO FINANCIAL STATEMENTS MAKE A DIFFERENCE?   205

Chapter 10
INTERNATIONAL FINANCIAL REPORTING   229

Chapter 1

Introduction

There may be differences of opinion as to what is "right."[1]

The success of investors, executives, students, and others is highly dependent on the ability to analyze and understand financial statements. This ability is as much an art form as it is an application of standard technical analyses. The primary goal of this book is to guide the reader in developing both artistic expertise and technical expertise in interpreting financial statements. To accomplish this purpose, an emphasis is placed on viewing the accounting process—which culminates in financial statements—as a social science rather than as a set of technical rules that unambiguously categorize financial transactions.

The technical analysis of financial statements is straightforward. A variety of common financial ratios have been designed to produce information and to provide insight into the financial condition of a corporation and the results of corporate operations. Financial ratios are computed easily by selecting financial statement amounts and entering them into a formula for each financial ratio.

Calculated ratios for two companies can result in identical numbers. However, an informed analyst may have different interpretations of the information conveyed through the financial ratios for each company. This is due to the artistic dimension of the analytical process. The artistic dimension is important because the accounting process relies to a great extent upon the application of judgment.

Judgment, which necessarily introduces subjectivity, is used in the accounting process to reflect the economic consequences of transactions. Different, yet valid, views and interpretations of the economic consequences of a specific transaction often exist. An analyst must be

---

[1]Doctor Macphail to Mr. Davidson when discussing the actions of Ms. Sadie Thompson in the movie *Rain*, based on Somerset Maugham's novel.

1

able to interpret accounting decisions and their implications on the financial statements and to recognize erroneous judgments made during the accounting process.

Users of financial statements quite often believe that the statements are a result of a precise measurement-and-valuation process. An objective of this book is to clarify this misconception, which is probably the result of a combination of factors, including the financial statements themselves. Net income and other financial statement information may be reported in a manner that implies preciseness. For example, the annual report of Bogert Oil Company for 1983 reports total revenues and net income in the amount of $11,877,812 and $1,051,359, respectively. Total assets are valued at $27,322,896. Because financial information is often estimated at the financial reporting date, measurement to a specific dollar amount conveys a degree of accuracy that is not necessarily present.

There is additional evidence that users of financial statements wrongly perceive the information contained in financial statements. This evidence is the so-called *perception gap*. The perception gap primarily concerns the audit report and what it signifies. The audit report contains information that is an integral part of the financial statements. For several reasons, users of financial statements perceive the auditor's examination to be more than it is. Chapter 2 contains an in-depth discussion of the objective of the audit function performed by independent auditors, the perception gap, and the accounting profession's attempts at dealing with this problem.

PURPOSE AND OBJECTIVES OF FINANCIAL REPORTING

Financial statements are prepared with the intention of accomplishing several broad objectives. In order to alleviate misconceptions, users should become acquainted with these objectives. *Statement of Financial Accounting Concepts No. 1 (SFAC 1)* explains that the broad objective of financial reporting is to provide useful information for making decisions to those individuals external to the reporting entity. Primary external users are identified by *SFAC 1* as present and potential investors and creditors of the reporting entity and as those individuals who advise the investors and creditors. Investors, creditors, and other external financial statement users may have different investment goals. However, financial reporting is not directed toward satisfying the needs of a specific group of external users; instead, it is considered general-purpose financial reporting, which is directed toward the common interests of various user groups. External users are identified as the primary beneficiaries of financial reporting because they "lack the authority to prescribe the financial information they want from an enterprise and therefore must use the information that management communicates to them."[2]

In order for financial statements to be useful to external users, the financial statements must be understandable. *SFAC 1* emphasizes, though, that financial statements are prepared on the assumption that users have a relatively sophisticated level of knowledge.

> Financial information is a tool and, like most tools, cannot be of much direct help to those who are unable or unwilling to use it or misuse it. Its use can be learned, however, and financial reporting should provide information that can be used by all—nonprofessionals as well as professionals—who are willing to learn to use it properly.... Financial reporting should not exclude relevant information merely because it is difficult for some to understand.[3]

Thus, an appropriate level of knowledge is a prerequisite for financial statement analysis. Furthermore, as the economy and the financial transactions become more complex, the degree of sophistication required for financial analysis becomes more crucial.

As previously mentioned, the broad objective of financial reporting is to provide information that is useful in decision making. This objective is important because a capitalist economy relies upon the idea that if the market is provided with sufficient reliable information, resources will be allocated in a manner that produces a higher standard of living in the economy than could be attained if resources are directed on some other basis. It is, therefore, presumed that, if the objectives of financial statements are fulfilled, a broader purpose will be accomplished:

> ...Saving and investing in productive resources (capital formation) are generally considered to be prerequisite to increasing the standard of living in an economy. To the extent that financial reporting provides information that helps identify relatively efficient and inefficient users of resources, aids in assessing relative returns and risks of investment opportunities, or otherwise assists in promoting efficient functioning of capital and other markets, it helps create a favorable environment for capital formation decisions.[4]

---

[2]SFAC 1 (Stamford, Conn.: FASB, 1978), par. 28.
[3]Ibid., par. 36.
[4]Ibid., par. 33.

It should be apparent that the auditor's role is very important. External users are relying on financial statements prepared by management. Because of the self-interested motivations (discussed in detail in Chapter 7) that are attendant in any economic circumstance, the auditor's role is to act as an independent party and to express an opinion about the fairness of the financial statements in reflecting the economic consequences of the reporting entity's transactions. This role provides users with the confidence that financial statements are useful for decision-making purposes.

However, as discussed in the next section, there are inherent limitations in accounting and financial reporting. In order to properly understand financial statements, an analyst must fully appreciate their limitations. To accomplish this objective, this book develops a basic, yet comprehensive, theoretical and practical foundation of accounting principles.

The first phase of this foundation begins in Chapter 3 which introduces the reader to accounting conventions and the elements of financial statements. Chapter 4 discusses basic financial statement analysis and utilizes conventional financial statement ratios to illustrate the framework on which analysis is initiated. Chapter 5 enriches the theoretical foundation by introducing the idea that accounting principles are purposely designed to accommodate various scenarios so that financial statements reflect the reality of the economic consequences of management decisions.

THE ROLE OF JUDGMENT ON FINANCIAL STATEMENTS

Because of the designed flexibility in accounting principles, their application is predicated on judgments of *when* and *how* to record transactions. Namely, accounting principles and standards are not governed by consistent laws of nature. A chemist, for example, knows that, when two parts of hydrogen are combined with one part of oxygen, the result will be water. However, when a corporation issues a negotiable security with clauses that reflect characteristics of both ownership in the corporation and debt obligations for the corporation, some accountants would say that the corporation has issued a debt security, while other accountants would claim that the corporation has issued an equity security. An equity security is fundamentally different from a debt security.

Since the accounting records must reflect the security as either debt or equity, a judgment must be made on how to view the security. This decision will have implications for various elements of financial statements. Consequently, financial statement ratios will differ, depending on which view is accepted as appropriate. Since an analyst external to the firm may not have all the facts, it may not be obvious to that analyst that an alternative view is possible.

Because financial transactions are not governed by consistent laws of nature, published financial statements are a consensus of the management's and the independent auditor's opinions about the fairness of reported results for operations, financial condition, and other aspects of financial statements. When alternative views of the consequences of transactions are possible, the ultimate choice is made by a group composed of management and independent auditor. This group makes decisions concerning when revenue should be recognized and when and how costs should be allocated to expense. There are various alternatives concerning when and how revenue and expense should be recognized, all of which may be considered by the accounting profession as proper. If the makeup of the group (management and auditor) changes, the group consensus may also change. Furthermore, two virtually identical companies may publish financial statements that differ significantly simply because the two groups forming the consensus opinion view specific situations differently.

This does not mean that the application of judgment results in financial statements that are products of arbitrary decisions. Financial statements are the end product of the accounting process, which is confined to the use of generally accepted accounting principles. However, there are *alternative* generally accepted accounting principles from which to choose, because the objective of accounting is to capture the economic reality of financial transactions. Based on the judgment of an individual or a group of individuals, an accounting principle is chosen to record a financial transaction so as to reflect fairly the economic consequences of that transaction, given the circumstances present. Hence, financial statements reflect accounting choices that are not arbitrary, but rather are chosen from alternatives within the boundaries of acceptable practices.

At this point, it should be obvious why this chapter began with the quote from *Rain*. The concept concerning differences of opinion as to what is "right" is an easy one to intellectualize. Yet, because of the misconceptions concerning accounting and preciseness, it is often difficult for financial statement users to apply this concept to financial reporting.

These circumstances leave users of financial statements in an awkward position unless they understand that acceptable, alternative views of the same fact situation can and often do exist. That is, financial statement analysis is, in a real sense, a search for the *truth*. Therefore, users of financial statements should understand, that financial statements are not precise, nor are they absolutely accurate documents. This important theme is integrated throughout this book.

Examples of Different Views

Examples of how different views of the truth arise and how they are justified are briefly discussed at this point to provide the reader with an initial insight into the problem. Ultimately a uniform view of the truth emerges once all facts are known. Although it may take years for all the facts to become known, an interpretation of the most current facts is still necessary because financial statements are prepared at least on an annual basis.

Periodic financial reporting is necessary because financial statement users require timely information so that financial information is *relevant* for decision making. Relevant information is information that has the capacity to make a difference in the decision-making process. Furthermore, financial information should be *reliable* in order to assist financial statement users in their decision-making process. Reliability in this context does not imply precision. Reliability, as used in accounting, is linked to the concept of *representational faithfulness*. Representational faithfulness is defined as "correspondence or agreement between a measure or description and the phenomenon it purports to represent."[5] Reliability assumes that financial statement users understand "that the information provided by financial reporting often results from approximate, rather than exact, measures involving numerous estimates, classifications, summarizations, judgments, and allocations."[6]

The following examples provide a brief glimpse into the problems of providing timely information and of using judgment to present relevant and reliable information. A deeper discussion of the implications and consequences of these and other examples is provided in Chapters 5 and 6.

---

[5]*SFAC* 2 (Stamford, Conn.: FASB, 1980), par. 28.
[6]Ibid., par. 64.

Revenue Recognition. The recognition of revenue, which can occur at various points during the production-and-sales process, depends on the interpretation of the facts. For example, it is considered proper under certain circumstances to recognize revenue during production (i. e., prior to sale of the product) and at other times to delay revenue recognition until some point after the sale. As discussed in Chapter 5, revenue recognition is often deferred beyond the point of sale because of uncertainties associated with the transaction. Obviously, an individual contemplating investment in one of two companies should be careful to heed the effects of different revenue-recognition policies on the standard financial ratios and analyses.

Moreover, estimates are often made for revenue when it is initially recognized in the accounting records as earned. For example, many retail stores sell to customers on credit. Since some customers do not pay their debts, an estimate is made of the amount of sales that will ultimately be collected in order to properly recognize revenue. Given identical facts, one company's management and auditor may be more adept at estimating revenues than another company's management and auditor. Therefore, reported revenues can be significantly different, depending on the group consensus opinion formed by each company's management and auditor.

Asset and Expense Recognition. Companies must also adopt approaches for allocating costs. All assets are consumed eventually, although it is not always apparent when an asset has been consumed or how much of an asset has been consumed at any point in time. There are various acceptable approaches to determine when and how much of an asset has been consumed. Most of these cost-allocation approaches involve an estimate or assumption. Therefore, many cost allocations are necessarily imprecise and even arbitrary. For example, consider the purchase of a truck. The truck is an asset when purchased, but eventually it becomes worthless (or nearly so). Therefore, the cost of the truck should be allocated to expense in the years that the truck is used. Since the amount of the truck that is "used up" is not obvious and since periodic financial statements are prepared, the amount of cost allocated to expense must be based on some estimate.

Since there are various acceptable approaches to cost allocation, the impact on financial ratios and analyses of different companies may not be readily apparent. That is, some companies may allocate the cost of trucks to expense earlier than other companies because of differences in management and auditor judgments about how and when trucks become worthless.

Another factor involved in expense recognition is the question of whether an expenditure has resulted in an asset, which does not immediately affect net income, or an expense, which does immediately affect net income. For example, in the case of the oil and gas industry, some companies have adopted the successful efforts method of accounting, which expenses the costs of unsuccessful wells immediately. Other companies have adopted the full cost method, which does not expense the costs associated with unsuccessful wells but accounts for these expenditures as an asset. Consequently, the financial statements of companies using two different costing methods cannot be directly compared.

Liability Recognition. Likewise, there may be a question about whether an expenditure has satisfied an obligation, or liability. For instance, if cash is transferred to an irrevocable trust to be used solely to satisfy specific debt obligations as they are due, should the debt be removed immediately from the balance sheet of the corporation as if the debt had been entirely satisfied? If Company A follows this policy and removes the debt, can Company A be compared to Company B, that, under identical circumstances, does not utilize a trust to "dispose" of the debt?

Hopefully, it is becoming clear that the accounting process, and therefore financial reporting, is not a precise science. This process becomes more complex as the structure of financial transactions become more complicated and the securities issued by entities becomes more exotic:

> The financial statements of a business enterprise can be thought of as a representation of the resources and obligations of an enterprise and the financial flows into, out of, and within the enterprise—as a model of the enterprise. Like all models, it must abstract from much that goes on in a real enterprise....In real life, it is necessary to accept a much smaller degree of correspondence between the model and the original....[7]

Thus, the accounting model allows the use of accounting alternatives when circumstances differ, so that a more representationally faithful financial picture can be presented. Chapter 6 investigates the implications of the alternatives afforded by accounting principles and the inherent problems of subjectivity attendant to judgments. Examples gleaned from the financial press are used to illustrate that the implications of the theoretical framework outlined in Chapters 3 through 5 have consequences in a practical context. Obviously, these conse-

---

[7]Ibid., par. 76.

quences are important in forming conclusions during the analytical process.

ENVIRONMENTAL AND POLITICAL INFLUENCES AND THEIR IMPACT ON FINANCIAL STATEMENTS

The second part of this book includes a discussion of the influential and interactive processes that impact financial reporting, and an investigation of whether or not financial statements are useful to investors and other users in capital markets. Financial statements are not prepared, nor are accounting standards formed, in a vacuum. The environment and the private agendas (hidden, or otherwise) of groups or individuals help to shape the ultimate consequences of transactions on financial reporting.

Accounting, therefore, is a social science. Accordingly, financial statement analysis must incorporate human and environmental factors in order to develop a complete picture of the entity under analysis. These influences are particularly important because they are not always obvious in an economic context. There is, apparently, a tendency to believe that accounting principles are set in a sterile environment. However, human characteristics pervade all occupations. Human reactions are relatively uniform; we are normally considered to be resourceful, evaluative, maximizing individuals.[8]

When there are alternative accounting principles that may result in different reported accounting numbers for a specific transaction, it is natural to expect resourceful, evaluative, maximizing individuals to choose the principle that results in the most favorable interpretation of events from their individual perspectives. Because various constituencies may be affected by the alternative selected and because different constituencies may have different interests in the interpretation due to the projected effects of the interpretation, competing interests may emerge.

Politics, the media, regulatory bodies, and Congress have all become involved in an attempt to influence the accounting profession and, particularly, the standard-setting bodies within the accounting profession. As explained in the next section, the standard-setting body within the accounting profession is the Financial Accounting Stan-

---

[8]W. H. Meckling, "Values and the Choice of the Model of the Individual in Social Sciences," *Schweizerische Zeitschriff für Volkswirtschaft und Statistik* (December 1976), 545.

dards Board (FASB). The FASB has adopted a due-process approach to the setting of accounting standards. This process, explained in detail in Chapter 7, allows all interested parties the opportunity to present their views before the FASB in public hearings.

The interested parties can be classified into five general categories: managements, auditors, resource providers (investors and creditors), the Securities and Exchange Commission (SEC), and investment advisors. Normally, at each public hearing, members from each of the five categories present their views on the subject under discussion. In general, members of a particular category are expected to lobby for specific types of standards.

For example, managements normally argue for standards that allow revenue to be recognized earlier, rather than later, in the earnings process. This is because a major criterion for judging managements' effectiveness is the amount and trend of net income. On the other hand, auditors may lobby for deferring the point at which revenue is recognized. This is because auditors are often sued because of the overstatement of revenue by managements that caused resource providers to invest in a company that subsequently went bankrupt. Auditors generally believe that conservative revenue-recognition approaches to accounting decrease the likelihood of lawsuits.

Also, managements of different companies may disagree on the appropriate accounting treatment because of the natures of their companies and because of the perceived effects of a particular accounting standard. For example, managements of some oil companies believe that if they must account for the cost of unsuccessful oil wells as expenses rather than assets, then they may be unable to raise money from investors. This is because most oil wells are not successful, and, therefore, high levels of expenses will be a disincentive for investment. However, managements of other oil companies believe that the costs of unsuccessful wells do not represent assets and should be expensed in order to reflect the high degree of risk associated with the oil industry.

The theory of FASB due process is that, after all sides have presented their arguments, the FASB will arrive at a fair conclusion with regard to any specific accounting standard. The adoption of fair accounting standards will allow for financial reporting to fulfill its societal role:

> The role of financial reporting requires it to provide evenhanded, neutral, or unbiased information. Thus, for example, information that indicates that a relatively inefficient user of resources is efficient or that investing in a particular enterprise involves less risk than it does and information that is directed toward a particular goal, such as encouraging the reallocation

of resources in favor of a particular segment of the economy, are likely to fail to serve the broader objectives that financial reporting is intended to serve.[9]

The FASB due-process approach provides the opportunity for political interaction as well. Chapter 7 presents an example where standard-setting bodies have been impacted by the political process.

The accounting profession is attempting to resolve many of the foregoing accounting problems and questions, and others as well. Some, in fact have been resolved already. The accounting theory involved in the resolution of specific problems is discussed briefly in Chapter 8.

Chapter 9 examines whether financial statements actually make a difference in the analytical process. For example, if the same facts can be interpreted differently, does this render financial statements useless? Chapter 9 addresses this issue and investigates evidence of the usefulness of financial statements.

Finally, because of increased international commerce and the concomitant increase in competition for capital from resource providers, financial statement users need an understanding of international financial reporting limitations. Chapter 10 briefly examines the issues involved in international financial reporting by multinational companies.

AN HISTORICAL PERSPECTIVE OF ACCOUNTING STANDARD SETTING

In order to fully understand the influences affecting the accounting profession, a brief discussion of the development of the standard-setting bodies within the accounting profession is needed. The profession recognized the importance of establishing standards as early as the 1930s. Standards require a more consistent treatment of transactions, thereby establishing continuity and comparability of financial statements. The first standard-setting body to evolve from within the accounting profession was the Committee on Accounting Procedure (CAP), which was composed of practicing certified public accountants(CPAs). The CAP was in existence from 1939 to 1959 and published 51 *Accounting Research Bulletins* (*ARBs*) that addressed specific problems or controversies.

---

[9];*SFAC 1*, par. 33.

In 1959, the American Institute of Certified Public Accountants (AICPA) established the Accounting Principles Board (APB). The APB not only addressed the treatment of specific problems through the issuance of 31 APB *Opinions* (*APBOs*), but it also began recognizing the need to form a consistent, normative theory from which to derive standards.

Early on, the APB ran into political problems, both from within and from outside the accounting profession, with the passage of *APBO 2*, which specified the accounting for the investment tax credit. Furthermore, the APB never fully formulated a theoretical foundation from which to derive standards.

Because of continued criticism of the APB, the AICPA formed a committee chaired by Francis M. Wheat, a former SEC chairman. The Wheat Committee completed a report that recommended the formation of the Financial Accounting Standards Board (FASB) to replace the APB. The structure of the FASB would be different from the APB; it would be semiautonomous with full-time members who are not required to be CPAs. The AICPA accepted the Wheat Committee's recommendations and formed the FASB in 1973.

The FASB has adopted a due-process approach, whereby a topic is identified, and numerous public memorandums, hearings, exposure drafts, and comments are solicited before a *Statement of Financial Accounting Standards* (*SFAS*) is issued. More than 100 *SFASs* have been issued since 1973. Moreover, the FASB has developed a conceptual framework from which to derive a set of consistent standards. To date, six *Statement of Financial Accounting Concepts* (*SFACs*) have been issued.

ARBs, *APBOs*, and *SFASs* form the foundation of *generally accepted accounting principles* (GAAP). GAAP actually means those principles that have substantial authoritative support. While substantial authoritative support has never been officially defined, GAAP has come to mean principles supported by the pronouncements of the CAP, the APB, the FASB, and the SEC, and by commonly followed business practices. GAAP is important because Rule 203 of the *Code of Professional Ethics* of the AICPA prohibits an auditor who is a member of the AICPA from expressing an opinion on financial statements that are not prepared in accordance with GAAP. (There are rare circumstances where Rule 203 does not apply.) However, interpretive problems arise when alternative GAAP exists. This occurs when the same transaction can be recorded differently and still be within the guidelines of GAAP.

The FASB approach to standard-setting, which attempts to incorporate as much input as possible, actually increases the potential for political influence. A constituency may prefer to have a particular transaction or event reported in a manner that has the most favorable impact on that constituency. It is now understood that accounting standards can be and have been influenced by particular interest groups. Among examples that will be discussed later are *SFAS 19* and *SFAS 25*, which cover accounting for oil and gas producing companies.

GLOSSARY

Accounting principles. A set of rules and methods used to transform financial data into useful financial statements.

Accounting standards. A set of rules promulgated by authoritative bodies within the accounting profession.

Audit report. A report attached to the financial statements, which is designed to communicate the auditor's opinion of the fairness of the financial statements, the character of his or her examination, and the responsibility of auditor and management. The audit report usually contains three paragraphs that communicate this information.

Cost allocation. The process of determining the amount of an asset that has expired and become an expense.

Elements of financial statements. Each is defined briefly here. (See Chapter 3 for more formal definitions.)

>   **Asset.** A right or property, owned by an entity.
>   **Liability.** A debt, or obligation, to another entity that is not an owner.
>   **Stockholders' equity.** The owners' net interests in the assets after subtracting liabilities.
>   **Revenue.** An inflow of assets due to the sale of products or services.
>   **Expenses.** The outflow of assets in the production of revenue; an expired cost. (See *cost allocation*.)

Financial statements. A set of reports that provides financial information on an entity's financial condition, results of operations, cash flows, and changes in stockholders' equity. (See Chapter 3)

Financial statement users (external). Individuals, groups, or others outside of the entity who make use of accounting information.

Generally accepted accounting principles (GAAP). Rules and standards promulgated by authoritative bodies as well as evolved practice that has been accepted as appropriate.

Going-concern assumption. Assumption that an entity will continue to operate indefinitely in the absence of evidence to the contrary.

Independent auditor. A CPA retained by management and required by the SEC to provide an independent opinion about the fairness of financial statements of publicly traded companies.

Management. Employees of a company that establish overall policy. The term is usually used to describe top-level management, such as president, chief financial officer, and so on, that act as a team to direct company efforts.

Materiality. A concept used to describe an amount of financial statement error or misstatement large enough to cause external users to draw an incorrect conclusion.

Negotiable security. A financial instrument issued by a corporation that can be bought and sold on the open market. A negotiable security can be of two general types:

> **Debt.** A loan to the corporation from the security holder (e.g., bonds.).
>
> **Equity.** An investment in the corporation by the security holder. An equity security represents an ownership interest (e.g. common stock).

Recognition of revenue. The recording of revenue in the accounting records. This is done at the point in time that revenue is considered to have been earned.

Results of operations. A financial statement that calculates net income by subtracting expenses from revenues. Sometimes called an **income statement.**

Statement of financial condition (position). A financial statement that contains a listing of assets, liabilities, and stockholders' equity with recorded values. Sometimes called a **balance sheet.** (See Chapter 3)

Chapter 2

Auditing and the Attest Function

The typical auditor is a man past middle age, spare,
wrinkled, intelligent, cold, passive, non-committal,
with eyes like a codfish, polite in contact, but at the
same time, unresponsive, cold, calm and damnably
composed as a concrete post or plaster-of-paris cast; a
human petrification with a heart of feldspar and
without charm of the friendly germ, minus bowels,
passion, or a sense of humor. Happily, they never
reproduce and all of them finally go to hell.[1]

Many individuals perceive auditors as indicated in this quote. This perception may arise from the employees of a company under audit, who often believe that it is the auditor's function to burrow through accounting records in a molelike manner to discover clerical errors.

However, the auditor's function is much broader, and it fulfills a profound social need. As noted in Chapter 1, there are alternative methods of reporting similar transactions. Company management may have an inherent bias to select the method that reflects most favorably on the company and itself. Hence, creditors, investors, and others can be misled concerning the economic consequences of transactions, especially if they are without the intervention of an independent party with the expertise to determine whether events are reported fairly.

The primary theme of this book is that, financial statements, due to the inherent limitations of the accounting process, are not precise reflections of the economic consequences of transactions. Accountants

---

[1]Elbert Hubbard quoted by W. Wallace in *Auditing Research Monograph No. 2.* (New York: Macmillan, 1985), 61–62.

are aware of this problem and have attempted to communicate the limitations of financial statements to users. Because of these limitations and others discussed in this chapter, independent auditors can only provide reasonable assurance to users that the financial statements they review are not *materially* misleading.[2]

THE SOCIAL NEED FOR INDEPENDENT AUDITORS

In a capitalist economy, individuals make decisions concerning the allocation of individual resources. In order for the economy to operate efficiently, individual investors and creditors must be able to rely on the financial information that is provided to them. An independent auditor fulfills a social need of a capitalist economy by providing an opinion concerning the *fairness* of the financial statements prepared by company management. Such an opinion provides credibility to financial statements because, as already mentioned, management's motivations may run counter to investor interests.

This social need is fulfilled by auditors through the *attest function*. In performing the attest function, the auditor provides an opinion regarding the overall fairness and dependability of financial statements. The auditor's opinion is the culmination of a two stage investigative process. In the first stage, the auditor gathers evidence from company records and discussions with management. In the second stage, the auditor evaluates the evidence obtained as the basis for a judgment concerning the overall fairness of the company's financial statements. The judgment made by the auditor is expressed as an opinion contained in the auditor's report, which is included with the company's financial statements.

However, it is important to understand that the auditor is merely expressing an *opinion* on financial statements that have been prepared by the management of the company. That is, the auditor does not prepare the financial statements. As noted in Chapter 1, the auditor may have input into management's decision as to the particular accounting principles applied. Nevertheless, the ultimate decision rests with management.

AN HISTORICAL PERSPECTIVE OF AUDITING

In order to understand the auditor's role and the apparent misperceptions attributed to users, an historical perspective of the development of

---

[2]The concept of *materiality* is briefly explained beginning on page 23.

auditing and the audit report follows. There has always existed a need for assessment of stewardship when one entity has maintained a fiduciary responsibility for the property or investment of others.

> Whenever the advance of civilization brought about the necessity of one man being entrusted to some extent with the property of another the advisability of some kind of check upon the fidelity of the former would become apparent.[3]

There is evidence that ancient civilizations established organized government and businesses in approximately 4,000 B.C. Ancient civilizations recognized this stewardship concept; surviving records indicate that the Babylonians created "carbon" copies by enclosing a sun-dried clay tablet with an outer coating of clay which duplicated the original document.[4]

Stewardship, in a modern sense, has been defined as follows:

> Management of an enterprise is periodically accountable to the owners not only for the custody and safekeeping of enterprise resources but also for their efficient and profitable use....[5]

Modern requirements for audits evolved with the corporate form of ownership, which enabled owners to be absent from the operation of the company. Laws passed in England beginning in 1845 stimulated the development of accounting standards and independent audits. The primary purpose of these audits was to verify stewardship of management and to detect fraud. Initially, audits consisted of a transaction-by-transaction, detailed examination.

As the economy became more complex and business transactions increased, the emphasis of the audit evolved to the expression of an opinion concerning the overall fairness of the financial statements. This was a natural evolution if audits were to remain cost effective. Because of the increased complexity and number of transactions, auditors were forced into the practice of testing, or sampling, rather than investigating the propriety of each transaction.

As auditors began to change the nature and conduct of an audit, there is evidence that the public was unaware that the focus had shifted from a detailed examination and detection of fraud to the expression of an opinion concerning the overall fairness of financial statements. The

---

[3]R. Brown, *A History of Accounting and Accountants* (New York: Augustus M. Kelly Pubs., 1971), 74.

[4]M. Chatfield, *A History of Accounting Thought* (New York: Krieger Pub. Co., 1977), 4.

[5]"Objectives of Financial Reporting by Business Enterprises," *SFAC 1* (Stamford, Conn.: FASB, 1978), par. 50.

reason for this misperception has not always been clear to auditors because it was believed that the audit report was worded in such a manner as to clearly express the function of the auditors. However, part of the confusion may have stemmed from old audit reports that used words such as *certify*, which imply a verification function. It should be noted that the term *certify* has been deleted from audit reports since the early 1930s.

Nevertheless, financial statement users continued to place a responsibility on auditors for detecting errors and fraud, thus perceiving auditors as a type of guarantor of financial statements. Surveys have also confirmed that this misperception exists.[6] Furthermore, in the early 1980s, as business failures increased, the public apparently embraced the notion that auditors should provide early warning of business failure.[7]

The reduction of the so-called *expectation gap* became a priority of the accounting profession. Hopefully, this reduction has been accomplished with a strategy of informing users about the nature of an audit by a change in the wording of the audit report and by changes in auditing standards that provide for increased auditor responsibilities.

THE CURRENT AUDITOR RESPONSIBILITIES

While auditors have accepted the increased responsibilities, they still are not held responsible for predicting future outcomes such as business failures. The prediction of future outcomes is the responsibility of analysts, and it is the end product of the analytical process. However, the analysis is performed with the assumption that auditors are providing an independent and objective opinion about the fairness of the financial statements.

The assumption of independence and objectivity is a necessary condition for the fulfillment of the societal need for audits. There have been valid concerns that auditors are not "independent" if they are being paid by the company under audit. Auditors respond that their professional code of ethics addresses the question of independence and resolves the matter to the extent possible.

---

[6]C.D. F. Baron, et al., "Uncovering Corporate Irregularities: Are We Closing the Expectation Gap?" *Journal of Accountancy* (October 1977), 56–66.

[7]J. D. Sullivan, "A Program for Progress in Standards Setting," *In Our Opinion* (October 1985), 1–2.

Furthermore, auditors can be held liable to third-party users. Hence, while the responsibility for the financial statements rests with management, absolving auditors of any responsibility for misleading financial statements would undermine the social need for audits. Auditors are subject to human pressures. If management wants a particular interpretation of an event because that interpretation reflects more favorably upon the financial statements, an auditor may become sensitive to management's interpretation. This is because management can decide to retain another auditor who agrees with management's interpretation, which results in a loss of revenue to the initial auditor. However, the integrity of the auditor and the threat of third-party lawsuits deter an auditor from blindly accepting management interpretations.

Auditors can be held liable if they are negligent in the conduct of the audit. Unfortunately, there have been several audit "failures" for which auditors have been responsible.[8] An audit failure results when an auditor does not detect material misstatements.[9] By failing to exercise due diligence or by failing to retain his or her independence and objectivity, an auditor violates the public trust and subverts the purpose of an audit. In cases where investors have relied on audited financial statements and auditors have been negligent, investors have been awarded damages by the courts. Fortunately, the vast majority of audits are conducted in a responsible manner by ethical and competent auditors.

An additional consideration is the evolved nature of audits. Auditors are unable to examine each transaction. Obviously, if auditors are examining transactions on a test basis, there are inherent limitations built into the audit. Namely, auditors are drawing conclusions from a sample of evidence that is assumed to be representative of all the transactions. While there are procedures that can be instituted to increase the probability that the sample used is representative, the possibility always exists that the sample is not representative. From a statistical standpoint, the auditor will not have an indication of whether inferences are being drawn from a nonrepresentative sample.

The implications of sampling are obvious. Auditors are constantly at risk of providing an audit report that indicates no material distor-

---

[8]For the details of a famous and spectacular case see L. J. Seidler, et al., *The Equity Funding Papers: The Anatomy of a Fraud* (New York: Wiley, 1977).

[9]A material misstatement is an error or distortion (intentional or unintentional) in the financial statements that causes the financial statements to be misleading or unfair.

tions in the financial statements when, in fact, material distortions exist. This is an unavoidable risk, especially given the evolved nature of audits and business. Because the public relies on the audit report, when an auditor fails to detect material misstatements, society's need for audits may be undermined, resulting in an inefficient allocation of resources. However, given imperfect knowledge and the uncertainties associated with business, this is a fundamental problem with no cost-effective solution at this time.[10]

Therefore, financial statement users should read the audit report contained in financial statements in order to comprehend the auditor's communication to the financial statement user. Users also should be aware of the inherent limitations of audits.

THE INDEPENDENT AUDITOR'S REPORT AND THE MANAGEMENT'S DISCUSSION

The independent auditor's report is the end product of the audit. The attest function performed by the auditor culminates with the issuance of the report. Because the purpose of the attest function is to provide an opinion concerning the overall fairness of the auditee's financial statements when taken as a whole, the auditor's report contains an opinion by the auditor that addresses this question. The opinion expressed in the audit report addresses only the financial statements and the accompanying notes to the financial statements. In addition to financial statements and notes, most annual reports include the "Management's Discussion," to which the auditor's opinion does *not* extend. It is through this discussion that the company president explains significant events of the past fiscal year and also explains the outlook for the company's future.

Because of the expectation gap, the wording of the standard audit report was changed recently. The change in wording is intended to inform users of the responsibilities and obligations of the auditor. The standard audit report is now worded as follows. (NOTE: emphasis has been added.)

---

[10]Further discussion of these problems are beyond the scope of this book. The reader should refer to the Reading List at the end of this chapter for additional information.

Date

Independent Auditor's Report
To the Directors and Stockholders of
EFG Corporation:

We have audited the consolidated balance sheets of EFG Corporation as of September 30, 19XY, and the related consolidated statements of income, stockholders' equity, and cash flows for the year then ended. These financial statements are the *responsibility of the Company's management. Our responsibility is to express an opinion* on these financial statements based on our audits.

We conducted our audits in accordance with generally accepted auditing standards. Those standards require that we plan and perform the audit to obtain *reasonable assurance* about whether the financial statements are *free of material misstatement*. An audit includes examining, on a *test basis*, evidence supporting the amounts and disclosures in the financial statements. An audit also includes assessing the accounting principles used and significant estimates made by management, as well as evaluating the overall financial statement presentation. We believe that our audit *provides a reasonable basis for our opinion*.

In our opinion, the financial statements referred to above *present fairly, in all material respects*, the financial position of EFG Corporation as of September 30, 19XY, and the results of its operations and its cash flows for the year then ended in conformity with generally accepted accounting principles.

Gordon & Gordon, CPAs
Address

This new report concisely explains what the auditor is accomplishing and communicates this to the financial statement user.

The standard audit report is used only when it is appropriate. It is referred to as an *unqualified opinion*, and it is intended to communicate a favorable signal to users concerning the overall fairness of the financial statements. This type of report is the audit opinion that management wants.

Unfortunately, there are circumstances where an unqualified report is not appropriate. Inappropriate circumstances usually involve material distortions in the financial statements, limitations in the scope of the auditor's engagement, or a lack of sufficient evidence for the auditor to form an opinion.

Note that distortions in the financial statements must be material to cause an unqualified opinion to be inappropriate. The concept of *materiality* is easy to understand, but often difficult to apply. In an audit context, materiality might be defined as the smallest error or distortion that could make a difference in the decision-making process of a user. Obviously, this is a very subjective concept, as one person's opinion of materiality, given the same facts and circumstances, may be entirely different from another person's opinion.[11] Furthermore, in a quantitative sense, materiality is directly dependent on the size of the firm. For example, the threshold for determining materiality in a nationally recognized corporation the size of IBM would be much higher than the threshold for materiality of a locally owned grocery store chain.

While further discussion of materiality is beyond the scope of this book, a basic conceptual understanding is necessary to comprehend what is communicated in audit reports. If the auditor detects a material distortion in the financial statements, it is appropriate to issue a *qualified opinion*. A qualified opinion uses the words *except for* to describe the effect of the particular matter causing the material distortion.

In general, financial statements are considered to be materially misstated if they depart from GAAP. From the accounting profession's viewpoint, the application of GAAP results in a more fair presentation than the use of alternative non-GAAP principles.

Some financial statements can contain a material distortion so significant that a qualified opinion is inappropriate. Under such circumstances an *adverse opinion* is provided in the audit report. An adverse opinion states that the distortions are so material that they cause the financial statements to be unfair and misleading.

In some situations, the auditor may be unable to gather sufficient evidence to form an opinion. This can result from limitations placed on the auditor by the management of the auditee or by particular circumstances outside of the control of the auditee or auditor. If the scope of the audit has been restricted by company management to the extent that the auditor has been unable to gather sufficient evidence to form an opinion, it is appropriate for the auditor to *disclaim* an opinion. Namely, the auditor does not express an opinion and explains why in the audit report. If the scope restriction was not imposed by company management, but by other circumstances, generally a qualified opinion is appropriate, although a disclaimer of opinion can be used if the restriction significantly reduced the auditor's ability to obtain evidential matter on which to base an opinion.

---

[11]For a discussion of auditor differences in materiality judgments, see W. J. Read, "Planning Materiality and SAS No. 47," *Journal of Accountancy* (December 1987), 72–79.

Finally, under certain circumstances, an auditor's report may contain an unqualified opinion issued with explanatory or modifying language. One of the most important reasons for such an unqualified, but modified, report concerns an entity's ability to continue in business indefinitely. Thus there is an assumption incorporated into the accounting model that a business will continue as a *going-concern* entity for an indefinite period. However, because of poor economic conditions, in general or specific to an industry, some companies may experience severe financial difficulties that create concerns about whether they will continue indefinitely. Auditors are required to evaluate going-concern status in every audit and to include modifying language in the audit report to point out that there is evidence that calls into question an entity's ability for continued existence.[12] If that evidence is very strong, such as the commencement of bankruptcy proceedings, the auditor may even give a disclaimer of opinion. The types of audit reports are listed in Table 2-1.

TABLE 2-1

TYPES OF AUDIT REPORTS

	Unqualified	*Qualified*	*Adverse*	*Disclaimer*
		Materiality Continuum		
Differences discovered through the auditing process	Immaterial			Very Material
Opinion disclosure	Modifying or explanatory language if necessary	Lack of supporting evidence Scope restriction GAAP departure	GAAP departure	Lack of supporting evidence Scope restriction Going concern in doubt

---

[12]Under no circumstances is the auditor attempting to predict bankruptcy or financial failure. The auditor is simply notifying the user that doubt exists concerning the entity's ability to remain a going concern.

As noted earlier, company management desires an unqualified opinion, because there are negative connotations implied by the other types of audit reports. However, an unqualified opinion does not indicate the lack of problems; it only indicates that, through the testing process, the auditor discovered no material errors or distortions. The audit report actually received will be dependent on the auditor's evaluation of the characteristics and on the materiality of the problems detected.

Auditors' Responsibility for Fraud Detection and Illegal Acts

One additional subject that should be discussed is fraud. In the past, the public has presumed that the auditor was responsible for fraud detection. Notice that there is no acceptance of such a responsibility by the auditor in the audit report. Furthermore, the auditor communicates this lack of responsibility for fraud detection directly to company management through written documents that provide an understanding between the auditor and the management about the responsibilities of each. However, the audit profession has tried to narrow the expectation gap through changing audit standards. As previously discussed, one change dealt with a revision of the audit report. The purpose of this revision was to communicate to the user a better understanding of the audit function and the nature of an audit, which should reduce the expectation gap from the user side. The auditing profession has also attempted to reduce the expectation gap from the auditor side by changing audit standards to require the auditor to assume more responsibility for detecting fraud by employees of the auditee and to adopt an attitude of increased professional skepticism. Under generally accepted auditing standards, the auditor has the responsibility to design the audit in order to provide reasonable assurance that, material fraud, if present, will be detected by the auditor. This is a greater burden on the auditor than existed before the revision of audit standards.

Furthermore, auditors are responsible for designing the audit in order to provide reasonable assurance that illegal acts of the auditee will be detected. However, auditors make no warranty that, if illegal acts have been committed by the auditee, they will be detected. All publicly traded companies are subject to regulatory laws imposed by Congress and the SEC. A large portion of regulatory rules were promulgated by the Securities Exchange Acts of 1933 and 1934. These laws were passed as a result of the stock market crash of 1929, and they were designed to protect investors and creditors of publicly traded companies that may present fraudulent, misleading, or manipulated financial statements.[13] The SEC requires that all publicly traded companies undergo independent audits. This requirement formalizes the notion that auditors are fulfilling a social need.

Another prominent law that causes auditors concern is the Foreign Corrupt Practices Act of 1977, which makes it unlawful for companies to bribe foreign officials to obtain and/or retain business. The law also established requirements for accurate accounting records and sound internal accounting control, which, presumably, will expose the aforementioned illegal payments.

SUMMARY

The purpose of requiring audited financial statements is to provide users with an independent and objective opinion regarding the fairness of financial statements when taken as a whole. This requirement presumes that fair presentation will provide users with information that can accommodate efficient allocation of resources. Therefore, auditors fulfill a societal need.

The user of financial statements should be aware that there are significant inherent limitations to an audit. First, the auditor is forming an opinion that is based on a sample of evidence presumed to be representative of all transactions. If the sample is not representative, the auditor may not have an indication of an existing material misstatement. Second, company management, through collusive acts, may deceive the auditor. History has shown that clever manipulation by a management team that acts in concert to deceive the auditor can be successful.

The limitations just discussed relate to gathering sufficient, competent evidence to form an opinion. There are additional limitations regarding audited financial statements. The evidence gathered during the audit process enables the auditor to obtain reasonable assurance about whether financial statements are free of material distortion.

---

[13]There are those who claim that there is little evidence that the stock market crash resulted from fraudulent financial statements, but that the Securities Exchange Acts of 1933 and 1934 were simply political "solutions" to the public's demand that the government respond to the crash. See D. R. Carmichael, "Internal Accounting Control—It's the Law," *Perspectives in Auditing*, 4th ed., D. R. Carmichael and J. J. Willingham, eds. (New York: McGraw-Hill, 1985), 198–204.

Both reasonable assurance and material distortion are subjective concepts that create additional limitations. Also, recall from Chapter 1 that financial statements are models (i.e., abstractions) that purport to represent economic reality.

Furthermore, users should understand that financial statements are prepared as general-purpose financial statements to meet the needs of a variety of users. These statements are prepared on the assumption that any user has a relatively sophisticated knowledge of business and financial concepts and should not rely solely on the auditor's report in making investment decisions.[14]

Therefore, users should be cautious in interpreting financial statements at face value. Furthermore, as discussed briefly in Chapter 1, the accounting process may not be capable of capturing the truth, particularly since there may be alternative interpretations of economic reality.[15] Do these collective limitations render financial statements meaningless for analytical purposes? This question is addressed in later chapters after a deeper foundation of accounting concepts has been developed.

Chapters 1 and 2 have made continual reference to financial statements. What actually composes the financial statements, and what do they purport to show? Chapter 3 addresses these questions.

READING LIST

Baxter, W. T. "The Accountant in Our History: A Bicentennial Overview." *In The House of Hancock.* Cambridge, MA.: Harvard Univ. Pr., 1945.

Bernstein, L. A., "The Concept of Materiality.", *The Accounting Review* (January, 1967): 86–95.

Charles, I. "Materiality: A Factor to Consider." *Accountancy* (April 1990): 8–91.

Greene, R., ed. "Crime and Punishment." *Forbes*, September 10, 1984, 114–116.

Mautz, R. K. "Self-Regulation—Criticisms and a Response." *Journal of Accountancy*, (April, 1984): 56–66.

---

[14]*SFAC 1*, pars. 34, 36.

[15]These problems are discussed in greater detail in Chapter 5.

Mednick, R. "Independence: Let's Get Back to Basics." *The Journal of Accountancy* (January, 1990): 86–93.

Reckers, P. M., Kneer, D. C., and Jennings, M. M. "Concepts of Materiality and Disclosure." *The CPA Journal* (December 1984): 20–30.

Saunders, L. "Too Little Is Not Enough." *Forbes*, November 7, 1983, 106.

Seidler, L. J., Andrews, F., Epstein, M. J. *The Equity Funding Papers: The Anatomy of a Fraud*, New York: Wiley, 1977.

Wood, A. M., and Sommer, Jr., A. A. "Peer Review and the Public Oversight Board: Doing the Job." *Journal of Accountancy* (May 1985): 122–131.

Wright, G. B., and Taylor, R. D. "Reporting Materiality for Investors." *Journal of Accounting, Auditing, and Finance* (Summer 1982): 301–309.

STUDY QUESTIONS

1. Audits are required by the SEC of all publicly traded companies. In the absence of such a requirement, why would an investor desire an audit?
2. An old college chum has moved to Australia and has asked you to provide the seed capital for a fast-food restaurant serving Koala burgers. You live in Dallas, Texas, and operate a gift boutique. He has suggested that the two of you split profits after he receives a 10 percent bonus of net income prior to the profit split. Assuming you agree to invest, do you believe that it will be in your interest to require an audit? Justify your response.
3. Materiality is a concept that pervades the accounting and auditing process.
   A. What is the definition of materiality?
   B. A quantitative definition of materiality is usually determined based as a percentage of some financial statement element— for example, 10 percent of net income or 5 percent of total assets. Given the definition of materiality, what is your idea(s) of percentages based on financial statement elements?
4. An audit is a two-stage investigative process. In the first stage, auditors gather evidence to provide the basis for their opinion. An important procedure in the evidence-gathering stage is the observation of physical inventory. This procedure provides evidence that the inventory exists at the date of financial statement. If an auditor is unable to observe inventory at that date, will this have an effect on the audit report? If so, what effect will it have?
5. Assume the following facts: ABC Corporation has a trend of declining revenues and increasing expenses over several years; there are large loans coming due within the next few months, and cash balances are declining. What type of audit report is the auditor likely to provide?
6. Since auditors are only inspecting a sample of transactions on which to base their audit report, if they are sued by third parties, can they use this as a defense?
7. Should the auditor place more emphasis on fraud detection?
8. What are the benefits of an audit to an auditee? To society?

Chapter 3

Financial Statements and Accounting Conventions

*Banker to prospective borrower: "Now then, we will
need a financial statement from you."
Borrower to banker: "All right, let's see....How's
about 'A fool and his money are soon parted.'"*[1]

*I*n order to understand basic financial statement analysis, the analyst
must first comprehend some basic definitions that relate to the elements of financial statements. These elements have been defined
formally for business enterprises, and they consist of the following:[2]

- . Assets
- . Liabilities
- . Equity
- . Revenues
- . Expenses
- . Gains
- . Losses

Assets are generally known as tangible or intangible properties
owned by an entity. However, this definition does not address the true
nature of assets. *Statement of Financial Accounting Concepts No. 3 (SFAC
3)* has defined assets as "probable future economic benefits obtained or
controlled by a particular entity as a result of past transactions or
events."[3] Readers may be concerned initially by the inclusion of the

---

[1]From the cartoon "The Born Loser," Nacogdoches Daily Sentinel (November 18,
1989: NEA, Inc.).
[2]*SFAC 6* (Stamford, Conn.: FASB, 1985), ix–x.
[3]*SFAC 3* (Stamford, Conn.: FASB, 1980), par. 19.

term *probable* in the definition. However, this term is used in order to convey that business activities are conducted in an environment that is characterized by uncertainty. This idea is directly related to the premise advocated in this book; namely accounting and financial reporting are necessarily imprecise. All assets are consumed eventually and become expenses or the rights represented by the asset expire. However, determining *when* an asset has come into existence and has expired is not always obvious. This will become more clear in Chapter 5, as the discussion of when assets come into existence and expire is expanded.

Liabilities are known generally as obligations or debts that are owed to nonowners of the entity. Namely, liabilities are claims to the assets by nonowners. *SFAC 3* defines liabilities as "probable future sacrifices of economic benefits arising from present obligations of a particular entity to transfer assets or provide services to other entities in the future as a result of past transactions or events."[4] Once again, the reader should take note of the term *probable* in the definition.

Equity is a term used to refer to the net worth of the entity; it represents the claims to the assets by the owners. *SFAC 3* defines equity as "the residual interest in the assets of an entity that remains after deducting its liabilities. In a business enterprise, the equity is the ownership interest."[5] In other words, equity is the residual claim to the assets after nonowner claims have been recognized, and it is often referred to as the *net assets* (i.e., assets minus liabilities).

Revenues represent the gross amounts received from the sale of a product or service. This definition begs the question: When is a "sale" a sale? Initially, it appears to be a simple question to answer. The formal definition promulgated in *SFAC 3* is that "revenues are inflows or other enhancements of assets of an entity or settlements of its liabilities (or a combination of both) during a period from delivering or producing goods, rendering services, or other activities that constitute the entity's ongoing major or central operations."[6] By definition, the recognition of revenue is tied to the recognition of assets. The implications of this interconnection are important, and they are further developed in Chapter 5.

Expenses are the costs associated with generating revenues. *SFAC 3* formally defines expenses as "outflows or other using up of assets or incurrence of liabilities (or a combination of both) during a period from delivering or producing goods, rendering services, or carrying out

---

[4]Ibid., par. 28.
[5]Ibid., par. 43.
[6]Ibid., par. 63.

other activities that constitute the entity's ongoing major or central operations."[7]

Gains and *losses* are essentially the same as revenues and expenses, except that they are the result of activities not associated with the entity's ongoing operations. An example would be the disposal of an automobile by an entity that is not a car dealership. *SFAC 3* defines gains as "increases in equity (net assets) from peripheral or incidental transactions of an entity and from all other transactions and other events or circumstances affecting the entity during a period except those that result from revenues or investments by owners."[8] Losses, then, are decreases in equity for similar reasons.

Having defined the elements that compose financial statements, it is important to understand what is usually included in the term *financial statements*. Financial statements normally are composed of the following:

- . Balance sheet (statement of financial condition or position)
- . Income statement (profit and loss statement)
- . Statement of stockholders'equity (capital statement)
- . Statement of cash flows.

BALANCE SHEET (STATEMENT OF FINANCIAL CONDITION OR POSITION)

A *balance sheet* provides information concerning the financial position (or condition) of the entity at *a point in time*. It is simply a listing of the assets, liabilities, and equity. The balance sheet is an expression of the accounting equation:

$$\text{Assets} = \text{Liabilities} + \text{Stockholders' Equity.}$$

Assets and liabilities can be further divided between current and noncurrent items. Generally, *current assets* are those assets that will be converted into cash, sold, or consumed within one year or during the operating cycle, whichever is longer.[9] Some examples are cash, marketable securities, accounts receivable, inventories, and prepaid expenses.

---

[7]Ibid., par. 65.

[8]Ibid., par. 67.

[9]The operating cycle is defined as the time period between acquisition of inventory until conversion of the inventory to cash. Normally, the operating cycle is less than one year.

Current Assets

Cash is the basic medium of exchange, and it is the measurement basis for recording transactions. While the layperson may think of several types of assets as cash, to be reported on the balance sheet as cash, the asset must be readily available for expenditure without any restrictions. For example, a certificate of deposit maturing in six months is not readily available, nor is it free of contractual restriction. To gain access prior to maturity, the corporation will pay a penalty. Therefore, many companies report cash and *cash equivalents*, which include assets such as short-term certificates of deposit.

Marketable securities are investments in stock or other securities issued by other corporations or investments in securities issued by governmental entities. For an investment to be classified as a marketable security, the nature and intent of the investment must be short-term.[10] That is, the investment is usually made with the intention of absorbing an excess in cash balances required for operations or for some other temporary purpose; there is no intention by the investor company to acquire enough securities to gain control or exercise significant influence on the investee company. These securities are listed on the balance sheet at the lower-of-cost-or-market value.[11]

Accounts receivable are assets that represent customers' promises given at the time of sale to pay cash at a future date (i. e., purchase by customers on credit). Often these assets are referred to as *trade receivables*. Accounts receivable are reflected on the balance sheet at their estimated (or net) realizable value, which is the amount of cash expected to be received ultimately. Usually, there is a difference between the gross amount of receivables and their net realizable value because some customers, unfortunately, do not make good on their promises to pay. The valuation at net realizable value is accomplished through the deduction of an allowance for doubtful accounts, which is an estimate of the total receivables that are uncollectible.[12] The estimated realizable value can be referred to as *net receivables*.

Inventory is an asset bought with the intention of selling that asset to the company's customers or of using it in the manufacture of another

---

[10]Used in this context, the word *short-term* is synonymous with *current*; the asset is expected to be consumed or sold within one year.

[11]There will be additional discussion of this valuation approach in Chapter 5.

[12]Obviously this is an estimate, and *specific* worthless accounts are unknown; otherwise, they would not be a part of gross receivables. The calculation of the estimate, which is based on various factors, is beyond the scope of this discussion.

product to be sold. Manufacturing companies usually report at least three types of inventories on their balance sheets, each reflecting the stage of completion of the product. These types of inventories are raw materials, work-in-process, and finished goods.

Prepaid (or *deferred*) *expenses* are assets that represent rights that have not yet been consumed. A common example is property insurance purchased for a one-year period, on which the premiums have been paid in advance. By paying in advance for insurance protection, the entity has the right to such protection and, therefore, reflects an asset on the balance sheet until the right has expired.

Noncurrent Assets

Sometimes referred to as long-lived assets, *noncurrent assets* are those assets that will not be converted into cash or consumed within one year or during the operating cycle, if longer; that is, benefits are expected to be received from these assets for a period of more than one year. Noncurrent assets usually are classified as property, plant, and equipment; intangible assets; investments; and other assets.

Assets classified as *property, plant, and equipment* are those long-lived assets currently being used to generate revenue or to manufacture a product, and not being held for resale. Although these assets are recorded at their cost, their utility decreases with usage and time. This decreased utility is recognized through depreciation, which must be estimated. The accumulated depreciation, when deducted from the cost, results in a *book value*, which is reported on the balance sheet.
It should be noted that book value and market value are two different concepts. *Book value* is an estimate of the decreased utility of the asset based on original cost. *Market value* is the amount that can be received upon the sale of the asset. It is affected by the general purchasing power of the dollar and specific attributes of the asset.

For example, consider a building purchased in downtown Manhattan in 1970 for $1 million. Because of inflation, it may take $2 million in today's dollars to acquire the same building. Assuming the building is in a desirable location, the market value of the building may have increased beyond $2 million. Assuming the building had an estimated life in 1970 of 40 years, the book value as of 1990 might be approximately $500,000 (i.e. original cost less half of the original cost, which represents the decreased utility through 20 years usage). Obviously, there can be a significant difference between book value and market value.

Investments are assets that are purchased with the intention of retaining the investment for more than one year and that are not currently being used to generate revenue or manufacture a product. Equity securities of corporations are often purchased with the intention of gaining control or exercising significant influence over the issuing corporation.[13] Note the distinction between the assets that are classified as marketable securities (discussed earlier) and the assets that are classified as investments; the difference lies in their basic natures and in the intentions behind the purchases of the assets.

Additionally, there are often other assets that are classified as investments that are not securities. For example, an entity may acquire a tract of undeveloped land that is properly classified as an investment. This classification is proper whether the purpose of the acquisition is to speculate or to use the land for future expansion. The key is whether the asset is idle or is actively being used to generate revenues.

Intangible assets are assets that do not have a physical existence, yet impart rights of ownership. Some examples of intangible assets include patents, copyrights, trademarks and goodwill.[14] Most intangible assets have a legal life that can be different from their useful life. For example, a patent has a legal life of 17 years, but its useful life is often shorter due to expected future technological advances that make the patent obsolete. The utility of an intangible asset decreases with time. This decrease, which is recognized in the accounting records, is referred to as *amortization*. On the balance sheet, intangible assets are reported at their cost net of accumulated amortization. Amortization is the same concept as depreciation, but amortization relates to the decline in service utility of intangible assets.

Other assets are long-lived assets that cannot be categorized in the foregoing classifications. Some examples of other assets include long-

---

[13]There are two major types of securities that corporations issue; namely, debt and equity. Equity securities (stock) denote an ownership interest in the issuing corporation and often provide the holder of the securities with voting rights in electing the board of directors. The board of directors, in turn, establishes overall policies, hires, and directs the management of the corporation. Therefore, the greater the number of equity securities owned, the greater the degree of influence through voting rights. Debt securities (bonds) do not provide ownership interest, but evidence an obligation of the issuing corporation to an outside party. The terms of repayment of principal and payment of interest by the corporation are contained in the debt instrument.

[14]Goodwill is a special type of intangible asset that does not have a legal life. An explanation is provided in Chapter 6.

term prepaid expenses or types of assets that arise under certain circumstances when there is a difference between taxable income and financial income.

Current Liabilities

Generally, *current liabilities* are those liabilities that are due within one year or that are satisfied with a payment from current assets. Examples include accounts payable, notes payable, and accrued liabilities.

Accounts payable, sometimes referred to as *trade payables*, are debts owed to suppliers who supply services, goods, or inventory used in daily operations. Accounts payable are differentiated from *notes payable* because notes payable are evidenced by written promissory notes, which usually state an interest rate on the debt. *Accrued liabilities*, or other current liabilities, include such items as amounts owed but not yet paid, to employees for work performed, as well as amounts owed to local, state, and federal governments for various taxes. When prepayment has been received from a customer and it has not yet been earned, as with prepaid magazine subscriptions, the company recognizes a *deferred revenue*. Any portion of the deferred revenue that will not be earned within the year is classified as noncurrent.

Noncurrent Liabilities

Noncurrent liabilities include all other amounts owed that are not classified as current liabilities; that is, the debts will not mature until at least one year from the balance sheet date. These can include the same types of liabilities already discussed that are classified as current because of the maturity date. A common type of noncurrent liability is *bonds payable*. Bonds are debt securities issued by a corporation. However, any portion of noncurrent (or long-term) debt that is coming due within the coming year is classified as current.

The proper classification of assets and liabilities is critical for financial statement analysis. This will become quite evident in Chapter 4, as the classification of assets and liabilities directly impacts the assessment of liquidity of the company. *Liquidity* is a relative term that refers to an entity's ability to meet current debts as they come due, and it is important to an analyst. One common measure of liquidity is the comparison of current assets to current liabilities. Liquidity increases as current assets increase relative to current liabilities.

Because an analyst does not have access to an entity's records, he or she must rely on the independent auditor's ability and integrity to ensure proper classification of assets and liabilities by management. In some instances, the auditor may come under pressure by the entity's management to favor management's interpretation of the appropriate classification of assets or liabilities in order to present a favorable picture of the company's liquidity. It is imperative that the auditor remain independent and objective in determining whether or not management's classification results in a fair picture of liquidity. Otherwise, the auditor is not fulfilling the social need that the SEC has recognized as so important.

Initially, it may appear that determining the classification as either current or noncurrent is a simple, straightforward task. However, it is important that the economic consequences of an asset or a liability are reflected by the classification because this affects the analysis. One example of interpretive problems associated with classification is short-term debt that is expected to be refinanced with the issuance of long-term debt. Assume that a debt issue is maturing on June 1, 1993, and that the financial statements for the year ended December 31, 1992, are being prepared. Ordinarily, this debt issue would be classified as short-term because the maturity date is within 12 months from the balance sheet date. However, if the maturing debt issue is to be paid with the proceeds of the sale of other debt securities that are to be classified as long term, and if the intention is appropriately supported by the ability to accomplish this refinancing, the debt maturing on June 1 may be classified as long-term on the balance sheet as of December 31, 1992. This interpretation is premised on the assumption that the maturing debt is essentially being rolled over into long-term debt.[15] If the debt coming due can be classified as long-term rather than as short-term, there is a beneficial effect on liquidity measures of the entity. This is because a reclassification from short term to long term will increase liquidity measures, since current assets remain unchanged.

Before proceeding to other financial statement elements, note a symmetry between some assets and liabilities of two entities. For example, the accounting records of Company A, which is a supplier to Company B, will reflect an asset (account receivable) for amounts sold to its customer, Company B. Conversely, the accounting records of Company B will reflect a liability (account payable) for the amounts owed to its supplier, Company A.

---

[15]*FASB Interpretation No. 8* (Stamford, Conn.: FASB, 1976), par. 9–11.

Equity — Contributed Capital

As noted earlier, *equity* is a concept that refers to ownership interest in an entity. There are various forms that entities can take: sole proprietorships, partnerships, and corporations. For our purposes, the corporate ownership form will be assumed. Ownership in a corporation is evidenced by a stock certificate, which is exchanged by the corporation for cash or other assets of the investor.[16] The owner of the stock certificate, or the stockholder, has certain rights that enable the that person to influence the operations of the corporation. (See Footnote 13.)

The equity portion of a corporation's balance sheet is usually entitled Stockholders' Equity, or some similar title, and it is not divided between current and noncurrent items. All the items in this section of the balance sheet are considered to be noncurrent. The stockholders' equity section of the balance sheet is generally divided into the following components: *capital stock* (legal capital or contributed capital), *additional paid-in capital* (sometimes called other contributed capital) and *retained earnings*. An understanding of the items listed in this portion of the balance sheet requires a basic understanding of the sale of stock certificates. Many states require corporations to issue stock that has a *par value*, which merely indicates the amount of *legal capital* and has no necessary correlation to market value. Legal capital is a minimum amount of capital that state law mandates a corporation to maintain for the protection of creditors. Other states allow for the issue of no-par stock; the sales price of no-par stock can represent the amount of legal capital. Because market value (the sales price) is usually higher than par value, the portion of the sales price that represents the par value is designated as legal capital. The excess of sales price over par value becomes designated as other contributed capital (additional paid-in capital, or paid-in capital in excess of par).[17]

Different types of stock certificates can be issued by corporations. Those certificates that allow the holder to vote at stockholders' meetings and to exercise a degree of influence over corporate operations are

---

[16]Entities are incorporated under laws of the state in which the incorporation takes place. These laws are relatively uniform, but further discussion is beyond the scope of this discussion. However, the reader should note that corporations may also be subject to SEC rules and regulations, which are federal requirements.

[17]There are other ways to impact these components, but these transactions are beyond the discussion at this point.

called *common stock*. Conceivably, various classes of common stock with different rights and privileges can be issued; thus, not all common stock has voting rights.

Another type of stock is called preferred stock. Preferred stock gives the holder preferences as to dividends, as well as other preferential rights. However, preferred stockholders do not have voting rights. This raises questions about whether preferred stock actually exhibits equity characteristics, since it provides no voting rights. Regardless, preferred stock generally is included in the stockholders' equity section of the balance sheet.

Equity — Earned Capital

Retained earnings (or earned capital) is the third component of stockholders' equity. The amount reflected as retained earnings may give an unknowing reader the impression that there is a correlation between cash retained and retained earnings. Retained earnings is defined as total net income less dividends and net losses since the date of incorporation.[18] *Net income* is a positive number defined as revenues plus gains and less expenses and losses. *Net loss* is calculated in the same manner, except the resulting number is negative. Almost all *dividends* consist of two types: cash or stock. Stock dividends have no impact on total equity and will be discussed later. Cash dividends are payments of cash to stockholders, and they reduce assets because cash is being paid by the corporation. Since assets are reduced through payment of cash to owners, equity is also reduced because it represents the owners' claims to the assets.

Cash and retained earnings do not correlate because net income is defined on an *accrual basis,* as opposed to a *cash basis.* Namely, revenue is recognized when earned for financial accounting purposes, rather than when cash is received. Also, expenses are recognized when incurred, rather than when cash is disbursed. For example, Company A may sell a product or service to Company B; and as part of the sales terms, Company B promises to pay cash to Company A at a future date. As discussed earlier, this transaction produces an asset (account receivable) for Company A. Company A recognizes revenue at this time because the concept of accrual accounting considers and records the economic consequences of the transaction once they are known or

---

[18]There are other transactions that can affect retained earnings that are beyond the discussion at this point.

estimable, rather than focusing on the activity of actual cash payment or receipt. The payment or receipt of cash is a result of the original underlying transaction. Of course, accrual accounting and cash accounting will provide the same results when the original underlying transaction and the payment or receipt of cash occur simultaneously.

Additionally, retained earnings and cash retained are not equal because many cash expenditures or receipts do not impact net income directly. For example, when cash is received from loans or from the issuance of securities, the reason for receipt of the cash does not meet the definition of revenue and, therefore, does not affect net income, but it does affect cash.

INCOME STATEMENT
(PROFIT AND LOSS STATEMENT)

An income statement is a listing of total revenue and gains, less total expenses and losses recognized over a given period of time not to exceed 12 months. After each 12 month period, a new period for calculating net income commences. A balance sheet, prepared as of a specific point in time, is analogous to a photograph of the financial condition of an entity. An income statement, prepared for a period of time, can be related to a motion picture in terms of providing information over time.[19] These two financial statements provide complementary information.

Companies that sell or manufacture a product prepare a more complicated income statement because a special type of expense must be calculated. This expense, entitled *cost of goods sold* or *cost of product sold*, is exactly that—the cost of the inventory that has been sold and whose sales revenue is recognized in the current income statement. The difference between the sales price and the cost of goods sold is the *gross profit* (sometimes referred to as the *gross margin*). Selling, administrative, and other expenses are then subtracted from gross profit to calculate net income.

An income statement links or explains certain changes in balance-sheet items. This linking process is called *articulation*. Net income (or net loss), which results largely from operations of the business, is added to or subtracted from equity, specifically from retained earnings. Retained earnings is the balance-sheet item that links the results

---

[19]*SFAC 3* (Stamford, Conn.: FASB, 1980), par. 14.

of operations (net income or net loss) to the balance sheet. In other words, articulation between the two financial statements is accomplished through retained earnings.[20] It should be remembered that equity represents the residual interests, or claims to the assets, of the owners. Therefore, a business enterprise operating at a profit (net income) will increase net assets (assets minus liabilities). This increase is reflected in retained earnings, a component of stockholders' equity. In other words, net income represents the *change* in equity over time as a result of business operations.

Therefore, the income statement will indicate the *rate* of change in the net assets, as well as the *direction* for a period of time, whereas the balance sheet indicates the *amount* of net assets (equity) at a specific point in time. Obviously, financial statement users should know not only the rate of change in net assets, but also the absolute amount. The relationship and articulation of the balance sheet and income statement can be related to a bathtub filling with water.[21] The water level in the tub, measured at a point in time, represents the amount of net assets. The water level (net assets) will increase or decrease depending on the rate that water flows in through the faucet as compared to the rate it flows out through the drain. The water flowing in through the faucet represents revenues, and the water flowing out through the drain represents expenses. Thus, the rate of increase or decrease represents net income, and, as with any rate, it can only be measured over a period of time.

STATEMENT OF STOCKHOLDERS' EQUITY (CAPITAL STATEMENT)[22]

A *statement of stockholders' equity* reflects all changes that have occurred in equity for a period of time. As discussed earlier, the basic items that will change equity are net income, sale of stock by the corporation (investment by owners), and net loss or cash dividends (payments to owners). The first two items cause an increase in equity, and the last two items cause a decrease in equity.

---

[20]A more in-depth discussion of articulation is contained in Chapter 4.

[21] M. H. Granoff, *Accounting for Managers and Investors* (Englewood Cliffs, NJ: Prentice-Hall, 1983), 28–30.

[22]The term *capital* has many different connotations. It is sometimes used in particular accounting or business contexts to represent the concept of equity or ownership interest. In other contexts, it is used to represent cash or equipment.

It is important for a financial statement user to understand all the reasons why net assets (equity) changed during a particular period. This information will provide deeper insight into the reasons for the rate and direction of changes and for the absolute amount of equity. In this way, the analyst is provided with a clearer picture of the overall financial situation of the company.

For example, if a company has experienced a series of net losses, equity will decrease. However, a company may offset losses by sale of stock that provides inflows of assets to maintain equity. If this is the case, the analyst has information that, at least in the past, the company has been able to raise funds and maintain equity despite financial losses. This information may be quite helpful to the analyst in his or her decision-making process.

STATEMENT OF CASH FLOWS

As discussed earlier, the calculation of net income is based on accrual accounting concepts. These concepts recognize that it is the economic substance of a transaction that determines the timing of accounting recognition rather than the activity of receipt or payment of cash. Therefore, financial statements are necessarily defined and constrained by accrual accounting concepts.

However, while accrual accounting concepts are considered theoretically superior in measuring economic consequences, there may be only a slight correlation between cash flows and equity changes. Namely, while the results of operations (net income) may be quite good when calculated on an accrual basis, actual cash flows could be negative. For example, the Charter Company, a *Fortune* 100 company in 1983, reported earnings in excess of $50 million in 1983. However, the company filed for bankruptcy soon after the issuance of its 1983 financial statements. An analysis of cash flows for 1983 reveals the company had a *negative* cash flow from operations (i. e., the amount of cash outflow exceeded the amount of cash generated through net income) of approximately $90 million for the same period.[23] The statement of cash flows was not a required part of the financial statements in 1983. In 1984, the Charter Company filed for bankruptcy. Some financial statement users could have been misled about the future prospects of the Charter Company in this instance because no cash flow statement was available.

---

[23]R. Kochanek and C. Norgaard. "Analyzing the Components of Operating Cash Flow: The Charter Company," *Accounting Horizons*, (March 1988): 58–66.

The importance of cash flows is recognized as an overriding concern. Net income is an important measure of performance, but it may provide little information concerning the resources required to maintain or increase the present level of performance.

Consequently, the *statement of cash flows* is considered an important component of financial statements. Furthermore, the insight provided by knowledge of cash flows can be enhanced if cash flows are segregated by origin. Therefore, the statement of cash flows reflects net cash flows from three origins: operations, financing, and investing activities.

Cash flows from operations represent the net cash flow as a result of operations, which essentially converts accrual accounting net income (or net loss) to a cash basis. *Net cash flows from investing activities* provides information from such things as purchase and sale of assets. *Net cash flows from financing activities* provides information on net cash proceeds from the sale and, perhaps, repurchase of the entity's own securities.

Through segregating cash flows by origin, an analyst is permitted additional insight. For example, cash balances may have increased during the year, but the increase may not be due to cash generated through net income. In fact, the Charter Company example indicates that the opposite is true. Assume that the increase is a result of the sale of assets (investing activities). While the increase in cash is a positive factor, the sale of assets may reduce the entity's ability to generate additional revenue in the future and may even place the long-term future of the entity in jeopardy. Therefore, an analyst should be aware of *why* cash balances changed.

The statement of cash flows should provide the last overall key to interpretation of the financial situation of an entity. The information provided by one financial statement alone is not sufficient for most decisions. However, the information provided by the *set* of financial statements, which contains all four statements, should provide the analyst with sufficient information, especially when considered in light of the other factors. That is, financial statements are only one source of information needed for an informed decision. For example, an analyst should consider general economic conditions, industry economic conditions, developments that have occurred since the balance-sheet date, political events, and so forth. The integration of these factors into the analytical process is discussed later.

ACCOUNTING CONVENTIONS AND ASSUMPTIONS

Having defined and identified what constitutes financial statements and their elements, it is important to understand the underlying bases for measuring and valuing each financial statement element. The measurement-and-valuation process is dependent on the accounting method employed, which, in turn, is dependent on the conventions and assumptions adopted by the accounting profession. Therefore, to fully understand financial statements, it is necessary to understand the fundamental bases on which they are prepared.[24]

Financial statements purport to represent the economic consequences of results of the operations and the financial position of a specific entity. In this book, the entity is assumed to be a corporate entity, although other forms of ownership are possible. A corporation and its owners (stockholders) are separate legal and accounting entities and are accounted for as such. In other words, transactions between a stockholder (one entity) and a corporation (a separate entity) are recorded separately by each. Furthermore, transactions between the corporation and a nonstockholder entity are not recorded by stockholders.

In order to make financial statements meaningful and to determine responsibility for results of operations and financial condition, it is necessary to account for economic activities as being associated with specific and separate entities. However, this assumption can often be modified to capture the economic consequences of transactions and to assign responsibility for results. For example, it is possible for Corporation A to acquire stock in Corporation B, which enables Corporation A, as an owner, to influence the policies of Corporation B. Therefore, one or more corporations, all separate legal and accounting entities, can come under the effective control of one entity. For financial reporting purposes, it may be more meaningful to prepare one set of financial statements for the group of companies, as the group is essentially one *economic* entity composed of several legal and accounting entities. Such a situation results in *consolidated* financial statements.

---

[24]The implications and modifications of these assumptions are discussed in greater detail in Chapter 5. At this point the reader is provided with an elemental understanding of these assumptions so that a basic analysis of financial statements can be initiated.

An assumption that affects the measurement of financial statement elements is that all transactions should be initially recorded in terms of *historical cost*, or the exchange price. For instance, if the contract price of a building bought for use by the entity is $500,000, the accounting records reflect that amount as the appropriate measure regardless of current or subsequent market value.[25] Therefore, as previously discussed, the valuation for accounting purposes may not coincide with market value. The justification for using historical cost is that it is objective and verifiable.

Closely tied to the assumption of historical cost is the idea that the dollar is the appropriate *measurement unit*. This is a logical assumption. However, if the economy is experiencing inflation, the purchasing power of the dollar changes over time. This can cause interpretive problems because assets will be acquired and liabilities incurred at different times when the measurement unit has changed in value. The resulting measurement differences are not obvious to a financial statement user. Typically, no adjustments are made in the accounting records for these measurement differences.

Another important accounting convention is the preparation of financial statements at predefined intervals. This provides financial-statement analysts with relatively current information about operations and financial condition and enables the analyst to make informed decisions. These predefined reporting intervals normally do not exceed a 12-month period; namely, the *fiscal year*. The fiscal, or accounting, year may begin and end at any point in the calendar year. For example, a fiscal year might begin on July 1, 1992 and end on June 30, 1993.

Business transactions are often characterized by a great degree of uncertainty. This uncertainty, coupled with the convention of reporting results of operations for a predefined interval, creates additional measurement problems. For example, suppose, that sales have been made to customers who have promised to pay the seller cash at a future date. Further suppose past experience has indicated that, despite credit-screening practices, there are always some customers who do not ultimately pay. Which sales will actually be converted to cash will not be known until a future date. Because financial statements must be prepared at the end of a predefined time interval, some method must be established for estimating the value of the "good" sales and the corresponding "good" promises to pay for the sales.

---

[25]Historical cost is adjusted for depreciation, but the depreciation is based on original cost.

The above description is only one example of when estimation is required. Several other examples will be discussed in Chapter 5. Estimation techniques used to value financial statement elements are also required so that revenues and expenses can be recognized in the appropriate time interval. The *matching* concept is incorporated into the accounting model for the purpose of linking revenues with the associated expenses that were incurred in an effort to generate the revenues. Because net income is defined as revenue less expenses, net income will be distorted if the expenses incurred in generating revenues are not matched with the time interval in which the revenues were generated.

Another assumption used in preparing financial statements is the *going-concern* assumption. Financial statements are prepared on the premise that business entities will continue in existence for an indefinite period. This is one reason why assets and liabilities are classified as current and noncurrent. If there is evidence that the entity will not continue as a going concern (e.g., because of bankruptcy proceedings), there is no need to classify assets and liabilities as noncurrent, since they are expected to be converted within the near future to satisfy claims of creditors. Furthermore, it is appropriate in these circumstances to value assets at their *liquidation* value, rather than at their historical cost. Liquidation value also may be different from market value in these circumstances because potential buyers are aware of the desperate cash needs of an entity in bankruptcy.

Full disclosure is another accounting convention. The numbers reflecting the measurement of assets, liabilities, revenues, and expenses often do not provide enough information to allow users to make informed decisions. Therefore, narrative and additional numerical disclosures, sometimes called *footnotes* to the financial statements, are included as an integral part of the financial statements. These disclosures reveal information to users that provides additional insight into the meaning of the numbers reflecting asset measurement and so forth. Without these disclosures, financial statements can be misleading. Hence, the auditor is responsible for judging the adequacy and fairness of the footnote disclosures.

A final convention used in preparing financial statements is *conservatism*. The accounting profession has adopted the attitude of applying the most conservative of interpretations to economic events when there is more than one possible interpretation. The more conservative interpretation is the one that results in the lowest recorded values for assets and revenues and/or the highest recorded values for liabilities and expenses. It is believed that this kind of interpretation results in a higher quality of financial reporting. However, conservatism should not be interpreted as a deliberate understatement of assets and revenues.

> Conservatism is a prudent reaction to uncertainty to try to ensure that uncertainties and risks inherent in business situations are adequately considered. Thus, if two estimates of amounts to be received or paid in the future are about equally likely, conservatism dictates using the less optimistic estimate....[26]

SUMMARY

The term *financial statement* actually incorporates at least four different statements. A balance sheet provides information on the financial condition of an entity as of a point in time. It is a listing of assets, liabilities, and stockholders' equity. The income statement is a listing of total revenues, less expenses over a period of time and it presents net income or net loss, which are measures of performance. Net income increases and net loss decreases the stockholders' equity, or claim to assets. Retained earnings, a component of stockholders' equity, links the balance sheet and the income statement.

Certain accounting conventions and assumptions are used in recording transactions and measuring financial statement elements. They help to provide general guidance in establishing perspectives when interpretation of economic events are made. The result is to establish a more uniform perspective used by all accountants, which enhances comparability of different companies' financial statements since they are prepared by different accountants. However, the use of these conventions and assumptions builds in limitations to financial statements.

The statement of stockholders' equity and the statement of cash flows completes the set of financial statements. The statement of stockholders' equity reflects all changes that have occurred in the components of stockholders' equity over a period of time. The statement of cash flows enables an analyst to determine the reasons for changes in cash balances. All four financial statements are considered important to achieve the necessary insight needed for analysis of an entity.

---

[26]*SFAC 2* (Stamford, Conn.: FASB, 1980), par. 95.

STUDY QUESTIONS

1. What is the difference between a revenue and a gain? An expense and a loss?
2. A U.S. dollar is the unit of measurement employed in preparing financial statements. From an analyst's viewpoint, what problems are created by this?
3. Requiring annual financial statements seems to create problems of measurement and of deciding when revenue or expense should be recognized. Why do you suppose *annual* financial statements are required?
4. A pencil sharpener is acquired for use in a business. Consider the definitions of elements of financial statements. A pencil sharpener should fall into what category?
5. A company that manufacturers plastic toys is gearing up for the production of toys for the Christmas season. Several ingredients used in making plastic come from petroleum. Because of Middle East tensions, the price of these ingredients has increased, and the president of the company fears that supplies of the ingredients may decrease and that the price may increase even further. Accordingly, the company enters into a fixed-price contract with its supplier for a firm commitment to acquire 5 tons at $2.50 per pound. Subsequent to fiscal-year end, the market price of the ingredients decreases to $1.50 per pound. What implications does this commitment have for the financial statements?
6. What is legal capital, and why is it important?
7. Are the four financial statements described related, or unrelated?

Chapter 4

Financial Statement Analysis — The Basics

All things are numbers.[1]

As noted in Chapter 1, financial statement analysis is more of an art form than a routine technical series of calculations. Nevertheless, the beginning point in financial statement analysis is the application of a series of standard calculations. Therefore, this chapter's objective is to familiarize the reader with the purely quantitative aspects of analysis. The remainder of the book is devoted to cautioning the reader that the results derived from the standard approach must be qualified, depending on a multitude of factors.

Ratios and percentages are used in financial analysis because they enable the analyst to normalize financial characteristics of companies. Absolute measures may have little or no meaning when taken by themselves. For example, assume that Company A and Company B are in the same industry and that they report net income of $1 billion and $1 million, respectively. In absolute terms, Company A is more profitable. However, if Company A maintains $10 billion in total assets and Company B maintains $2 million, the reader may draw the conclusion that Company B is more profitable in a relative sense.

Therefore financial analysis is a relative, not an absolute, concept. The use of ratios and percentages places financial statement amounts in the appropriate context by focusing attention on relationships between financial statement items. The purpose is to normalize financial characteristics so that companies can be compared.

---

[1]Attributed to Pythagoras.

COMMON-SIZE ANALYSIS AND TRENDS

Common-size analysis is a technique that enables an analyst to determine the component makeup of a company's balance sheet and income statement in relation to a critical component. When this technique is used in conjunction with the balance sheet, all balance sheet items usually are represented as a *percentage of total assets*. When used in conjunction with the income statement, all items usually are represented as a *percentage of net sales or revenues*.[2] This type of analysis can give important clues about financial condition and operations. For example, it might be believed that it is in a company's best interest to maintain a high percentage of total assets in cash, inventory, or receivables, since such a strategy increases liquidity. However, the real question is, What is the appropriate percentage to maintain? Too high a proportion in cash can indicate an inadequate deployment of cash. Too high a proportion in inventory can indicate obsolete inventory. Too high a proportion in receivables may indicate inappropriate credit policies. The ultimate decision concerning the appropriate percentages of asset make-up depends on individual judgment and on the specific circumstances of an entity and its industry.

The financial statements for RJR Nabisco (RJR) for the fiscal year ended December 31, 1987 are reproduced in the appendix. The basic analysis discussed in this chapter is exemplified by using the financial statements for RJR. A common-size balance sheet (as a percentage of total assets) in Figure 4-1 and income statement (as a percentage of net sales) in Figure 4-2 are presented for December 31, 1987.

Common-size analysis can be either vertical or horizontal. The preceding discussion and example concerned *vertical* common-size analysis because income statement or balance sheet components are expressed as percentages of another critical component that is expressed at 100 percent on the same financial statement. *Horizontal* common-size analysis develops trends of balance sheet or income statement components over time. A particular year is considered the base year, and the absolute amount of any component for that year is expressed as 100 percent. Subsequent years are related to the base year in terms of base-year percentages. In other words, if, in the year subsequent to the base year, sales rise 5 percent, sales in the subsequent year will be expressed as 105 percent. In this manner, trends can be discerned.

---

[2]Net sales are gross (total) sales less sales returns and allowances. Sales returns are goods that have been sold to and then returned by the customer, and allowances are sales prices that have been reduced because the customer was dissatisfied. Net sales should not be confused with net income.

FIGURE 4-1

VERTICAL COMMON-SIZE BALANCE SHEET

Current Assets:		
Cash and investments	6.5 %	
Receivables	10.3	
Inventories	15.9	
Prepaid expenses	2.0	
Total current assets		34.7 %
Long-Term Assets:		
Property, plant, and equipment (net)	34.7	
Goodwill	26.8	
Other	3.8	
Total long-term assets		65.3
Total Assets		100.0
Liabilities and Stockholders' Equity		
Current Liabilities:		
Notes	2.6	
Accounts payable	18.9	
Current maturities, long-term debt	1.0	
Taxes	2.0	
Total Current Liabilities		24.5
Long-Term Liabilities:		
Long-term debt	23.0	
Other	10.7	
Deferred income taxes	5.0	
Total long-term liabilities		38.7
Redeemable preferred stock		1.0
Common Stockholders' Equity:		
Common stock	1.5	
Paid in capital	1.8	
Retained earnings	32.9	
Other[3]	0.4	
Total common stockholders' equity		35.8
Total Liabilities & Stockholders' Equity		100.0

---

[3]Note that the RJR balance sheet in the appendix indicates a negative amount for "treasury stock." Treasury stock refers to stock of the issuing corporation (RJR in this instance) that has been reacquired. This is often done in order to have stock on hand to issue to employees under stock option agreements. Treasury stock is not considered outstanding; therefore, the acquisition of treasury stock will have a favorable impact on earnings per share. Treasury stock is discussed later in this chapter.

Also included in the percentage for "Other" is the cumulative translation adjustment. This adjustment to stockholder's equity is a result of value changes in the dollar relative to other currencies. RJR is a multinational company that often enters into transactions denominated in foreign currencies. Because of exchange rate changes subsequent to the initiation of the transaction, RJR experiences gains or losses when the results of the transaction are translated into dollars. Calculation of the translation adjustment is complicated and beyond the scope of this discussion. As of December 31, 1987, RJR reports net gains of $86 million due to translation adjustments. See Chapter 10 for further discussion of this topic.

FIGURE 4-2

VERTICAL COMMON-SIZE INCOME STATEMENT

Net sales		100.0 %
Deductions:		
Cost of product sold	(52.1)	
Selling, advertising, general and admin.	(31.7)	
Restructuring	(1.6)	(85.4)
Operating income		14.6
Interest		(3.1)
Income before provision for income taxes		11.5
Provision for income taxes		(4.7)
Income from continuing operations		6.8
Loss from discontinued operations	0.0	
Gain from sale of discontinued operations	1.4	1.4
Income before extraordinary items		8.2
Extraordinary loss		(.5)
Net income		7.7

FIGURE 4-3

HORIZONTAL COMMON-SIZE BALANCE SHEET (1986 AS BASE YEAR)

	1987	*1986*
Total Current Assets	108	100
Total Assets	101	100
Total Current Liabilities	101	100
Total Common Stockholders' Equity	114	100

FIGURE 4-4

HORIZONTAL COMMON-SIZE INCOME STATEMENT (1986 AS BASE YEAR)

	1987	*1986*	*1985*
Net Sales	104	100	77
Operating Income	98	100	83
Income before Taxes	102	100	93
Net Income	114	100	94

In the interest of brevity, only major classifications of items are used (from the RJR financial statements) to illustrate horizontal analysis. The analyst will benefit from a more detailed approach that discloses trends in more detailed components.

In summary, common-size analysis reduces absolute numbers to percentages of components in the financial statements at one point in time or to percentages of change in components over time. Both types of analysis are needed to provide insight into the company's current status and direction and the rate of change of important components. Therefore, the analyst obtains an idea of the interactive relationships of the financial statements' component parts. Moreover, since these relationships have been normalized through percentages, one company can be evaluated *vis-a-vis* another.

RATIO ANALYSIS

Financial statements are analyzed with a primary purpose in mind. Ordinarily the primary purpose of the analysis is related to the type of financial statement user and his or her objectives. For example, a bank lending officer considering a six-month loan to a company is concerned primarily with the company's ability to meet near-term obligations, or liquidity. In contrast, an institutional investor interested in acquiring a company's debt securities (bonds) that will mature in 20 years has a different focus in the analytical process—namely, the company's ability to pay its long-term debts. A potential investor considering an investment in equity securities (common stock) may have an even different focus during the analytical process.[4]

Consequently, the remainder of this chapter is divided into ratio groups with a particular focus. These groups represent liquidity, ability to pay long-term debts, profitability, and equity-investor analysis. However, simply because an analyst has one main objective does not imply that he or she has considered only one ratio group during the analytical process.

Essentially, the analyst is attempting to gain as much insight as possible into the entity undergoing analysis. Because of the interrelationships and articulation of the financial statements, it is important to consider more than one ratio within a group, or even more than one group of financial ratios. The insight gained by investigating more than one group of ratios is similar to viewing an object that appears to be a square in two dimensions. When a third dimension is added, the square may actually be a cube. Therefore, additional ratio groups

---

[4]SFAC 1, par. three, established that financial statements should be prepared for use by a variety of different user groups and that they are considered "general purpose" financial statements.

provide additional perspectives, thereby increasing the analyst's probability of arriving at a more correct conclusion.

Furthermore, the analytical ratios developed should not be taken completely at face value. Additional considerations are discussed in Chapter 6. At this point, it is sufficient to understand that the analyst looks at changes in ratios from year to year and then investigates the reasons for changes in the ratios.

Each of the ratios in the following sections is illustrated by using data from the December 31, 1987, financial statements for RJR. The numbers in brackets are indexed to items from the RJR financial statements that are presented in the appendix to this chapter. The result of each calculation is provided in parentheses to the right of the formula for calculating the ratio.

Liquidity Ratios

Liquidity refers to the entity's ability to meet short-term debts as they come due. The ratios in this section are designed to provide the analyst with information to accomplish this objective. Short-term debts can be satisfied with cash or through the conversion of assets to cash and subsequent payment of the obligation. Generally, current assets are more easily converted into cash than are noncurrent assets. In fact, the sale of long-term assets can disrupt the achievement of a company's long range goals and objectives. For this reason, liquidity ratios focus on the relationship among current assets, current liabilities, and revenues.

Current and Quick Ratios. These ratios are commonly applied to obtain a relative measure of the firm's liquidity by comparing current assets (or a group of current assets) to current liabilities. Their calculation is as follows:

$$\text{Current Ratio} \; = \; \frac{\text{Current Assets} \quad [5]}{\text{Current Liabilities} \quad [14]} \qquad (1.4)$$

$$\text{Quick Ratio} \; = \; \frac{\begin{array}{c}\text{Cash and Short - Term Marketable Securities}\\ \text{+ Net Accounts Receivable} \quad [1] + [2]^*\end{array}}{\text{Current Liabilities} \quad [14]} \qquad (0.70)$$

---

*Index number [2] refers to net accounts receivable in the amount of 1745 for 1987. Index number [2a] refers to the allowance for accounts receivable (61 for 1987). Therefore, gross receivables is equal to net receivables plus the allowance.

By excluding inventories that take longer to convert to cash than other current assets, the quick ratio provides a more conservative view of liquidity.

There is no standard number that an analyst should look for in this calculation; it should depend on the industry and the results of other analyses. All things equal, a higher number is indicative of greater liquidity. However, is the maintenance of higher liquidity sacrificing profitability by the improper deployment of cash or other current assets? The answer depends on the analyst's judgment, after considering other factors.

Cash Ratio. The cash ratio is a very conservative measure of liquidity in order to indicate immediate liquidity problems. It is defined as follows:

$$\frac{\text{Cash and Short – Term Marketable Securities} \quad [1]}{\text{Current Liabilities} \quad [14]} \qquad (0.26)$$

The resulting number usually is below 1.0 because most companies will not retain high cash balances; to do so would be inefficient. However, the appropriate ratio is once again a matter of judgment after considering all other factors.

Working Capital. Working capital is closely related to the current ratio, but it is an absolute number. It is defined as follows:

$$\text{Current Assets} \quad [5] – \text{Current Liabilities} \quad [14] \qquad (1717)$$

The ability to maintain or increase the level of current operations is directly dependent on the amount of working capital. This is because current and near-term operations use current assets and require the payment of current liabilities. Ordinarily, the larger the company, the greater the demand for working capital in absolute terms. When comparing companies of different sizes, absolute amounts can be misleading. Therefore, working capital is generally used in conjunction with the current ratio.

Both the trend in working capital changes from year to year and the change in components of working capital must be considered. For example, if working capital is increasing, but cash balances are decreasing and inventories are increasing, then the reason for this should be investigated. Consider the following:

	Year 2	Year 1
Cash	$1,000	$5,000
Accounts receivable	10,000	7,000
Inventory	15,000	10,000
Total current assets	26,000	22,000
Current liabilities	<10,000>	<10,000>
Working capital	$16,000	$12,000

The Year 2 increase in working capital appears to be favorable. However, note that the composition of working capital has changed. The decrease in cash and increase in less liquid assets may indicate collection problems with customers and/or inefficient inventory management or obsolete inventory. These possibilities should direct the analyst's efforts toward investigating the reason for these changes.

Cash Flow. Cash flow is an important measure for all user groups. With regard to liquidity, the important measure is cash flow divided by current liabilities. In applying this ratio, the analyst must be careful to segregate cash flows into the categories provided by the statement of cash flow[5]. The most conservative view is to use cash flows from operations, probably the most constant amount available. (Recall the discussion of origins of cash flows from Chapter 3.) The analyst should remember that cash flows from financing and investing activities reported on the statement of cash flows can vary. Therefore, use caution to prevent the analysis of the statement of cash flows in any one year from adversely influencing the analyst's conclusions.

$$\frac{\text{Cash Flow from Operations} \quad [43]}{\text{Current Liabilities} \quad [14]} \qquad (0.43)$$

---

[5]The statement of cash flows was not a required part of the financial statements until 1988. Prior to this date, the statement of changes in financial position was required. Note that the 1987 financial statements of RJR include the Statement of Changes in Financial Position on p. 54 of the financial statements that is reproduced on page 86 of the appendix.

In 1988, RJR was bought by a private investment group. Hence, annual reports are no longer required to be made public. However, SEC requirements mandate that RJR file certain forms, which are public documents. Included in the appendix are the Statements of Cash Flows from the Form 10-K filed with the SEC, for the year ended December 31, 1987. It is used for the cash-flow data in this section.

$$\frac{\text{Net Cash Flow} \quad [46]}{\text{Current Liabilities} \quad [14]} \qquad (0.06)$$

Receivables and Inventory. Since receivables and inventories are current assets that may be converted to cash relatively easily and quickly, they have a direct impact on a firm's liquidity.[6] The absolute amounts for these assets can be placed into several different contexts to develop additional insight into their effect on liquidity.

Days' sales in receivables is a measure of the average daily credit sales in receivables. It is a measure of the collection period for credit sales and can be used to determine the effectiveness of the firm's credit policies. It is calculated as follows:

$$\text{Days' Sales in Receivables} = \frac{\text{Gross Receivables} \quad [2] + [2a]}{\text{Net Sales} \div 365 \quad [25] \div 365 \text{ days}} \qquad (41.8 \text{ days})$$

Gross receivables, rather than the net realizable value, is used because net sales contain both collectible and uncollectible sales. Once a specific account receivable has been deemed uncollectible, the accounting procedure to recognize the bad debt does not affect sales.

Other ratios that can accomplish the same objective of evaluating the liquidity of receivables are as follows:

$$\text{Accounts Receivable Turnover} = \frac{\text{Net Sales} \quad [25]}{\text{Average Gross Receivables}[7] \quad [2] + [2a]} \qquad (8.9 \text{ times})$$

$$\text{Turnover in days} = \frac{\text{Average Gross Receivables} \quad [2] + [2a]}{\text{Net Sales} \div 365 \quad [25] \div 365 \text{ days}]} \qquad (41.1 \text{ days})$$

Accounts receivable turnover expresses the relationship between sales and average receivables. RJR turned over its receivables 8.8 times. Turnover in days indicates that, approximately every 41 days, RJR turns over, or collects, receivables. Generally, a higher turnover is indicative of greater liquidity. Note that the analyst should use only credit sales (sales on account) in these ratios. Hence, cash sales should be excluded, since they have no impact on receivables. However, it may not be possible to determine credit sales from the

---

[6]The term receivables represents only trade receivables in this section.

[7]Average gross receivables may be estimated by adding receivables at the beginning of the current year (end of previous year) and end of the current year and dividing the sum by 2.

financial statements. In such instances, the analyst must remember that, if both cash and credit sales are used, the resulting measure of liquidity will be overstated because it will include cash sales.

Similar ratios can be used to evaluate the liquidity of inventory. The specific objective of this analysis is to evaluate the firm's inventory maintenance policy, which directly influences liquidity. The ratio also provides information concerning management's effective use of resources. For example, management should maintain sufficient inventory to prevent stockouts. *Stockouts* result when sales exceed production or purchases to the point that inventory is depleted. Stockouts can cause customers to switch to a competitor, thus causing loss of sales.

On the other hand, maintaining excessive inventory levels is inefficient because assets could be deployed in other areas. Furthermore, there are costs associated with holding, storing, and ordering inventory. All of these variables and consequences can be quantified by management to create an efficient inventory-maintenance policy. That policy, which directly impacts inventory liquidity, can be evaluated through the following ratios:

$$\text{Days' Sales in Inventory} = \frac{\text{Ending Inventory} \quad [3]}{\text{Cost of Goods Sold} \div 365 \quad [26] \div 365} \quad (118.9 \text{ days})$$

$$\text{Inventory Turnover} = \frac{\text{Cost of Goods Sold} \quad [26]}{\text{Average Inventory}^8 \quad [3]} \quad (3.1 \text{ times})$$

$$\text{Inventory Turnover in Days} = \frac{\text{Average inventory} \quad [3]}{\text{Costs of Goods Sold} \div 365 \quad [25] \div 365} \quad (117.6 \text{ days})$$

Recall that the operating cycle is the length of time it takes to purchase inventory, sell the inventory and convert the sale into cash. Current assets are defined as those assets that will be consumed within one year or within the operating cycle, whichever is longer. Note that the operating cycle of RJR can be estimated by adding the days' sales in receivables (42) to the days' sales in inventory (119), which is 161 days. On average, this means that a dollar of cash invested today in inventory will return to RJR (with profit) 161 days later.

In general, the longer the operating cycle, the greater the strain on cash. Cash is required to pay operating expenses, such as payroll,

---

[8]Average inventory for 1987 can be estimated by summing the inventory amounts for 1987 and 1986 and dividing by 2.

between the investment in inventory and the receipt of cash through collection of receivables. If the operating cycle increases in length, the cash strain can become acute, thereby causing financial problems. For example, a recession is likely to increase the operating cycle as sales and collections slow. Without sufficient cash reserves, the resulting cash strain can prevent the company from meeting financial obligations.

An important additional consideration in analyzing liquidity ratios is the business cycle of the company in relation to the company's fiscal year end. For example, consider the financial statements of two toy manufacturers. Company A has a fiscal year end of September 30, and Company B has a fiscal year end of December 31. Because both companies' sales are seasonal due to the high demand for toys at Christmas, financial statement amounts can be distorted.

To illustrate this point, assume that both companies operate at full capacity from late summer until the end of October in order to build up inventories for seasonal sales to retail stores, which begin in October. Since Company A prepares financial statements as of September 30, inventories are expected to be relatively high and receivables, relatively low. On the other hand, Company B prepares its financial statements as of December 31—after the seasonal peak. At this point, inventories will be relatively low and receivables, relatively high. At the financial statement date, neither company's financial statement amounts are representative of average amounts during the year. This can cause a distortion in the financial ratios and can result in an incorrect conclusion, especially if the analyst is not aware of these possibilities.

Ability to Pay Long-Term Debts

The previous section dealt primarily with an entity's ability to satisfy current debts as they come due. The objective of this section is to evaluate an entity's ability to satisfy debts coming due in the relatively distant future (i.e., beyond 12 months from the balance sheet date).

An important consideration in debt-paying ability is cash flow. A ratio of cash flow to long-term debt can be calculated. However, cash flow must be evaluated in terms of its origins: operating, investing, or financing activities. It should be remembered that operating cash flows normally will recur in a more constant fashion than will cash flows from investing or financing areas.

Repayment of debt takes two forms: repayment of principal and repayment of interest. Furthermore, repayment ability can be viewed from either an income statement (profitability) perspective, or from a balance sheet perspective. The concept of profitability provides a longer-term view of the entity's ability to repay debts because profitable operations over time generally are considered to be a necessary condition for the entity's indefinite continued existence.[9]

The balance sheet perspective provides information concerning the nature of the existing capital structure of the entity as of a point in time.[10] This structure is important to analyze because it provides information concerning relative risk that has been assumed by stockholders and creditors. As long term debts increase relative to stockholders' investment, the risk borne by creditors increases because creditors have provided a larger proportion of resources from which they expect a payback in principal and interest. As risk increases, the creditors expect higher interest in order to offset the higher risk.

The deliberate manipulation of the capital structure by management of a corporation can produce interesting results through a concept known as *leverage*. When a corporation desires an immediate increase in resources, it can sell stock (equity securities) or bonds (debt securities) or it can borrow from a lending institution. If the entity uses the cash proceeds of borrowing to increase net income, the excess resources accrue to the benefit of stockholders. Therefore, positive leverage is the result and stockholders have used non-owners' cash to increase their equity. Furthermore, because the cost of debt capital (interest) is a deductible tax expense and the cost of equity capital (dividends) is not, the effect of positive leverage becomes even more beneficial from an after-tax perspective.

Unfortunately, leverage also can have undesirable effects. If total invested resources provided by debt do not generate sufficient cash to cover total interest charges, then it has a negative impact on owners' equity.

---

[9]Debt is, of course, normally repaid with cash. Since net income (one measure of profitability) is calculated on an accrual basis, in the short term, profit and cash flows are not necessarily correlated. However, in the long run, a correlation between operations cash flows and accrual net income will emerge as receivables are collected and payables are paid. Nevertheless, there will always be a difference due to the use of noncash expenditures, such as depreciation, in the calculation of net income.

[10]Note the use of the term *capital* in this context. It does not refer to the owner's equity, but rather to the entire long-term structure of claims against the assets. That is, it refers to stockholder's equity and long-term debts owed to nonowners.

The foregoing discussion of leverage has focused on what may be viewed as project specific leverage. Namely, it is revenue generated from specific borrowing dedicated to a particular project compared to the interest costs associated with the specific borrowing. Leverage can also be viewed from an overall sense, in which case it is referred to as *financial leverage*.

Financial leverage uses debt as a fulcrum to lever percentage changes in net income up or down beyond changes in earnings. The effects of financial leverage follow, assuming the corporation issued bonds in Year 1:

	Year 1	Year 2 Assuming 10% Increase in Earnings	Year 2 Assuming 10% Decrease in Earnings
Income before Interest and Taxes	$10,000,000	$11,000,000	$9,000,000
Interest	1,000,000	1,000,000	1,000,000
Earnings before Taxes	$9,000,000	$10,000,000	$8,000,000
Tax 50%	4,500,000	5,000,000	4,000,000
Net Income	$4,500,000	$5,000,000	$4,000,000

A 10 percent increase in earnings translates into an increase of 11.1 percent in net income [($5,000,000 - $4,500,000)/ $4,500,000 in Year 2]. Assuming an earnings decrease of 10 percent, net income decreases by 11.1 percent [($4,000,000 - $4,500,000)/$4,500,000 in Year 2].

The *degree of leverage* can be calculated as follows:

$$\frac{\text{Earnings before Interest and Taxes (Operating Income)}}{\text{Earnings before Taxes   [31]}} \qquad (1.27)$$

For Year 1 in the above table, the degree of leverage is 1.11. Note that the degree of leverage changes as earnings before interest and taxes change. The degree of leverage is the factor by which operating income changes as compared to the change in earnings.

Financial leverage can be measured by the *debt/equity ratio*, which indicates the proportion of the capital structure provided by creditors relative to stockholders. It is calculated as follows:

$$\frac{\text{Total Long-Term Debt}^{11} \quad [15] + [16] + [18]}{\text{Total Common Stockholders Equity}^{12} \quad [24]} \quad (0.97)$$

From the creditors' standpoint, the lower this ratio, the better.

The *debt ratio* indicates the relationship between total long-term debt and total assets. Essentially, this provides the same information as the debt/equity ratio, since equity is one of two sources of claims against total assets. It is calculated as follows:

$$\frac{\text{Total Long-Term Debt} \quad [15] + [16] + [18]}{\text{Total Assets} \quad [9]} \quad (0.35)$$

From the creditor viewpoint, the smaller this ratio, the better.

Obviously, it is in the stockholders' best interests for a corporation to utilize leverage if the corporation can generate more than sufficient revenues from the borrowed funds to repay the principal and interest. However, there are limits to its use; as more debt capital is used, more risk is shifted to creditors. As risk to creditors rises, not only do interest rates associated with the additional debt rise, but also creditors reach a point where no additional funds will be loaned due to existing high-debt levels.[13] Therefore, both creditors' and owners' interests act as countervailing forces in the market to retain an appropriate balance, given the specific circumstances of a particular industry and company. Nevertheless, given the uncertainties present, market forces sometimes become imbalanced and one potential result is bond default.

An additional ratio that focuses on profitability and interest repayment is *times interest earned*:

$$\frac{\text{Income before Taxes + Interest Expense} \quad [31] + [30]}{\text{Interest Expense} \quad [30]} \quad (4.7)$$

Interest expense should be added back to net income in the numerator in order to prevent distortion of the ratio by 1.0. Ordinarily, the higher

---

[11]Redeemable preferred stock is included as part of long-term debt because it is subject to mandatory recall by RJR as of a specific date. This, in essence, makes the nature of this type of preferred stock more akin to debt than equity.

[12]Some analysts prefer to add all debt, including short-term debt, to the numerator, on the basis that short-term debt is constantly turning over and, in essence, is permanent debt.

[13]L. H., Clark, Jr., and A. L. Malabre, Jr., "Takeover Trend Helps Push Corporate Debt and Defaults Upward", *The Wall Street Journal*, March 15, 1988.

the ratio, the better. A computed ratio of 1.0 would indicate that earnings are just sufficient to cover interest charges. However, since earnings are calculated on an accrual basis, net cash flows from operations could be used as a surrogate numerator.

Profitability

Profitability is an income statement concept. It is extremely important to all users of financial statements. However, as discussed earlier, keep in mind that profitability and cash flows are not necessarily correlated in the short run. In general, the higher the profitability ratios, the better.

Earnings per share (EPS) is a statistic that is required to be calculated and presented on the face of the income statement by the reporting entity.[14] Therefore, the analyst is not required to compute EPS. However, the analyst should understand what the statistic represents, as a great deal of attention has been given to it.

EPS purports to represent the amount of earnings available to common stockholders.[15] Therefore, the basic computation is as follows:

$$\frac{\text{Net Income} - \text{Preferred Stock Dividends} \quad [38] - [39]}{\begin{array}{c}\text{Weighted Average Number of}\\ \text{Common Shares Outstanding} \quad [42]\end{array}} \qquad (\$4.70)$$

Preferred stock dividends are subtracted from earnings because the objective is to determine the amount of earnings available to common stockholders. The sale of common stock produces cash proceeds that are invested to generate additional income. The denominator is weighted average shares. If common stock was sold *during* the year, then the proceeds would only be available to the entity to generate earnings for the portion of the year that the stock was outstanding. Therefore, use of an absolute number of shares in this case would unfairly distort EPS. EPS for RJR, as reported on the face of the income statement for 1987, is $4.70.

---

[14]Accounting Principles Board Opinion No. 15, (Accounting Principles Board, 1969), par. 12.

[15]Earnings "available" to common stockholders is terminology commonly used in an EPS context. However, there is no suggestion that this amount is available for dividends or for distribution in cash. Recall that earnings and cash balances are not necessarily correlated.

Prior to the issuance of *APBO 15* (Footnote 14) the investing public appeared to have anchored on this one statistic. Apparently, the general public was searching for one all-encompassing statistic to reflect profitability. As corporations recognized this reliance, a number of exotic securities were issued that were not common stock, yet had common stock characteristics. Therefore, in computing EPS, corporations were able to exclude these securities from the denominator, but use the proceeds from the sale of the securities in generating earnings that became a part of the numerator. Consequently, EPS of these companies was favorably distorted.

This was the primary reason for the issuance of *APBO 15*, which, in most cases, required a dual presentation for EPS. *Primary* earnings per share (PEPS) is calculated in the manner above. *Fully diluted* earnings per share (FDEPS) is calculated in a highly complex series of computations, which are beyond the scope of this discussion.

Because of the recent emphasis on cash flows, another useful calculation used in conjunction with EPS is *cash flow per share*, which provides information on the cash generated per share. Unlike EPS, this measure is not required to be computed and published with the financial statements. Cash flows from operations should be used, although cash flows from other origins could be added to operations for a total. The calculation is as follows:

$$\frac{\text{Cash Flow - Preferred Dividends} \quad [43] - [39]}{\text{Common Stock Outstanding} \quad [42]} \qquad (\$6.93)$$

If possible, the denominator may be adjusted as in PEPS and FDEPS. However, in most cases this will not be possible without data that is not normally published by the entity. Cash flow per share is an excellent complement to EPS for a short-run measure of profitability, since earnings and cash flows normally will not correlate in the short run.

Return on investment is a traditional measure of the degree of efficiency with which management of the corporation is using its resources. Generally, return on investment measures profitability (net income) relative to resources used to generate net income. There are several ratios that can be used to accomplish this purpose; each ratio analyzes the return from a slightly different perspective.

Resources of the firm are generated internally or externally. Internally generated resources come from operations (net income), which become a part of stockholders' equity. Resources are generated externally through sales of securities that represent debt or equity. Therefore, in analyzing overall return on investment, all sources of capital should be used. *Return on total investment* (ROTI) is calculated as follows:

$$\frac{[38] + \{[30] \times (1.0 - 0.4)\}}{\text{Long Term Debt} + \text{Total Common Stockholders' Equity}}$$

$$\frac{\text{Net Income} + [\text{Interest Expense} \times (1.00 - \text{tax rate})]^{16}}{([15] + [16] + [17] + [18]) + [24]} \qquad (11.8\%)$$

The tax rate may be calculated by dividing income tax expense (or provision for income taxes) by net income before taxes. Net income is adjusted in the numerator to remove the complication of how the assets used to generate net income were financed. That is, the use of debt capital requires interest payments, which are tax deductible. Multiplying interest expense by the after-tax rate (1.00 minus tax rate) and adding the result to net income removes the effect that the issuance of long-term debt has on net income.

Removing this effect is necessary when comparing ROTI of companies because managements have different strategies for financing resources from which to generate net income. As mentioned earlier, resources can be financed internally or externally. There are two sources of external financing: debt or equity. The choice of debt or equity will affect net income because the cost of debt (interest) is an expense used in calculating net income, and the cost of equity (dividends) is not. By removing the tax effects of debt-financed resources, all financing is placed on an equal after-tax basis. Since the objective is to measure management's efficiency in generating profits from resources available and since profits will be affected by financing choices, the effect of the choice should be removed in order to compare efficiency.

Return on common equity (ROE) measures the efficiency with which corporate management is using common stockholders' investment. It is calculated as follows:

$$\frac{\text{Net Income} - \text{Preferred Dividends}}{\text{Total Common Stockholders' Equity}^{17}} \quad \frac{[38] - [39]}{[24]} \qquad (19.5\%)$$

---

[16]The effective tax rate was calculated by dividing income before taxes [31] by the provision for taxes [32].

[17]Total Commn Stockholders' Equity = Total Stockholders' Equity minus Preferred Stockholders' Equity.

Preferred equity and preferred dividends are deducted from total stockholders' equity and net income, respectively, since the calculation is based on common stock. *Return on total equity* also can be calculated by simply adding back the preferred equity and preferred dividends.

Note that a return-on-equity calculation provides results that focus on internally generated funds, as well as on equity capital. The difference between a return on equity calculation and ROTI is that the results from ROTI focus on all capital—internally generated capital and both sources of externally generated funds; namely, debt and equity capital. Therefore, a comparison of ROE to ROTI provides information about financial leverage. ROE for RJR is 19.5 percent compared to ROTI of 11.8 percent, which indicates positive financial leverage and effective use of debt capital.

Return on operating assets (ROA) is another traditional profitability ratio. It measures management's effectiveness in the utilization of operating assets:

$$\frac{\text{Operating Income} \quad [29]}{\text{Average Operating Assets}} \qquad (15\%)$$

Operating assets generally are defined as all assets less investments and other assets. The average can be approximated by adding the beginning and ending operating assets and dividing by 2.[18] Since the objective is to measure efficiency in utilizing operating assets, the appropriate profitability measure is operating income. Operating income excludes nonoperating revenue and expenses, which presumably would not be related to operating assets. This ratio provides a more specific measure that is directed at operations, rather than at an overall measure of profitability. *Return on total assets* (ROTA) can be calculated as well, but the profitability measure should be net income:

$$\frac{\text{Net Income} \quad [38]}{\text{Average Total Assets}^{19}} \qquad (7.2\%)$$

---

[18]Footnote 5 to the RJR annual report indicates that investments for 1987 are $786 million. Therefore, operating assets are $15,426 million ($16,861 [9] - $786 [RJR footnote 5] minus $ 649 [8]). For 1986, operating assets are $15,382 million, which is calculated in the same manner. Therefore, the average for 1987 is $15,404 [(15,426 + 15,382) / 2).

[19]Item [9] for 1987 (16,861 and for 1986 (16,701) summed and divided by 2 is average total assets.

Return on operating assets (ROA) can be affected by two components; namely, operating margin and operating asset turnover. *Operating margin* is a measure of profitability and is calculated as follows:

$$\frac{\text{Operating Income} \quad [29]}{\text{Net Sales} \quad [25]} \quad (14.6\%)$$

Operating asset turnover is a measure of management's efficiency in utilizing assets. It is equal to net sales divided by average operating assets. In other words, return on operating assets is equal to operating margin times operating asset turnover:

$$\frac{\text{Operating Income}}{\text{Net Sales}} \quad X \quad \frac{\text{Net Sales}}{\text{Operating Assets}}$$

Algebraically, net sales cancels out of each of the two ratios and the result is

$$\frac{\text{Operating Income}}{\text{Operating Assets}}$$

or return on assets.

By separating return on operating assets between components, the analyst is provided with reasons for changes in return on operating assets. Consider the following example:

	Year 1	Year 2
Operating Income	$1,000,000	$750,000
Average Operating Assets	$10,000,000	$9,000,000
ROA	10.0%	8.3%
Operating Margin	14.0%	15.0%
Operating Asset Turnover	0.7	0.6

This example indicates that, while ROA decreased to 8.3 percent, the basic reason was a decrease in operating asset turnover. Therefore, the decreased ability to generate sales dollars from operating assets is the reason for the decline in ROA.

ROTI and ROE provide insight into profitability in an overall sense. ROA focuses more specifically on operations. This information can be further supplemented by measures designed to provide additional specificity into profitability. For example, profit margins are also indicators of profitability. *Gross profit margin* provides basic information on the product markup. It is calculated as follows:

$$\frac{\text{Gross Profit} \quad [25] - [26]}{\text{Net Sales} \quad [25]} \quad (47.9\%)$$

Not all firms report gross profit, since some firms do not have inventories. Other firms maintain inventories, but they still do not report a separate amount for gross profit. Another profit margin calculation is *net profit margin*, which is calculated as follows:

$$\frac{\text{Net Income} \quad [38]}{\text{Net Sales} \quad [25]} \quad (7.7\%)$$

This ratio indicates the net income generated by each net sales dollar. The difference in the two profit margins is accounted for by the operating expenses and by other gains and losses that are used in calculating net income.

Equity-Investor Analysis

Many of the ratios previously discussed are used by investors in their analytical process. Those ratios are generally supplemented by the following additional ratios. A common approach to derive a market-determined benchmark for a particular company is to compute the *price/earnings* (P/E) *ratio*:

$$\frac{\text{Average Market Price per Share}[20]}{\text{Earnings per Share} \quad [41]} \quad (11.2)$$

Remember that EPS can be either primary or fully diluted and the analyst must be careful when making company comparisons to ascertain that the EPS calculation is consistent. The market price per share is the price per common share. The P/E ratio is relative to all other companies in the market.

This ratio is described as a market-determined benchmark because of the use of market price. Presumably, the market price at any point in time reflects all buyers' and sellers' collective decisions concerning the future prospects of this company. Consequently, this ratio is widely regarded as an indication of the firm's future earning power.

Because the P/E ratio is dependent on the market price, the analyst must be careful to consider that the market evaluation (through price)

---

[20]Average market price per share per year is calculated based on data found on page 51 of the annual report. It is calculated as follows: ($71.13 + $34.50) / 2 = $52.82.

may be incorrect at any point in time. If the market has placed a premium on price, the P/E ratio will be too high. That is, future prospects of the company are inflated by the market. If the analyst believes, based on other analytical procedures, that the P/E ratio is indeed too high, he or she should sell that particular stock, as the market will eventually correct to the appropriate price. Of course, determining the correct market price is based on many factors, and the overall market is right more often than wrong.

Another ratio indicative of growth potential is *percentage of earnings retained*. In percentage terms, this measures, the amount of net income that is not paid out in dividends:

$$\frac{\text{Net Income} - \text{Dividends} \quad [38 - ([39] + [40])]}{\text{Net Income} \quad [38]} \quad (61.1\%)$$

The higher the proportion of earnings that are retained, the greater the indication of the growth potential, as earnings retained represents resources available for growth as opposed to dividends paid out to investors. In the short run, however, earnings and cash flows may not be correlated.

A closely related measure is the dividend payout ratio:

$$\frac{\text{Cash Dividends per Common Share} \quad [40] + [42]}{\text{Earnings per Share} \quad [41]} \quad (37.3\%)$$

In general, the dividend payout ratio moves inversely to the P/E ratio and the percentage of earnings retained. That is, a company with a high P/E ratio usually has a relatively low dividend payout ratio, and vice versa. This is because high growth companies require as many resources as possible to feed anticipated growth. Therefore, dividend payments are relatively small which causes a low dividend payout ratio. On the other hand, low-growth companies typically are stable companies with higher dividend payouts and lower P/E ratios.

Investor objectives are important in the analysis process. Objectives associated with high appreciation of value are also associated with higher risk and are usually associated with high price volatility. Such investments usually are made in growth companies with high P/E ratios and low dividend payouts. On the other hand, objectives associated with lower risk and relatively fixed income usually require investments in low-growth companies with low P/E ratios and high dividend payouts.

Another perspective on dividend payout is provided by *dividend yield*:

$$\frac{\text{Cash Dividends per Common Share} \quad [40] \div [42]}{\text{Average Market Price per Share}^{21}} \quad (3.3\%)$$

This indicates, of course, the relationship between dividends and market price.

Book value per common share is often computed. However, book value and market value can be entirely different. Market value per share is the amount for which the entity's stock is selling on the open market. It is a value based on all buyers' and sellers' collective opinion concerning general economic and political factors, as well as a value based on expectations of the growth potential, earnings ability, and financial condition of a specific entity.

On the other hand, book value per share is simply the amount that would be received for each share owned by a stockholder in the event that assets and liabilities were liquidated at net costs with no gain or loss. Book value is computed as follows:

$$\frac{\begin{array}{cc}\text{Total Common} & \text{Preferred} \\ \text{Stockholders' Equity} \quad - \quad \text{Stockholders' Equity} \quad [24]\end{array}}{\text{Number of Shares of Common Stock Outstanding} \quad [42]} \quad (\$24.06)$$

Book value should be compared to market value (price) to determine the market's evaluation relative to book value. Often times stocks trade at an amount below book value. Since book value is based on historical costs, that is usually of little interest. Nevertheless, it is often discussed in the financial press.

SUMMARY

The analysis of financial statements begins with a routine calculation of ratios and a comparison of these ratios to past ratios of the same entity in order to discern a trend or change in trend. These ratios are compared with other companies and industry averages in order to obtain an idea concerning the relative position of the company *vis-a-vis* other companies.

---

[21]See footnote 20.

Different financial statement users have different primary interests or objectives in the analytical process. Hence, the ratios in this chapter have been divided into groups of primary objectives; namely, liquidity, long-term debt-paying ability, profitability, and equity-investor analysis. This is not to say, however, that a specific user group will only consider one group of ratios. An investor, for example, may be interested primarily in the equity-investor analysis, but may carefully consider other ratio groups, as these ratios enhance investor perspective.

However, there are limitations to accounting and financial statements that are necessarily incorporated into financial ratios. Consequently, the analytical process cannot terminate with the calculation of these ratios. The analyst must understand the cause and possible effects of the inherent limitations of accounting and financial reporting in order to properly evaluate the analytical product.

In other words, financial statement analysis is an art requiring that routine calculations be supplemented with knowledge that concerns a multitude of factors and their effects. The remaining chapters of this book concern many of these additional considerations and weaknesses that are inherent in financial reporting.

READING LIST

Boyer, P. A., and Gibson, C. H. "An inventory of Industry Average Financial Ratios," *Journal of Commercial Bank Lending,* (August, 1979): 59 - 64.

Conn, S. "Going With the Flow," *Inc.* (July 1986): 97 - 98.

Gibson, C. H. "Financial Ratios in Annual Reports," *The CPA Journal* (September 1982): 18-29.

Gibson, C. H. "How Industry Perceives Financial Ratios," *Management Accounting* (April 1982): 13-19.

Gibson, C. H. and Boyer, P. A. "Need for Disclosure of Uniform Financial Ratios," *Journal of Accountancy,* (May 1980): 78.

Throckmorton, J. J., and Talbot, J. "Computer-Supported Instruction in Financial Statement Analysis," *The Accounting Review* (January 1978: 186 - 191.

Wittington, G. "Some Basic Properties of Accounting Ratios," *Journal of Business Finance and Accounting* (Summer 1980): 219 - 232.

RJR Nabisco, Inc.
Consolidated Balance Sheets
December 31

(Dollars in Millions)		1987	1986
Assets			
	Current assets:		
[1]	Cash and short-term investments (Note 5)	$ 1,088	$ 827
[2]	Accounts and notes receivable		
[2a]	(less allowances of $61 and $67, respectively)	1,745	1,675
[3]	Inventories (Note 6)	2,678	2,620
[4]	Prepaid expenses and excise taxes	329	273
[5]	**Total current assets**	5,840	5,395
[6]	**Property, plant and equipment — at cost (Note 7)**	7,563	6,694
[6a]	Less accumulated depreciation	1,716	1,351
[6b]	**Net property, plant and equipment**	5,847	5,343
[7]	**Goodwill and trademarks**		
	(net of amortization of $326 and $207, respectively)	4,525	4,603
[8]	**Other assets and deferred charges**	649	644
	Net assets of discontinued operations (Note 3)	—	716
[9]		$16,861	$16,701
	Liabilities and Stockholders' Equity		
	Current liabilities:		
[10]	Notes payable (Note 8)	$ 442	$ 518
[11]	Accounts payable and accrued accounts (Note 9)	3,187	2,923
[12]	Current maturities of long-term debt (Note 10)	162	423
[13]	Income taxes accrued	332	202
[14]	**Total current liabilities**	4,123	4,066
[15]	**Long-term debt (Note 10)**	3,884	4,833
[16]	**Other noncurrent liabilities**	1,797	1,448
[17]	**Deferred income taxes**	846	751
	Commitments and contingencies (Note 11)		
[18]	**Redeemable preferred stock (Note 12)**	173	291
	Common stockholders' equity:		
[19]	Common Stock (Note 13)	251	251
[20]	Paid-in capital (Note 13)	312	320
[21]	Cumulative translation adjustments (Note 14)	86	(76)
[22]	Retained earnings	5,548	4,832
[23]	Treasury stock, at cost (Note 13)	(159)	(15)
[24]	**Total common stockholders' equity**	6,038	5,312
		$16,861	$16,701

RJR Nabisco, Inc.

Consolidated Statements of Income and Retained Earnings

For the Years Ended December 31

	(Dollars in Millions Except Per Share Amounts)	1987	1986	1985
[25]	**Net sales***	**$15,766**	$15,102	$11,622
	Costs and expenses:			
[26]	Cost of products sold*	8,221	7,920	6,024
[27]	Selling, advertising, administrative and general expenses	4,991	4,842	3,649
[28]	Restructuring expense, net (Note 1)	250	—	—
[29]	**Operating income**	**2,304**	2,340	1,949
[30]	Interest and debt expense (net of capitalized amounts of $19, $71 and $67, respectively)	**(489)**	(565)	(337)
	Other income (expense), net	**1**	7	51
[31]	**Income before provision for income taxes**	**1,816**	1,782	1,663
[32]	Provision for income taxes (Note 2)	735	757	746
[33]	**Income from continuing operations**	**1,081**	1,025	917
[34]	Income (loss) from discontinued operations, net of taxes (Note 3)	**(7)**	78	84
[35]	Gain (loss) on sale of discontinued operations, net of taxes (Note 3)	**215**	(39)	—
[36]	**Income before extraordinary item**	**1,289**	1,064	1,001
[37]	Extraordinary item — loss from early extinguishment of debt, net of taxes (Note 4)	**80**	—	—
[38]	**Net income**	**1,209**	1,064	1,001
[39]	Less preferred dividends	30	102	91
	Net income applicable to Common Stock	**1,179**	962	910
	Retained earnings at beginning of year	**4,832**	4,357	4,034
	Less:			
[40]	Cash dividends on Common Stock	**440**	378	357
	Retirement of Company's stocks	**23**	109	230
	Retained earnings at end of year	**$ 5,548**	$ 4,832	$ 4,357
	Income per common share:			
	Continuing operations	**$ 4.19**	$ 3.68	$ 3.27
	Discontinued operations	**0.83**	0.15	0.33
	Extraordinary item	**(0.32)**	—	—
[41]	**Net income**	**$ 4.70**	$ 3.83	$ 3.60
[42]	**Average number of common shares outstanding (in thousands)**	**250,612**	251,073	252,941

*Excludes excise taxes of $3,314, $3,057 and $2,640 for 1987, 1986 and 1985, respectively.

Source: RJR Nabisco 1987 Annual Report.

APPENDIX

RJR NABISCO, INC.

CONSOLIDATED STATEMENTS OF CASH FLOWS
For the Years Ended December 31

	1988	1987	1986
	(Dollars in Millions)		
[43]Cash flows from operating activities (Note 5)	$1,840	$1,769	$1,718
Cash flows from investing activities:			
Capital expenditures	(1,142)	(936)	(1,022)
Deposits on fresh fruit vessels	(126)	—	—
Proceeds from sale of capital assets	52	48	59
Proceeds from dispositions of businesses	489	1,597	1,321
Acquisitions of businesses and minority interests	(189)	(72)	—
Collections of notes receivable	19	92	128
[44] Net cash flows (used in) from investing activities	(897)	729	486
Cash flows from financing activities:			
Dividends paid	(494)	(474)	(514)
Proceeds from the issuance of long-term debt	1,435	1,288	1,125
Payments to retire long-term debt	(236)	(2,680)	(960)
Increase (decrease) in notes payable	9	(89)	(121)
Proceeds from issuance of Company's stocks	22	11	12
Repurchase of Company's stocks	(1,380)	(317)	(1,467)
[45] Net cash flows (used in financing activities	(644)	(2,261)	(1,925)
Effect of exchange rate changes on cash and cash equivalents	38	24	1
[46] Net change in cash and cash equivalents	337	261	280
Cash and cash equivalents at beginning of year	1,088	827	547
Cash and cash equivalents at end of year	$1,425	$1,088	$ 827

Source: From RJR Nabisco, Inc., Form 10-K

RJR Nabisco, Inc.
Selected Five-Year Financial Data
For the Years Ended December 31

(Dollars in Millions Except Per Share Amounts)	**1987**	1986	1985	1984	1983
Results of Operations					
Net sales	**$15,766**	$15,102	$11,622	$8,200	$7,565
Operating income (1)	**2,304**	2,340	1,949	1,412	1,205
Interest and debt expense	**489**	565	337	166	177
Income from continuing operations	**1,081**	1,025	917	747	626
Net income (2)	**1,209**	1,064	1,001	1,210	881
Preferred dividends	**30**	102	91	56	62
Net income applicable to Common Stock	**1,179**	962	910	1,154	819
Income from continuing operations per common share	**4.19**	3.68	3.27	2.46	2.00
Net income per common share (2)	**4.70**	3.83	3.60	4.11	2.90
Other Data					
Dividends on Common Stock	**$ 440**	$ 378	$ 357	$ 360	$ 345
Dividends per common share	**1.76**	1.51	1.41	1.30	1.22
Dividend payout percentage (3)	**37.3%**	39.3%	39.2%	31.2%	42.1%
Common Stock price range:					
High	**$ 71⅛**	$ 55⅛	$ 35	$ 29	$ 25⅜
Low	**34½**	31	24¾	21⅛	18
Number of common shares outstanding at year end (in thousands)	**247,357**	250,395	250,566	258,383	283,183
Number of stockholders at year end	**112,879**	114,121	155,138	114,220	126,889
Number of full-time employees of continuing operations at year end	**120,334**	122,395	127,404	79,234	78,266

Prior years have been restated to report the Company's former spirits and wines business as discontinued operations (see Note 3 to the Financial Statements). The 1985 amounts include the operations of Nabisco Brands from July 2, 1985 (see Note 16 to the Financial Statements).

(1)   Operating income includes the effects of net restructuring expense incurred in 1987 of $250 million (see Note 1 to the Financial Statements).

(2)   The 1987 and 1984 amounts include net gains on the sale of the Company's discontinued operations of $215 million or 86 cents per share and $275 million or 98 cents per share, respectively. In addition, the 1987 amounts include an extraordinary loss from the early extinguishment of debt of $80 million or 32 cents per share. (See Notes 3 and 4 to the Financial Statements.)

(3)   Dividends on Common Stock as a percentage of net income applicable to Common Stock. The 1987 and 1984 dividend payout percentage would be 45.6 and 41.0 percent, respectively, excluding the gain on the sale of discontinued operations.

**Consolidated
Net Sales**
(Dollars in Billions)

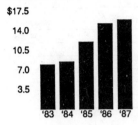

**Consolidated
Operating Income**
(Dollars in Millions)

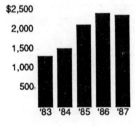

**Consolidated Income
from Continuing Operations**
(Dollars in Millions)

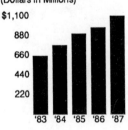

Management's Discussion and Analysis

The operations of the Company's former spirits and wines business have been reported as discontinued operations, and prior years have been restated (see Note 3 to the Financial Statements). The Company now classifies its continuing operations into two lines of business, tobacco and food.

Results of Operations

Consolidated

Consolidated net sales for 1987 increased 4 percent over the prior year to $15.8 billion. Both the tobacco and food lines of business contributed to the increase. The tobacco gain was due principally to price increases together with favorable foreign currency exchange rates and international tobacco unit volume growth. The food gain was due to new product introductions and volume gains.

Operating income increased in both lines of business principally due to the factors noted above; however, the improvements were more than offset by the $250 million special charge for net restructuring expense (see Note 1 to the Financial Statements).

The 1987 income from continuing operations increased $56 million, or 5 percent, and income from continuing operations per share increased 51 cents, or 14 percent, to $4.19. These increases were mainly due to the sales increases noted above and decreased interest and debt expense resulting from the early extinguishment of $1.6 billion of high-interest debt in the first quarter of 1987 (see Note 4 to the Financial Statements).

Net income for 1987 rose $145 million to $1.2 billion and net income per share increased 23 percent to $4.70. The higher net income and net income per share were primarily the result of improved income from continuing operations and the $215 million gain on the sale of discontinued operations (see Note 3 to the Financial Statements), partly offset by the extraordinary loss of $80 million on the early extinguishment of debt. During 1987, the Company repurchased 3.6 million shares of its Common Stock and 1.2 million shares of its

Series B Cumulative Preferred Stock (see Notes 12 and 13 to the Financial Statements).

Consolidated net sales for 1986 increased 30 percent over the prior year to $15.1 billion. The improvement was principally due to the inclusion of Nabisco Brands, which was acquired on July 2, 1985 (see Note 16 to the Financial Statements). Tobacco operations also contributed to the sales gain through volume and price increases.

Consolidated operating income for 1986 increased 20 percent, or $391 million. The increase was primarily the result of the Nabisco Brands acquisition, and contributions from tobacco operations. Partially offsetting these increases was a charge of approximately $94 million related to the streamlining of the corporate office functions in connection with the planned relocation of the corporate headquarters to Atlanta, Georgia in 1987.

The 1986 income from continuing operations increased $108 million, or 12 percent, and income from continuing operations per share increased 41 cents, or 13 percent, to $3.68. These increases were mainly due to the improved operating income noted above. Partially offsetting these increases were higher interest and debt expense, mainly related to the Nabisco Brands acquisition, the corporate streamlining noted above, the early retirement of high-cost debt and the reversal of investment tax credits as a result of the Tax Reform Act of 1986.

Net income for 1986 rose $63 million to $1.1 billion and net income per share increased 6 percent to $3.83. The higher net income and net income per share were primarily the result of improved operating income. The percentage contributions of each of the Company's lines of business to net sales and operating income during the last five years were as follows:

	1987	1986	1985	1984	1983
Net Sales					
Tobacco	**40%**	39%	47%	63%	64%
Food	**60**	61	53	37	36
	100%	100%	100%	100%	100%
Operating Income*					
Tobacco	**67%**	67%	73%	88%	90%
Food	**33**	33	27	12	10
	100%	100%	100%	100%	100%

*Contributions by line of business computed without effects of corporate and restructuring expense (see Note 1 to the Financial Statements).

Tobacco

The tobacco line of business includes the operations of R.J. Reynolds Tobacco USA and R.J. Reynolds Tobacco International, which manufacture and sell tobacco products, principally cigarettes. Products are manufactured in the United States and in 33 foreign countries and territories by subsidiaries or licensees, and are sold throughout the United States and in more than 160 markets around the world. Also included are the operations of RJR Archer, a packaging company.

Sales for the tobacco operations were $6.3 billion for 1987, up $480 million over the prior year. The sales increase for the year was due to higher manufacturers' selling prices, record international unit volume growth and favorable foreign currency rates.

Domestic market share for 1987, measured on a manufacturer's shipment basis, increased to 32.5 percent. While the total industry volume declined 2.0 percent, R.J. Reynolds Tobacco USA once again outperformed the industry with a decline of only 1.6 percent to 185.3 billion units.

The gain in international unit volume, to 98.9 billion units compared with 89.7 billion units in 1986, was the highest rate of growth among major multinational tobacco companies. This was achieved through advances in

the Company's three primary international brands: CAMEL, SALEM and WINSTON. At the same time, growth was achieved in all major geographic regions including Europe, Asia, Canada and Latin America. R.J. Reynolds Tobacco International increased or maintained its share of market in all of its top 20 markets.

Operating income was $1.8 billion for 1987, or 10 percent higher than last year, excluding restructuring expense. The improvement in operating income was the result of the sales gains noted above, improved operating efficiencies and continuing cost-control efforts. These factors more than offset increased expenses designed to strengthen marketing and selling activities.

Sales for the tobacco operations were $5.9 billion for 1986, up $444 million over the prior year. The sales increase for the year was due to improved volumes, favorable foreign currency effects and increased selling prices.

Domestic market share for 1986, measured on a manufacturer's shipment basis, increased to 32.4 percent, and unit volume increased to 188.3 billion units, despite an overall industry decline. Market share also improved at the consumer level due to strong performance from established brands and volume from new brands.

International volume for 1986 was up 3.3 percent to 89.7 billion units, with CAMEL volume up 8 percent. CAMEL held or increased its share of market in 9 of its top 10 markets and reached a 3.6 percent share of the European market. WINSTON and SALEM also performed well in their respective regions of emphasis.

Operating income was $1.7 billion for 1986, or 12 percent higher than in 1985. The improvement in operating income resulted from the higher prices and volumes and foreign currency effects noted above as well as continuing cost-control efforts.

Consolidated Income from Continuing Operations Per Common Share
(Dollars)

$4.75
3.80
2.85
1.90
0.95

'83 '84 '85 '86 '87

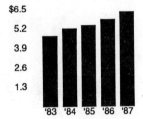

Tobacco Sales
(Dollars in Billions)

$6.5
5.2
3.9
2.6
1.3

'83 '84 '85 '86 '87

Tobacco Operating Income*
(Dollars in Millions)

$1,875
1,500
1,125
750
375

'83 '84 '85 '86 '87

*Excludes 1987 restructuring expense.

Food Sales
(Dollars in Billions)

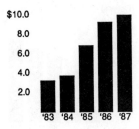

$10.0
8.0
6.0
4.0
2.0

'83 '84 '85 '86 '87

Food
Operating Income*
(Dollars in Millions)

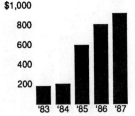

$1,000
800
600
400
200

'83 '84 '85 '86 '87

*Excludes 1987 restructuring expense.

Food

The food line of business includes the operations of Nabisco Brands and Planters LifeSavers, acquired in July 1985, and Del Monte. Food products are produced, marketed or distributed worldwide and include cookies, crackers, cereals, confectioneries, nuts, snacks, canned foods, beverages and fresh fruit.

Foods sales were $9.4 billion in 1987, an increase of $184 million over the prior year despite the loss of $639 million in sales from the divestment of certain Canadian and other food businesses in 1987 and 1986. New product introductions and volume growth in established brands resulted in higher United States market share in a number of product categories, such as cookies, crackers, cereal and margarine. Also contributing to the sales improvement were volume gains in the United Kingdom and other international markets.

Operating income increased to $915 million, excluding restructuring expense, compared with $820 million for the prior year, an increase of 12 percent, due principally to strong results from the Company's United States cookie, cracker, grocery products, hard-roll candy and gum businesses. The performance of Del Monte's tropical fruit business met expectations, although it was below the strong performance of 1986.

Food sales were $9.2 billion in 1986, an increase of 49 percent over 1985. This increase was principally due to the inclusion of the full-year results of Nabisco Brands. Partially offsetting this increase was the loss of sales from the dispositions of franchise beverages, vinegar and yeast, and frozen foods operations.

Operating income increased to $820 million for 1986 compared with $549 million for the prior year, an increase of 49 percent, due principally to the inclusion of a full-year's results of operations by Nabisco Brands. Also contributing to the operating income increase was a strong performance by the tropical fruit operations.

Restructuring Expense

During 1987, the Company incurred $250 million (net of nonrecurring gains) for restructuring expense (see Note 1 to the Financial Statements). These provisions were principally for the write-down of redundant equipment and facilities from the continuing modernization of domestic tobacco operations, implementation of a Voluntary Separation Incentive Program for tobacco employees, restructuring programs in its food subsidiaries and relocating

the Planters LifeSavers headquarters offices to Winston-Salem, North Carolina from New Jersey. As part of this program, the restructuring expenses were partially offset by nonrecurring gains from the sales of the Canadian coffee, margarine and confectionery businesses, sale of U.S. specialty tobacco brands, and premium refunds from a restructuring of insurance programs.

The R.J. Reynolds Tobacco Co.'s Voluntary Separation Incentive Program was implemented to increase operating efficiency and strengthen the Company's competitive position by reducing its work force. The Planters LifeSavers relocation, to occur in 1988, will take advantage of many common opportunities, in such areas as sales and distribution, with R.J. Reynolds Tobacco USA.

Interest and Debt Expense

Interest and debt expense (net of capitalized interest) for 1987 was $489 million, compared with $565 million and $337 million for 1986 and 1985, respectively. The 1987 decrease was principally due to the lower level of debt as a result of the early extinguishment of $1.6 billion of high-interest debt (see Note 4 to the Financial Statements) in the first quarter of 1987, while the 1986 increase was principally due to the higher level of long-term debt associated with the Nabisco Brands acquisition (see Note 16 to the Financial Statements).

Income Taxes

The FASB has issued a final statement, "Accounting for Income Taxes," which the Company expects to adopt in 1988. The new standard requires use of the liability method under which the effects on deferred taxes of changes in tax rates and laws are recorded as a component of tax expense in the period of change rather than the period of timing difference reversal as the current deferred method requires. The Company would realize, in the year of adoption, a one-time cumulative benefit to income from reductions of deferred income taxes resulting from lower income tax rates. The effect on annual income is not expected to be material.

The Company has chosen not to adopt this statement in 1987 to provide adequate lead-time for analyzing the effect of the new accounting standard.

RJR Nabisco, Inc.
Selected Five-Year Financial Condition Data

(Dollars in Millions Except Per Share Amounts)	1987 (1)	1986	1985	1984 (1)	1983
Funds provided by continuing operations	$ 2,124	$ 1,875	$ 1,447	$1,082	$ 943
Working capital	$ 1,717	$ 1,329	$ 1,617	$2,780	$2,853
Current ratio	1.4	1.3	1.4	2.5	3.3
Total assets	$16,861	$16,701	$16,414	$8,805	$8,776
Return on beginning total assets (2)	9.0%	8.5%	13.5%	14.8%	11.2%
Return on average total assets	8.9%	8.4%	9.4%	14.8%	11.2%
Total debt (3)	$ 4,488	$ 5,774	$ 5,628	$1,443	$1,444
Preferred stock	173	291	1,587	499	631
Common stockholders' equity	6,038	5,312	4,796	4,478	5,223
Total capital	$10,699	$11,377	$12,011	$6,420	$7,298
Return on beginning total capital (4)	13.2%	11.6%	18.5%	17.8%	13.6%
Return on average total capital	13.6%	11.9%	12.9%	19.0%	13.5%
Total debt as a percentage of total capital (5)	41.9%	50.8%	46.9%	22.5%	19.8%
Return on beginning common stockholders' equity (6)	22.2%	20.1%	20.3%	22.1%	17.2%
Return on average common stockholders' equity	20.8%	19.0%	19.6%	23.8%	16.4%
Capital expenditures	$ 936	$ 1,022	$ 946	$ 642	$ 492
Book value per common share	$ 24.41	$ 21.21	$ 19.14	$17.33	$18.44

Prior years have been restated to report the Company's former spirits and wines business as discontinued operations (see Note 3 to the Financial Statements). The 1985 amounts include the operations of Nabisco Brands from July 2, 1985 (see Note 16 to the Financial Statements).

(1) Net income for 1987 and 1984 includes a $215 million and $275 million gain, respectively, on the sale of the Company's discontinued operations. In addition, the 1987 net income includes an extraordinary loss from the early extinguishment of debt of $80 million. (See Notes 3 and 4 to the Financial Statements.)

(2) Net income plus after-tax interest and debt expense divided by beginning total assets.

(3) Total debt consists of notes payable and long-term debt (including current maturities).

(4) Net income plus after-tax interest and debt expense divided by beginning total capital.

(5) At December 31, 1987, 1986, 1985, 1984 and 1983, the sum of the total debt and redeemable preferred stock as a percentage of total capital was 43.6 percent, 53.3 percent, 60.1 percent, 30.2 percent and 28.4 percent, respectively.

(6) Net income applicable to Common Stock divided by beginning common stockholders' equity.

Funds Provided by Continuing Operations, Capital Expenditures and Cash Dividends
(Dollars in Millions)

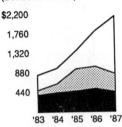

\$2,200

1,760

1,320

880

440

'83 '84 '85 '86 '87

☐ Funds Provided

▨ Capital Expenditures

■ Cash Dividends

Composition of Capital
(Dollars in Millions)

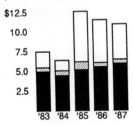

\$12.5

10.0

7.5

5.0

2.5

'83 '84 '85 '86 '87

☐ Total Debt

▨ Preferred Stock

■ Common Stockholders' Equity

Financial Condition

Funds Provided by Continuing Operations

Funds provided by continuing operations were \$2.1 billion in 1987 compared with \$1.9 billion in 1986 and \$1.4 billion in 1985. The increases in funds provided by continuing operations were due to higher levels of income and noncash charges. Internally generated funds from operations represent a major source of funds available to the Company.

During 1987, funds provided by continuing operations continued to be sufficient, as in prior years, to meet capital expenditures and cash dividends. Over the past five years, funds provided by continuing operations totaled \$7.5 billion and have increased at a compounded rate of 23 percent. These funds were principally used for capital expenditures and cash dividends, leaving \$1.2 billion of internally generated funds available for other Company purposes. In the future, the Company expects that internally generated funds will continue to be more than sufficient to meet projected capital expenditures and cash dividends. The Company has paid a dividend every year since 1900 and in the third quarter of 1987, increased the regular quarterly cash dividend on Common Stock by 20 percent to 48 cents per share.

Liquidity

At December 31, 1987, working capital was \$1.7 billion compared with \$1.3 billion at year-end 1986 and the current ratio was 1.4 for 1987 and 1986, respectively.

The Company believes that its continued favorable current ratio is an important indicator of its ability to meet short-term obligations. A further indication of the Company's favorable liquidity position is that 20 percent of current assets are LIFO inventories, which are carried at values substantially less than current cost. The current cost of inventories was \$1.3 billion more than the amounts at which they were carried on the 1987 Balance Sheet (see Note 6 to the Financial Statements).

During 1987, the Company's extinguishment of \$1.6 billion of high-interest debt (see Note 4 to the Financial Statements) and the issuance of \$1.3 billion of lower interest debt resulted in

a weighted average interest rate of less than 9% for debt outstanding at December 31, 1987. In addition, the Company maintained seasonal credit facilities with various banks, as well as a Eurodollar credit facility which expires in 1993 (see Notes 8 and 10 to the Financial Statements). The credit available through these facilities ensures the Company's access to credit markets and the availability of significant financial resources, as well as operational flexibility. Unused credit facilities totaled \$1.2 billion at year-end 1987, including \$550 million to support outstanding commercial paper. The Company utilizes commercial paper to fund seasonal working capital requirements as needed.

Capital Resources

Total capital was \$10.7 billion at December 31, 1987, compared with \$11.4 billion for the prior year end. The decrease was due principally to the early extinguishment of \$1.6 billion of high-interest debt (see Note 4 to the Financial Statements), retirement of substantially all of the short-term notes which were classified as long-term in the prior year, and the repurchase of a portion of its Common Stock and Series B Cumulative Preferred Stock. Through December 31, 1987, 3,103,400 shares have been repurchased under the Common Stock repurchase program which announced the repurchase of up to 5 million shares. The primary sources of funds for the above transactions were the proceeds from the sale of Heublein (see Note 3 to the Financial Statements), the issuance of \$1.3 billion of long-term debt and internally generated funds.

Consequently, total debt as a percentage of total capital at December 31, 1987, declined to 42 percent compared with 51 percent at year-end 1986, and the sum of total debt and redeemable preferred stock as a percentage of total capital decreased to 44 percent from 53 percent for the previous year.

The Company believes its financial position is strong, as indicated by continued favorable financial ratios, and that it has the ability to finance operations as necessary. The Company also believes that the debt-to-capital ratios will improve over time as internally generated funds are expected to exceed projected capital expenditures and cash dividends. Should the need for external financing arise, the Company expects to have continued access to short-term credit markets to fund seasonal working capital requirements and to have the ability to raise additional funds in the long-term debt market.

Capital Expenditures

Consolidated capital expenditures for 1987, 1986 and 1985 were $936 million, $1,022 million and $946 million, respectively. Tobacco capital expenditures accounted for 46 percent of the 1987 consolidated total, while food expenditures were 48 percent of the total.

Tobacco capital expenditures during 1987 were $433 million compared with $613 million for the prior year. The expenditures for both years were principally for a new manufacturing complex in North Carolina and for the expansion and modernization of facilities worldwide. The new cigarette plant began initial production in January 1986 and became fully operational by the end of 1987, supplying over 50 percent of the domestic tobacco production requirements.

Food capital expenditures totaled $445 million in 1987 compared with $344 million in 1986. The increase was primarily due to the modernization and cost reduction efforts of food operations.

Capital expenditures are currently projected to total $5.0 billion over the next three years compared with $2.9 billion for the last three years. The projected increase is principally due to the food businesses. Over this period, food capital expenditures are expected to increase to approximately 60 percent of the consolidated total, principally for the modernization and expansion of facilities in the Biscuit Division.

Foreign Currency

The Company has operations in many countries, utilizing 33 functional currencies in its more than 300 subsidiaries and branches. The major functional currency is the U.S. dollar. Significant foreign currency net investments are located in Canada, the United Kingdom, France, West Germany, Italy and the Philippines. Changes in the strength of these countries' currencies relative to the U.S. dollar result in direct charges or credits to the equity section on the Consolidated Balance Sheets. The Company also has significant exposure to foreign exchange sale and purchase transactions in currencies other than a functional currency.

The exposures include the West German mark, Japanese yen, U.S. dollar, French franc, British pound and Spanish peseta. The Company manages these exposures to minimize the effects of foreign currency transactions on its income.

Although fluctuations in the value of foreign currencies cause U.S. dollar translated amounts to change in comparison with previous periods, the Company cannot quantify in any meaningful way the effect of such fluctuations upon future income. This is due to the large number of currencies involved, the constantly changing exposure to these currencies, the complexity of intercompany relationships, the hedging activity entered into to minimize the effect of rate changes, and the fact that all foreign currencies do not react in the same manner against the U.S. dollar.

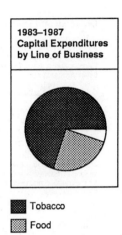

**1983–1987
Capital Expenditures
by Line of Business**

▨ Tobacco

▨ Food

☐ Corporate

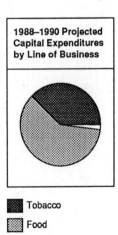

**1988–1990 Projected
Capital Expenditures
by Line of Business**

▨ Tobacco

▨ Food

☐ Corporate

Dividends and Stock Prices

The Company's Common Stock is listed on the New York Stock Exchange (trading symbol: RJR) and on stock exchanges in London, Geneva, Zurich, Basel, Frankfurt, Dusseldorf, Berlin, Amsterdam, Paris, Brussels, Antwerp and Tokyo. The number of common stockholders of record at December 31, 1987 was 104,720.

The Company's Series B Cumulative Preferred Stock is listed and traded only in the United States. The regular quarterly dividend per share is $2.87½.

The following table sets forth the dividends paid per share of Common Stock and the high and low sales prices, taken from the Composite Tape as reported by the Wall Street Journal, for the common and preferred stock during the last two years:

**Net Income Per
Common Share and
Dividends Per Common Share**
(Dollars)

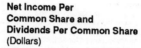

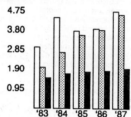

□ Net Income

▨ Net Income from Continuing Operations

■ Dividends

Quarters	Common Stock		Series B Cumulative Preferred Stock
	Dividends	Market Price (high-low)	Market Price (high-low)
1987			
First	$ .40	$65⅝ — 49	$125½ — 121
Second	.40	59⅛ — 47¼	124 — 117½
Third	.48	71⅛ — 52¾	123 — 117½
Fourth	.48	68⅝ — 34½	120 — 115¾
Year	**$1.76**	**$71⅛ — 34½**	**$125½ — 115¾**
1986			
First	$ .37	$44½ — 31	$121½ — 110⅜
Second	.37	54⅜ — 37	125⅜ — 120⅞
Third	.37	55⅛ — 44⅞	125¾ — 121¼
Fourth	.40	53⅝ — 47⅜	126¾ — 120¾
Year	$1.51	$55⅛ — 31	$126¾ — 110⅜

RJR Nabisco, Inc.

Consolidated Financial Statements

The Summary of Significant Accounting Policies below, the Notes to Consolidated Financial Statements on pages 56 through 62, and the Lines of Business and Geographic Data on pages 66 and 67 are integral parts of the accompanying financial statements.

Summary of Significant Accounting Policies

This summary of significant accounting policies is presented to assist in understanding the Company's financial statements included in this report. These policies conform to generally accepted accounting principles and have been consistently followed by the Company in all material respects.

Consolidation

The Company includes in its consolidated financial statements the accounts of the parent and all subsidiaries. The Company's former spirits and wines business is reported as discontinued operations, and prior years financial statements have been restated accordingly.

Inventories

In all of the Company's businesses, inventories are stated at the lower of cost or market. Various methods are used for determining cost as described below.

The cost of domestic inventories is determined principally under the LIFO method. The cost of remaining inventories is determined

under the FIFO, specific lot and weighted average methods. In accordance with recognized trade practice, stocks of tobacco, which must be cured for more than one year, are classified as current assets.

Depreciation

Property, plant and equipment are depreciated principally by the straight-line method.

Goodwill and Trademarks

Goodwill and trademarks are generally amortized on a straight-line basis over a 40-year period.

Other Income and Expense

The Company includes in "Other income (expense), net" items of a financial nature, principally interest income and gains and losses on foreign currency transactions.

Income Taxes

The Company uses the flow-through method in accounting for investment tax credits, whereby the provision for income taxes is reduced in the year the tax credits first become available.

Excise Taxes

Excise taxes are excluded from "Net sales" and "Cost of products sold."

RJR Nabisco, Inc.
Consolidated Statements of Changes in Financial Position
For the Years Ended December 31

(Dollars in Millions)	1987	1986	1985
Funds provided by continuing operations:			
Net sales	**$15,766**	$15,102	$11,622
Less operating costs and expenses which required the outlay of working capital	**13,642**	13,227	10,175
Total funds provided by continuing operations	**2,124**	1,875	1,447
Funds required by continuing operations:			
Change in working capital resulting from operations (see below)	**62**	(116)	(46)
Capital expenditures	**936**	1,022	946
Miscellaneous acquisitions of businesses	**78**	—	34
Miscellaneous dispositions of businesses	**(125)**	(376)	—
Disposals of property, plant and equipment	**(46)**	(62)	(58)
Cash dividends	**470**	480	448
Cumulative translation adjustments	**(88)**	(10)	15
Other	**108**	(172)	242
Total funds required by continuing operations	**1,395**	766	1,581
Net funds provided (required) by continuing operations	**729**	1,109	(134)
Funds provided (required) by financing transactions:			
Net change in current notes payable	**(76)**	(121)	429
Issuance of long-term debt	**1,288**	1,125	3,334
Retirements of long-term debt	**(2,545)**	(909)	(445)
Issuance of Company's stocks (Notes 12 and 13)	**24**	41	1,241
Repurchases of Company's stocks (Notes 12 and 13)	**(317)**	(1,469)	(403)
Extraordinary loss (Note 4)	**(80)**	—	—
Net funds provided (required) by financing transactions	**(1,706)**	(1,333)	4,156
Net change in funds related to discontinued operations (Note 3)	**1,238**	504	(85)
Net funds required for acquisition of Nabisco Brands, Inc. (Note 16)	**—**	—	(4,672)
Increase (decrease) in cash and short-term investments	**$ 261**	$ 280	$ (735)
Analysis of change in working capital resulting from operations:			
Funds required (provided) by the change in:			
Accounts and notes receivable	**$ 70**	$ (49)	$ 107
Inventories	**58**	(256)	(29)
Prepaid expenses and excise taxes	**48**	63	22
Accounts payable and accrued accounts	**(236)**	(154)	(418)
Income taxes accrued	**122**	280	272
Change in working capital resulting from operations	**$ 62**	$ (116)	$ (46)

RJR Nabisco, Inc.

Notes to Consolidated Financial Statements

(Dollars in Millions Except Per Share Amounts)

Note 1
Restructuring Expense, Net

Restructuring expense for 1987 included costs principally related to the write-down of redundant equipment and facilities from the continuing modernization of domestic tobacco operations ($135 million), the Voluntary Separation Incentive Program announced by R.J. Reynolds Tobacco Co. in June 1987 ($180 million), restructuring programs in the food subsidiaries ($134 million) and relocation of the Planters LifeSavers headquarters to Winston-Salem, North Carolina ($50 million).

This restructuring program included nonrecurring gains from the sales of the Company's Canadian coffee, margarine and confectionery businesses ($178 million), premium refunds from a restructuring of insurance programs and miscellaneous gains from the sale of specialty tobacco brands.

Note 2
Provision for Income Taxes

The provision for income taxes consisted of the following:

	1987	1986	1985
Current:			
Federal	$370	$305	$507
Foreign and other	312	228	177
	682	533	684
Deferred:			
Federal	84	178	25
Foreign and other	(31)	46	37
	53	224	62
Provision for income taxes	$735	$757	$746

Deferred income tax expense results from timing differences in the recognition of revenue and expense for book and tax purposes. The sources of these differences and the tax effect of each were as follows:

	1987	1986	1985
Excess of tax over book depreciation	$171	$178	$ 94
Restructuring items	(123)	—	—
Various other items	5	46	(32)
Deferred income taxes	$ 53	$224	$ 62

Pretax income from continuing operations for domestic and foreign operations is shown in the following table:

	1987	1986	1985
Domestic (includes U.S. exports)	$1,020	$1,209	$1,256
Foreign*	796	573	407
	$1,816	$1,782	$1,663

*Pretax income of foreign operations is income of all operations located outside the United States, some of which may also be currently subject to U.S. tax jurisdiction.

The differences between the provision for income taxes and income taxes computed at statutory U.S. federal income tax rates are explained as follows:

	1987	1986	1985
Income taxes computed at statutory U.S. federal income tax rates	$726	$820	$765
Taxes on foreign operations less than statutory U.S. federal income tax rates	(25)	(48)	(25)
State taxes, net of federal benefit	46	51	48
Investment tax credit	(14)	(46)	(60)
Goodwill amortization	48	58	25
Miscellaneous items	(46)	(78)	(7)
Provision for income taxes	$735	$757	$746
Effective tax rate	40.5%	42.5%	44.9%

At December 31, 1987, there was $2.2 billion of accumulated and undistributed income of foreign subsidiaries for which no provision for U.S. federal income taxes had been made. The undistributed income is intended to be reinvested abroad indefinitely or repatriated substantially free of additional tax.

There are a number of issues pending as a result of Internal Revenue Service audits. The resolution of these issues is not expected to have a material effect on the Company's financial position.

Note 3
Discontinued Operations

On March 6, 1987, the Company sold its spirits and wines business, conducted principally through Heublein, Inc., for $1.2 billion in cash. After provision for income taxes of $230 million, the gain on the sale was $215 million or 86 cents per share.

On October 1, 1986, the Company sold, for cash, its quick-service restaurant business, essentially Kentucky Fried Chicken, for $840 million. After provision for income taxes of $28 million, the loss on the sale was $39 million. The loss reduced 1986 net income per share by 16 cents.

Summarized information for discontinued operations is shown in the following table:

	1987	1986	1985
Net sales	$102	$1,896	$1,912
Operating income (loss)	(7)	208	214
Income (loss) before provision for income taxes	(10)	187	191
Provision (benefit) for income taxes	(3)	109	107
Income (loss) from discontinued operations	(7)	78	84
Gain (loss) on sale, net of tax	215	(39)	—
	$208	$ 39	$ 84
Discontinued operations per common share	$ .83	$ .15	$ .33

Note 4
Extraordinary Item

During the first quarter of 1987, the Company sustained an extraordinary loss as a result of the early extinguishment of $1.2 billion of the 11.2% Notes issued in the Nabisco Brands acquisition (see Note 16 to the Financial Statements), as well as 11.35%, 11.75% and 13.35% Debentures classified as short-term at year-end 1986. Proceeds from the sale of Heublein were used to extinguish the 11.2% Notes. A total of $1.6 billion of debt was extinguished at a premium of $80 million (after a tax benefit of $55 million), which decreased income per share by 32 cents.

Note 5
Cash and Short-Term Investments

Short-term investments at December 31, 1987 and 1986, valued at cost (approximate market), totaled $786 million and $675 million, respectively. Short-term investments at December 31, 1987 principally consisted of certificates of deposit.

Note 6
Inventories

The major classes of inventory and the amount of each at December 31 were:

	1987	1986
Leaf tobacco	$ 833	$ 945
Finished products	1,087	953
Raw materials	375	416
Other	383	306
	$2,678	$2,620

At December 31, 1987 and 1986, $1.2 billion and $1.3 billion, respectively, of the inventory was valued by the LIFO method. The balance of the inventory was valued by various other methods, principally FIFO.

The current cost of LIFO inventories at December 31, 1987 and 1986, was greater than the amounts at which these inventories were carried on the balance sheets by $1.3 billion in each year.

During 1987 and 1986, net income was increased by $20 million and $33 million, respectively, as a result of LIFO inventory liquidations. The LIFO liquidations resulted from management's plan to manage leaf tobacco inventory levels, consistent with its forecast of future operating requirements. The overall cost of recent leaf purchases at auction has been increasing, which results in higher cost of sales.

Note 7
Property, Plant and Equipment

Components of property, plant and equipment at December 31 are shown in the following table:

	1987	1986
Land and land improvements	$ 324	$ 296
Buildings and leasehold improvements	1,571	1,418
Machinery and equipment	5,064	4,373
Construction-in-process	604	607
	$7,563	$6,694

Note 8
Notes Payable and Related Information

Notes payable consisted of the following at December 31:

	1987	1986
Commercial paper	$283	$419
Notes payable, principally to domestic banks	159	99
	$442	$518

Unused lines of credit at December 31, 1987, totaled $1.2 billion and included $550 million to support outstanding domestic commercial paper. Of these lines at December 31, 1987, $639 million was in the form of seasonal credit facilities. The $550 million was in the form of a Eurodollar credit facility with various foreign banks and foreign branches of domestic banks which provides for commitments up to $600 million in borrowings. Under this facility agreement, the Company is obligated to pay a commitment fee of 8/100 of 1 percent per annum on the committed amount. It expires in 1993 (see Note 10 to the Financial Statements).

Note 9
Accounts Payable and Accrued Accounts

Accounts payable and accrued accounts consisted of the following at December 31:

	1987	1986
Trade accounts	$ 621	$ 532
Marketing and advertising	666	460
Payroll and employee benefits	489	444
Restructuring and relocation	255	—
Excise taxes	226	310
Other	930	1,177
	$3,187	$2,923

Note 10
Long-term Debt

	December 31, 1987		December 31, 1986	
	Due Within One Year	Due After One Year (1)	Due Within One Year	Due After One Year
Long-term debt consisted of the following:				
7⅜ – 9⅜% Debentures, with semiannual and annual sinking fund payments through 2017 (reduced by $79 million and $88 million of such debentures held by the Company on December 31, 1987 and 1986, respectively, for future sinking fund requirements)	$ 6	$1,454	$ 6	$ 483
11.35 – 13.35% Debentures	—	—	353	—
6⅞ – 9¾% Notes, due through 1994	100	351	—	250
10 – 10⅞% Notes, due 1988 to 1993	—	700	—	699
11.2% Notes, due 1997	—	—	—	1,199
7.61 – 10.88% effective interest rates, foreign currency debt, due 1990 to 2001 (2)	—	653	—	648
Zero Coupon Guaranteed Notes, due 1992, net of discount of $160 million and $202 million at December 31, 1987 and 1986, respectively, effective interest rate of 14.64%	—	205	—	198
Credit agreements with various banks, due 1993 (3)	—	50	—	877
Other indebtedness	56	471	64	479
	$162	$3,884	$423	$4,833

(1) The payment schedule of debt due through 1992 is as follows (in millions): 1989—$310; 1990—$274; 1991—$422; and 1992—$517.
(2) The Company has entered into hedging arrangements which will offset the effects of future exchange rate movements on these debt issues.
(3) At December 31, 1987, the Company's Eurodollar credit facility (see Note 8 to the Financial Statements) supported $50 million of short-term notes that have been classified as long-term based upon the Company's intention to continue that amount of debt in some form for more than one year.

Note 11
Commitments and Contingencies

Various legal actions, proceedings and claims are pending or may be instituted against the Company and its subsidiaries, including those claiming that lung cancer and other diseases have resulted from the use of the tobacco products of R.J. Reynolds Tobacco Co. (Reynolds). During 1987, 14 new such actions were commenced, and 42 such actions were dismissed or otherwise resolved in favor of Reynolds prior to trial. A total of 68 such actions were pending at December 31, 1987. Some of the foregoing involve or may involve claims for compensatory, punitive or other damages in substantial amounts. Litigation is subject to many uncertainties, and it is possible that some of the legal actions, proceedings or claims could be decided unfavorably to Reynolds.

The Company has product liability insurance covering only a portion of such legal actions, proceedings or claims, and the maximum insurance coverage available on reasonable terms and conditions is substantially less than the aggregate compensatory and other damages alleged in such actions, proceedings or claims.

The Company believes that the above actions, proceedings or claims, in the aggregate, should not have any material adverse effect on the Company's financial position.

At December 31, 1987, the Company had commitments totaling approximately $450 million for the purchase of machinery and equipment in connection with its facilities modernization programs.

Note 12
Redeemable Preferred Stock

The Company had one class of cumulative preferred stock (Series B) outstanding at December 31, 1987. The stock is senior to the Common Stock as to dividends and preferences in liquidation.

The Series B Stock is subject to mandatory redemption of 327,375 shares per year, commencing November 1, 1989, at a redemption price of $100 per share plus any accrued dividends. The Company has the noncumulative option to double the amount redeemed pursuant to such mandatory redemption in any year. The Company may elect to redeem all or part of the Series B Stock, in addition to the mandatory redemption requirement, at an initial optional redemption price of $111.50 plus accrued dividends on November 1, 1989. The optional redemption price declines thereafter on an annual basis to $100 plus accrued dividends on November 1, 1994, and thereafter. During 1987, the Company repurchased and retired 1,174,217 shares of the Series B Stock under a repurchase program to buy back up to 1,597,021 shares. Cumulative dividends are payable quarterly on the Series B Stock at an annual rate of $11.50 and aggregated $30 million in 1987, and $33 million in 1986 and 1985, respectively. Additionally, holders of the Series B Stock are entitled to one vote per share on all matters on which holders of Common Stock have the right to vote.

On March 1, 1986, the Company redeemed all remaining shares of its Series A Cumulative Preferred Stock at $48.50 per share plus accrued dividends. Dividends on Series A Stock were $1 million in 1986 and $9 million in 1985.

On December 1, 1986, the Company redeemed all remaining shares of its Series C Cumulative Preferred Stock at $135.23 per share plus $1.08 per share in accrued dividends. Dividends on Series C Stock were $68 million in 1986 and $49 million in 1985.

Changes in redeemable preferred stock are summarized in the following table:

	1987		1986		1985	
	Shares	**Amount**	Shares	Amount	Shares	Amount
Series A Cumulative Preferred Stock — **without par value** ($48.50 stated value):						
Balance at beginning of year	—	—	1,634,494	$ 79	7,053,478	$ 342
Shares redeemed and retired	—	—	(1,634,494)	(79)	(5,418,984)	(263)
	—	—	—	—	1,634,494	79
Less treasury stock:						
Balance at beginning of year	—	—	(41,809)	(2)	(2,801,856)	(133)
Shares purchased	—	—	—	—	(644,617)	(32)
Shares retired	—	—	41,809	2	3,404,664	163
	—	—	—	—	(41,809)	(2)
Balance at end of year	—	—	—	—	1,592,685	$ 77
Series B Cumulative Preferred Stock — **without par value** ($100 stated value—authorized 1,732,304 shares at December 31, 1987):						
Balance at beginning of year	**2,906,521**	**$ 291**	2,911,295	$ 291	2,899,112	$ 290
Shares issued upon conversion of 4 ½ % Convertible Subordinated Debentures	**—**	**—**	—	—	12,183	1
Shares retired*	**(1,174,217)**	**(118)**	(4,774)	—	—	—
	1,732,304	**173**	2,906,521	291	2,911,295	291
Less treasury stock:						
Balance at beginning of year	—	—	(4,774)	—	(4,774)	—
Shares retired	—	—	4,774	—	—	—
	—	—	—	—	(4,774)	—
Balance at end of year	**1,732,304**	**$ 173**	2,906,521	$ 291	2,906,521	$ 291
Series C Cumulative Preferred Stock — **without par value** ($125 stated value):						
Balance at beginning of year	—	—	9,750,095	$1,219	—	$ —
Shares issued in Nabisco Brands acquisition (see Note 16)	—	—	—	—	9,750,095	1,219
Shares redeemed and retired*	—	—	(9,750,095)	(1,219)	—	—
Balance at end of year	—	—	—	—	9,750,095	$1,219

*The aggregate cost to the Company, including all related fees and expenses, was $141 million in 1987 and $1,328 million in 1986. The excess of the cost of shares repurchased and retired over the stated value of $118 million and $1,219 million, in 1987 and 1986, respectively, has been charged to retained earnings.

Note 13
Common Stock and Paid-In Capital

	1987		1986		1985	
	Shares	**Amount**	Shares	Amount	Shares	Amount
Common Stock-no par ($1 stated value— authorized 600,000,000 shares at December 31, 1987):						
Balance at beginning of year	**250,698,401**	**$ 251**	250,698,401	$251	258,548,528	$259
Shares issued upon conversion of 4½% Convertible Subordinated Debentures	—	—	—	—	78,932	—
Shares repurchased and retired (1)	—	—	—	—	(7,929,059)	(8)
Balance at end of year	**250,698,401**	**$ 251**	250,698,401	$251	250,698,401	$251
Paid-in capital:						
Balance at beginning of year		**$ 320**		$332		$344
Common Stock repurchased and retired (1)		—		—		(10)
Other		**(8)**		(12)		(2)
Balance at end of year		**$ 312**		$320		$332
Treasury stock:						
Balance at beginning of year	**(303,468)**	**$ (15)**	(131,940)	$ (4)	(165,273)	$ (4)
Shares purchased (2)	**(3,633,200)**	**(176)**	(1,300,000)	(62)	(850,000)	(25)
Shares issued under incentive compensation plan awards, net	**595,432**	**32**	1,128,472	51	883,333	25
Balance at end of year	**(3,341,236)**	**$(159)**	(303,468)	$ (15)	(131,940)	$ (4)

(1) The aggregate cost to the Company, including all related fees and expenses was $248 million in 1985. The excess of the cost of shares repurchased and retired over the stated value has been charged to retained earnings, $230 million, and paid-in capital, $10 million.

(2) In October 1987, the Company announced its intention to repurchase up to 5 million shares of its Common Stock. At December 31, 1987, 3,103,400 shares had been repurchased under this program at an aggregate cost of $145 million.

The Company has three stock option plans that provide for the granting of options to purchase shares of the Company's Common Stock to certain officers and other employees. These plans permit the granting of incentive awards in the form of incentive stock options (ISOs), stock appreciation rights (SARs) and other stock options. The option price for outstanding options is the average quoted market price on the date of grant. Options that lapse or are cancelled are added back to shares authorized for future grants.

Under the 1982 Long-Term Incentive Plan, the maximum number of shares of Common Stock that may be granted is 12,500,000. As of December 31, 1987, there were 615,031 ISOs (37,201 of which have SARs attached) and 2,253,853 nonqualified options (1,341,928 of which have SARs attached) outstanding with expiration dates ranging from July 21, 1988 to June 18, 1996. The average exercise price was $34.18, and such options were held by 519 participants.

Under the 1977 Stock Option Plan, the number of shares of Common Stock granted, net of cancellations, was 5,325,548. No additional shares may be granted under this plan.

As of December 31, 1987, there were 749,105 nonqualified options/SARs outstanding with expiration dates ranging from September 21, 1988 to June 18, 1996. The average exercise price was $24.65, and such options/SARs were held by 168 participants.

Under the Career Executive Stock Plan, the total number of shares of Common Stock granted , net of cancellations, was 2,634,041. No additional shares may be granted under this plan. As of December 31, 1987, there were 10,425 nonqualified options/SARs outstanding with an expiration date of February 15, 1994. The average exercise price was $23.45, and such options/SARs were held by 6 participants.

The following table summarizes the changes in options outstanding and related price ranges for shares of Common Stock under options:

	1987	1986	1985
Options:			
Outstanding at beginning of year	**4,702,295**	4,918,294	4,136,785
1982 Long-Term Incentive Plan:			
Granted	**—**	1,242,900	1,305,278
Exercised	**(588,566)**	(959,213)	(396,523)
1977 Stock Option Plan:			
Granted	**—**	93,200	459,114
Exercised	**(210,204)**	(395,612)	(403,415)
Career Executive Stock Plan:			
Exercised	**(13,865)**	(51,050)	(45,201)
Cancelled	**(261,246)**	(146,224)	(137,744)
Outstanding at end of year	**3,628,414**	4,702,295	4,918,294
Price Ranges:			
Outstanding at beginning of year	**$12.19-49.06**	$11.81-31.55	$11.51-26.30
Granted under 1982 Long-Term Incentive Plan	**—**	49.06	26.19-30.55
Granted under 1977 Stock Option Plan	**—**	35.38-49.06	27.50-31.55
Options/SARs exercised (market prices ranged from $44.56-70.75 in 1987, $31.31-54.56 in 1986 and $25.25-34.88 in 1985)	**12.19-49.06**	11.81-31.55	11.51-26.30
Cancelled	**20.23-49.06**	18.48-49.06	17.28-31.55
Outstanding at end of year	**$12.19-49.06**	$12.19-49.06	$11.81-31.55

At December 31, 1987, options were exercisable as to 2,123,746 shares, compared with 2,172,799 shares at December 31, 1986, and 2,373,437 shares at December 31, 1985. As of December 31, 1987, options for 5,310,591 shares of Common Stock were available for future grants.

Note 14
Cumulative Translation Adjustments

The changes in this account are shown in the following table:

	1987	1986
Balance at beginning of year	$(76)	$(140)
Translation and other adjustments	159	34
Related income taxes	6	7
Sale of businesses	(3)	23
Balance at end of year	$ 86	$ (76)

Note 15
Retirement Benefits

The Company sponsors a number of non-contributory defined benefit pension plans covering most U.S. employees. Plans covering regular full-time employees in the tobacco operations (as well as hourly employees in the food operations) provide pension benefits that are based on the employee's length of service and final average compensation before retirement. Plans covering salaried employees of the corporate group and food operations were amended in late 1987 to provide for individual accounts which offer lump sum or annuity payment options, with benefits based on accumulated compensation and interest credits made monthly throughout the career of each participant, with an initial opening credit based on the value of retirement benefits accrued prior to the date of such amendment. The Company's policy is to fund the cost of current service benefits and past service cost over periods not exceeding 30 years to the extent that such costs are currently tax deductible. Additionally, the Company participates in several multi-employer plans, which provide defined benefits to certain of the Company's union employees.

Employees in foreign countries who are not U.S. citizens are covered by various post-employment benefit arrangements, some of which are considered to be defined benefit plans for accounting purposes.

The Company elected early adoption of FASB Statement No. 87, "Employers' Accounting for Pensions," for its United States pension plans in 1986 and for its Canadian pension plans in 1987. The effect of the 1987 adoption in Canada was not significant, while the 1986 adoption for U.S. plans reduced pension expense for that year by $21 million. Pension expense and related information presented for prior periods have not been retroactively restated. The Company intends to apply FASB Statement No. 87 to its other foreign plans in 1988, the effect of which is expected to be immaterial.

A summary of the components of net periodic pension cost for Company sponsored plans follows:

	1987	1986	1985
Defined benefit plans:			
Service cost— benefits earned during the period	**$ 82**	$ 69	
Interest cost on projected benefit obligation	**195**	167	
Actual return on plan assets	**(89)**	(281)	
Net amortization and deferral	**(132)**	96	
Total U.S. and Canadian plans	**56**	51	$60
Foreign plans	**18**	15	14
Net pension cost of defined benefit plans	**74**	66	74
Multi-employer plans	**29**	23	17
Total pension expense	**$ 103**	$ 89	$91

The following table sets forth the funded status and amounts recognized in the Consolidated Balance Sheets at December 31, 1987 and 1986 for the Company's United States and Canadian defined benefit pension plans, using the following assumptions:

	1987	1986
Weighted-average discount rate	**8.5%**	8.0%
Rate of increase in compensation levels	**6.5%**	6.5%
Expected long-term rate of return on assets	**9.0%**	9.0%

December 31, 1987	Plans Whose Assets Exceeded Accumulated Benefits	Plans Whose Accumulated Benefits Exceeded Assets
Present value of benefit obligations:		
Vested benefit obligation	**$ 1,050**	**$ 744**
Accumulated benefit obligation	**$ 1,247**	**$ 804**
Plan assets at fair market value	**$ 1,707**	**$ 676**
Projected benefit obligation	**(1,683)**	**(914)**
Projected benefit obligation (in excess of) or less than plan assets	**24**	**(238)**
Unrecognized net loss	**11**	**16**
Prior service cost not yet recognized in periodic pension cost	**11**	**24**
Unrecognized net assets at January 1, 1987, net of amortization	**(171)**	**(111)**
Net pension liability recognized in the balance sheet	**$ (125)**	**$(309)**
Net pension liability recognized in the balance sheet at December 31, 1986 (U.S. plans only)	$ (28)	$(329)

The projected benefit obligation includes $79 million related to the 1987 Voluntary Separation Incentive Program of R.J. Reynolds Tobacco Co.

At December 31, 1987, 82 percent of the plan assets were invested in listed stocks and bonds. The balance consisted of various income producing investments.

The actuarial present value of accumulated plan benefits for the United States defined benefit pension plans at December 31, 1986 was $1.8 billion, including vested benefits of $1.5 billion. The net assets available for benefits were $2.1 billion.

In addition to providing pension benefits, the Company provides certain health care and life insurance benefits for retired employees. Substantially all of its regular full-time employees, including certain employees in foreign countries, may become eligible for those benefits if they reach retirement age while working for the Company. The cost of retiree health care and life insurance benefits is generally recognized as expense when claims are paid. Claim payments and insurance premiums for retirees amounted to $28 million in 1987, $26 million in 1986 and $17 million in 1985.

Note 16
Acquisition

The Company purchased 50.2 percent of the outstanding shares of Nabisco Brands, Inc. Common Stock on July 2, 1985, for $85 per share. The acquisition was completed on September 10, 1985 upon the conversion of the remaining shares of Nabisco Brands, Inc. Common Stock into a combination of the Company's Series C Cumulative Preferred Stock and 11.2% Notes. (See Notes 10 and 12 to the Financial Statements.)

The total cost of the acquisition, which was accounted for as a purchase, was $4.9 billion. Excluding working capital acquired of $295 million, the investment was primarily for intangibles of $3.9 billion, property, plant and equipment of $1.8 billion, and long-term debt of $685 million.

If the acquisition had taken place as of the beginning of 1985, pro forma net sales, income from continuing operations and the related per share amount for 1985 would have been $14.5 billion, $899 million and $2.90, respectively.

Responsibility for Financial Statements

RJR Nabisco, Inc. is responsible for the preparation and accuracy of the financial statements and other information included in this report. The financial statements have been prepared in accordance with generally accepted accounting principles using, where appropriate, management's best estimates and judgment.

The Company's independent auditors, Ernst & Whinney, have examined the financial statements in accordance with generally accepted auditing standards and their report appears herein.

In meeting its responsibility for the reliability of the financial statements, the Company depends on its system of internal accounting controls. The system is designed to provide reasonable assurance that assets are safeguarded and transactions are executed as authorized and properly recorded. The system is augmented by written policies and procedures and an extensive internal audit program.

The Board of Directors of the Company has an Audit Committee which is composed entirely of directors who are neither officers nor employees of the Company. The Audit Committee meets regularly with management, the internal auditors and the independent auditors to discuss audit scope and results and to address internal control and financial reporting matters. Both independent and internal auditors have unrestricted access to the Audit Committee.

President and
Chief Executive Officer

Executive Vice President,
Finance, and Chief
Financial Officer

February 1, 1988

Report of Ernst & Whinney, Independent Auditors

RJR Nabisco, Inc.
Its Directors and Stockholders

We have examined the consolidated balance sheets of RJR Nabisco, Inc. and subsidiaries as of December 31, 1987 and 1986, and the related consolidated statements of income and retained earnings and changes in financial position for each of the three years in the period ended December 31, 1987. Our examinations were made in accordance with generally accepted auditing standards and, accordingly, included such tests of the accounting records and such other auditing procedures as we considered necessary in the circumstances.

In our opinion, the financial statements referred to above present fairly the consolidated financial position of RJR Nabisco, Inc. and subsidiaries at December 31, 1987 and 1986, and the consolidated results of their operations and the changes in their consolidated financial position for each of the three years in the period ended December 31, 1987, in conformity with generally accepted accounting principles applied on a consistent basis.

Ernst & Whinney

Atlanta, Georgia
February 1, 1988

RJR Nabisco, Inc.

Eleven-Year Financial Summary
For the Years Ended December 31

(Dollars in Millions Except Per Share Data)	1987	1986	1985	1984
Net sales	$15,766	$15,102	$11,622	$8,200
Operating income	2,304	2,340	1,949	1,412
Interest and debt expense	489	565	337	166
Income before provision for income taxes	1,816	1,782	1,663	1,353
Income from continuing operations	1,081	1,025	917	747
Net income	1,209	1,064	1,001	1,210
Preferred dividends	30	102	91	56
Net income applicable to Common Stock	1,179	962	910	1,154
Per share of Common Stock:				
Continuing operations	$ 4.19	$ 3.68	$ 3.27	$ 2.46
Net income	4.70	3.83	3.60	4.11
Dividends	1.76	1.51	1.41	1.30
Book value	24.41	21.21	19.14	17.33
Working capital	$ 1,717	$ 1,329	$ 1,617	$2,780
Capital expenditures	936	1,022	946	642
Depreciation expense	450	402	258	151
Property, plant and equipment, net	5,847	5,343	4,678	2,193
Total assets	16,861	16,701	16,414	8,805
Short-term debt	604	941	804	218
Long-term debt	3,884	4,833	4,824	1,225
Preferred stock	173	291	1,587	499
Common stockholders' equity	6,038	5,312	4,796	4,478
Average common shares outstanding (in thousands)	250,612	251,073	252,941	280,938
Number of employees at year end	120,334	122,395	127,404	79,234
Effective income tax rate	40.5%	42.5%	44.9%	44.8%
Current ratio	1.4	1.3	1.4	2.5

Prior years have been restated to report the Company's former spirits and wines business as discontinued operations (see Note 3 to the Financial Statements). The 1985 amounts include the operations of Nabisco Brands from July 2, 1985 (see Note 16 to the Financial Statements).

1983	1982	1981	1980	1979	1978	1977
$7,565	$7,323	$6,784	$6,061	$5,299	$3,250	$2,980
1,205	1,142	1,154	1,021	963	771	711
177	180	145	130	103	56	49
1,110	1,012	1,139	981	923	745	655
626	548	616	536	491	375	329
881	870	768	670	551	442	423
62	36	30	30	31	6	7
819	834	738	640	520	436	416
$ 2.00	$ 1.92	$ 2.24	$ 1.94	$ 1.79	$ 1.46	$ 1.27
2.90	3.13	2.81	2.45	2.02	1.72	1.64
1.22	1.14	1.00	0.87	0.78	0.72	0.67
18.44	16.93	15.05	13.24	11.84	10.83	9.79
$2,853	$2,008	$2,102	$1,795	$1,711	$1,278	$1,127
492	338	298	238	172	90	106
131	118	99	86	77	51	47
1,688	1,361	1,175	969	842	474	438
8,776	8,746	6,935	6,281	5,475	3,814	3,435
150	354	593	574	438	106	180
1,294	1,463	935	916	833	558	455
631	630	345	346	356	28	32
5,223	4,766	3,927	3,445	2,998	2,630	2,360
282,492	266,766	262,615	261,838	259,869	257,637	258,142
78,266	75,456	75,809	72,775	69,098	26,147	25,901
43.6%	45.8%	45.9%	45.4%	46.8%	49.7%	49.8%
3.3	2.2	2.4	2.3	2.5	3.3	3.0

RJR Nabisco, Inc.

Lines of Business Data

The Company classifies its continuing operations into two principal lines of business which are described in Management's Discussion and Analysis, beginning on page 45 of this report. Summarized financial information for these operations for each of the past three years is shown in the following tables. The 1985 amounts include the operations of Nabisco Brands from July 2, 1985 (see Note 16 to the Financial Statements).

(Dollars in Millions)	1987	1986	1985
Net sales:			
Tobacco	$ 6,346	$ 5,866	$ 5,422
Food	9,420	9,236	6,200
Consolidated net sales	$15,766	$15,102	$11,622
Operating income:			
Tobacco	$ 1,821	$ 1,659	$ 1,483
Food	915	820	549
Restructuring expense (1)	(250)	—	—
Corporate	(182)	(139)	(83)
Consolidated operating income	$ 2,304	$ 2,340	$ 1,949
Assets:			
Tobacco	$ 5,208	$ 4,882	$ 4,496
Food	10,117	9,822	9,598
Corporate (2)	1,536	1,281	863
	16,861	15,985	14,957
Net assets of discontinued operations	—	716	1,457
Consolidated assets	$16,861	$16,701	$16,414
Capital expenditures:			
Tobacco	$ 433	$ 613	$ 647
Food	445	344	279
Corporate	58	65	20
Consolidated capital expenditures	$ 936	$ 1,022	$ 946
Depreciation and amortization expense:			
Tobacco	$ 244	$ 205	$ 146
Food	380	376	195
Corporate	28	24	13
Consolidated depreciation and amortization expense	$ 652	$ 605	$ 354

(1) Restructuring expense for 1987 includes $(261) million, $18 million and $(7) million for Tobacco, Food and Corporate, respectively (see Note 1 to the Financial Statements).

(2) All cash and short-term investments are included in Corporate assets.

STUDY QUESTIONS

1. Assume that you are establishing an investment portfolio of stocks for retirement. Your objective is to acquire relatively safe and stable stocks. On what financial ratios will you primarily focus?
2. Note that the operating income for RJR decreased in 1987, but that the net income increased. Explain why.
3. Calculate the 1986 ratios for RJR to determine trends.
4. Why does an analyst want information on trends?
5. Why would return on stockholders' equity differ from return on total assets?
6. How is P/E ratio related to growth and risk?

Chapter 5

Two Great Mysteries: Net Income and Appropriate Balance Sheet Valuation

Some things in this world are not and yet appear to be. [1]

One of the primary objectives of this book is to dispel the notion that financial statements are precise and accurate. Apparently, many financial statement users have the impression that net income reported for the period under question is precise and that the valuation of assets and liabilities is accurate as of the balance sheet date. However, recall that auditors examine financial statements to evaluate whether they reflect *overall fairness*, rather than to evaluate the preciseness of the financial reporting of the company. One reason for this auditing approach is that accounting methods used to define net income and to value assets and liabilities necessarily lack the preciseness that is associated with them by many users.

In short, the results of business transactions have economic consequences that accounting procedures are designed to measure. The interactions and results of such transactions are often characterized by uncertainties.[2] There are no "laws of business nature" that assure the same result when given the same facts for any transaction. For example, when a truck is purchased by a business to assist in generating revenues for the company, it is known that the truck will eventually

---

[1] The Greek philosopher Epictetus quoted in D. E. Kieso and J. J. Weygandt, *Intermediate Accounting*, Kieso, 5th Ed. (New York: John Wiley and Sons, 1986), 540.

[2] Refer to the definitions provided (by *SFAC 6*) in the beginning of Chapter 3.

deteriorate. However, it is not known exactly when the truck will deteriorate or how much benefit (through revenues) the truck will contribute to the company's well-being. In fact, two companies can acquire identical trucks for the same price, yet it is conceivable that one of the trucks will be more productive than the other. At the time of the acquisition, however, this is not known, and it will become apparent only over time and through use. Nevertheless, because financial statements must be prepared periodically, accounting methods are adopted and utilized at the acquisition of the truck and during the period of use in order to measure net income and value assets and liabilities.[3] It is impossible to do so with precision given the uncertainties present.

Contrast this environment of uncertainty with the environment of the chemist, who combines two parts of hydrogen with one part of oxygen. Each time the chemist makes this combination, the result will be water. There are constant laws of nature that hold when given the same facts and circumstances. Consequently, most laymen think of science as precise and exact. Therefore, it comes as a surprise to read the "basic attitude of modern science—that all its concepts and theories are approximate."[4] If scientists have an approximation mindset even when given a relatively certain set of laws, surely financial statement users can understand that financial statements are imprecise because of the environment of uncertainty that characterizes business.

It is true that, *ultimately*, economic consequences of business transactions become known with relative preciseness. However, the measurement problem is exacerbated by the assumption that financial statements must be prepared periodically (i.e., at least on an annual basis). Return to the example of the truck acquired for use in a business. To properly value the truck as an asset on the balance sheet, between the date of acquisition and the date of disposal, the balance sheet should reflect remaining productive value. The question is, What is the productive value of the truck at this point in time?

Because of the articulation of the income statement and balance sheet, the estimate of remaining productive value reflected on the balance sheet will affect net income. The remaining productive value, reported on the balance sheet, is based on original cost less decline in

---

[3]The recorded depreciation of the truck will affect net income through expense and, through accumulation, will lower the book value of the truck on the balance sheet.

[4]F. Capra, *The Tao of Physics,* 2nd ed. (Pl. of Pub: New Science Library. 1985), 136.

utility, which is also based on original cost. Productive value defined in this manner may not be indicative of market value.[5]

Obviously, without the ability to see into the future, accountants must estimate productive values of assets between acquisition date and ultimate disposal of the asset. Since estimates are imprecise by definition, financial statements must also be imprecise, especially if estimates are utilized in defining net income and measuring assets and liabilities.[6] Furthermore, estimates are only one of several factors that contribute to the mysteries; What is net income? What are the proper balance sheet valuations?

ARTICULATION—
THE MEASUREMENT OF ASSETS AND LIABILITIES
AND RECOGNITION OF REVENUES AND EXPENSES

Chapter 3 used the analogy of a bathtub filling with water to describe the relationship between the income statement and the balance sheet. The water level represented the amount of net assets (assets less liabilities, which is equal to owners equity); and the rate of increase or decrease in water level was determined by the inflow of water (revenues) through the faucet relative to the outflow of water (expenses) through the drain. The net inflow (outflow) of water represented the net income (loss). This relationship between net income and net assets suggests that the measurement of assets and liabilities is dependent on the measurement of net income and vice versa.

In Chapter 3, there was a brief discussion of *articulation*, the manner in which the balance sheet and the income statement relate to one another. Articulation has been defined in the following manner:

> . . . The two statements [balance sheet and income statement] are mathematically defined in such a way that net income is equal to the change in owners' equity for a period, assuming no capital transactions or prior period adjustments.[7]

---

[5]The issues related to balance sheet valuation are discussed in greater detail later in this chapter.

[6]Estimates are an inherent part of the accounting process, and they are a necessity if financial statements are to be prepared periodically. The example used here is only one example. The reader will note in later discussions that estimates are used in recognizing revenues and expenses, as well as measuring assets and in liabilities. Therefore, equity is also composed of estimates.

[7]H. I. Wolk, J. R. Francis, and M. G. Tearney, *Accounting Theory: A Conceptual and Institutional Approach*, 2nd ed. (Boston: PWS-Kent Pub. Co., 1989), 264.

Capital transactions are transactions between the entity and its owners. Any such transaction will increase or decrease stockholders' equity, depending on the direction of transfer of assets. For example, a cash dividend paid to stockholders by the corporation will decrease equity. A sale of stock by the corporation to a stockholder will increase equity because cash is received from the stockholder in exchange for the corporation's stock. On the other hand, a *prior period adjustment* refers to the discovery of an error that occurred in a previous accounting year. The error is corrected by adjusting retained earnings, rather than by adjusting the effects of the error through the current period's net income. Along with current period net income or loss, a prior period adjustment is not a capital transaction.

To use this definition of articulation in the bathtub analogy, net income represents the change in the water level of the bathtub from one point in time to another point in time. In other words, net income is equal to the change in net assets (i.e., net assets are owners' equity) adjusted for capital transactions and prior period adjustments.

The articulation concept formalizes the idea that measurement of assets and liabilities is dependent on the determination of net income and vice versa. Therefore, there are two approaches to measuring balance sheet items and to determining net income. One approach focuses on the income statement and directly measures revenues and expenses through revenue and expense recognition principles, which are discussed later in this chapter. Under this approach, assets and liabilities are measured as a by-product of the measurement of revenues and expenses. In the context of the bathtub analogy, the rate of water flowing in through the faucet and out through the drain is the measurement focus, which will provide the answer to the water level (net assets) indirectly. The income statement approach has been the traditional approach. However, this approach burdens the balance sheet with the by-product of income measurement and sometimes results in items dubiously labeled as assets or liabilities.

In recent years, there has been a shift in focus to a balance sheet orientation, which directly measures assets and liabilities.[8] This approach places primacy on the balance sheet and indirectly determines

---

[8]Some recent examples are as follows: *SFAC 3* , par. 56, defines "comprehensive income" as the change in net assets; *SFAS 87* (Stamford, Conn.: FASB, 1985), on accounting for pensions, and *SFAS 96* (Stamford, Conn.: FASB, 1987), on accounting for income taxes, modified previous income statement approaches. The new standards place emphasis on measuring liabilities rather than expense.

net income as a by-product of the measurement of assets and liabilities. In the context of the bathtub analogy, the water level is measured at the beginning and end of a period, and the difference provides the answer for net income after adjusting for capital transactions.

The balance sheet approach is easier to justify because most assets and liabilities are tangible. Revenue and expense items, on the other hand, are intangible. In reality, both orientations are used.

Regardless of which approach is used to implement it, the articulation concept can be depicted in Figure 5-1.[9] Articulation requires that net assets affected by a single transaction should be measured in the same manner for both balance sheet and income statement purposes.

FIGURE 5-1

ARTICULATION CONCEPT

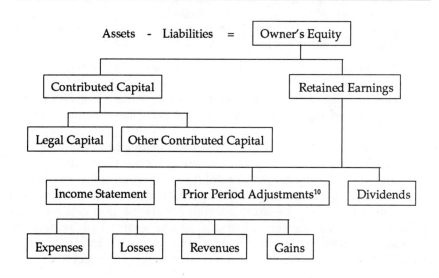

[9]Adapted from Wolk, Francis and Tearney , *Accounting Theory*, 265.

[10]Prior period adjustments are adjustments to retained earnings for errors affecting net income that are discovered in one fiscal year but have occurred in a previous fiscal year. It would distort the current year's net income if the error is adjusted through the income statement. There is another situation that qualifies as a prior period adjustment. See *SFAC 16* (Stamford, Conn.: FASB, 1977), par. 11, for additional information.

REVENUE RECOGNITION PRINCIPLES

Recall that revenue is intangible. Revenue can not be seen or touched, which makes it very difficult to define. Revenue is a concept founded on flows that may be characterized as "favorable" to the entity. Flows can be from several sources; and in order to be considered revenue, favorable flows should originate from the creation of goods or services. Because revenue is intangible, the flows are extremely difficult to measure and to determine when they begin or end.

Formal definitions of revenue have evolved over time through official pronouncements of the accounting profession. Although an early definition reflected a strict revenue-expense approach, the current definition, in accordance with recent trends, incorporates the asset-liability approach.[11]

> Revenues are inflows or other enhancements of assets of an entity or settlement of its liabilities (or a combination of both) during a period from delivering or producing goods, rendering services, or other activities that constitute the entity's ongoing major or central operations.[12]

Independent auditors scrutinize transactions that appear to embrace the definition of revenues in form, but not in substance. For example, consider a transaction evidenced by a sales contract for inventory that includes a clause committing the seller to repurchase the inventory from the buyer under certain conditions. While it may be in company management's best interest to interpret this transaction as revenue, the economic consequences are not necessarily equivalent to a sale; and, in fact, they may represent a financing arrangement (liability).[13] Due to different group make-ups (management and auditors) in different companies, the same substantive transaction can be interpreted as revenue by the consensus of one group and as debt by another.[14] However, the FASB is attempting to set guidelines that narrow the interpretations, given the same substantive facts.

---

[11]*Accounting Terminology Bulletin No. 2*, (American Institute of Certified Public Accountants, 1955), par. 5.

[12]*SFAC 6*, par. 78.

[13]Revenues should not be confused with gains. Gains have the same effect on net assets except that they result from transactions that, as stated in *SFAC 3, par. 67*, are not considered revenue or capital transactions. That is gains result from peripheral or incidental transactions, rather than the entity's central, profit-directed activities.

[14]See H.R. Jaenicke, *Survey of Present Practices in Recognizing Revenues, Expenses, Gains, & Losses*, Financial Accounting Standards Board. 1981.

Note that the definition of revenues does not address how or when to measure revenues. Defining revenues, a difficult task due to its intangibility, may be easier than determining how or when to measure revenues.

For financial accounting purposes, the exchange of cash should not be confused with the recognition of revenue:

> ... Revenues should be identified with the period during which the major economic activities necessary to the creation and disposition of goods and services have been accomplished, provided objective measurements of the results of those activities are available. These two conditions, i.e., accomplishment of major economic activity and objectivity of measurement, are fulfilled at different stages of activity in different cases, sometimes as late as time of delivery of product or the performance of a service; in other cases, at an earlier point of time.[15]

The recognition of revenue, therefore, is dependent on two factors: accomplishment of activity and objectivity of measurement. The determination of when the activity has been accomplished is open to interpretation in many cases.

Financial statements are prepared on a periodic basis so that users receive timely information. The application of different interpretations of *when* revenue is earned (and recognized) can affect reported net income in different periods. Hence, two companies with similar transactions can each interpret the facts of the transactions differently so that revenue is assumed as earned in different accounting years. Initially, it may appear that the question, When is a sale a sale? is actually not complicated. However, with the development of complex transactions, some of which are described later, the question, When is a sale a sale? is a real and difficult question to answer.

In most cases, revenue is recognized at the point of sale when there has been a "meeting of the minds" of seller and buyer. However, the point-of-sale concept may be modified by the idea that the earnings process must be completed before revenue should be recognized. Normally, revenue is recognized once an event that culminates the earnings process has occurred.

The second criterion for recognizing revenue is the ability to objectively measure or estimate revenue. This criterion depends on the ability to measure or estimate sales price, cash collections, and future costs for which the seller is responsible. Once again, because of the

---

[15]Sprouse, R. T. and M. Moonitz., "A Tentative Set of Broad Accounting Principles for Business Enterprises," *Accounting Research Study No. 3*, (1962): 47.

evolving complexity of sales transactions, many of these factors are not readily determinable at the point of sale.

Because both criteria (accomplishment of activity and objective measurement) must be met, revenue recognition may be deferred beyond the point of sale. While most transactions allow revenue to be recognized at the point of sale (when the earnings process has culminated), some alternative examples follow.

During Production Period

In some industries, long-term construction contracts are signed for projects that require several years to complete. Examples include the construction of large office buildings, bridges, commercial aircraft, and weapons systems. Deferring recognition of revenue until completion of the contract (point of sale) may distort net income and components of the balance sheet. In other words, the seller will incur ongoing operating costs, such as salaries and rent, during the period of construction. Consequently, if no revenue is recognized until the completion of the contract, the income statement will reflect an operating loss through the recognition of expenses without recognition of related revenue.

Therefore, when particular conditions are present in the project, accountants prefer to recognize revenue during production by using what is known as the *percentage of completion* revenue recognition method. Otherwise, the entire amount of revenue is recognized when the contract is completed under the *completed contract* method.[16] Ultimately, the same amount of revenue is recognized, but the timing of the recognition is different. Accordingly, the question What is net income? may be answered differently for companies within certain industries, depending upon the revenue recognition principle applied.

Completion of Production

Revenue recognition at the completion of production but prior to sale is another possible alternative. Examples of industries where this approach has been applied involve precious commodities or agricultural products with *assured market prices*. This approach is used when there is a ready market and an established price for a commodity with

---

[16]Approximately 6 percent of the companies making this choice in 1988 utilized the completed contract method. See Shohet, J. and Rikert, R. ed. *Accounting Trend and Techniques*, (AICPA: New York, 1990), 285.

a strong demand and when the product is interchangeable with relatively insignificant distribution costs. Companies involved in the mining of gold, platinum, or diamonds can justify the recognition of revenue upon mining (the point of production) and prior to the sale.

Cash Collection

To this point, the discussion of revenue recognition problems has involved only companies in the manufacturing or construction industries. Service industries are also concerned with revenue-recognition problems. One example of a revenue-recognition problem in a service industry involves the accounting treatment afforded the sale of "Lifetime Partnerships" by the PTL Club.

Briefly, the facts are as follows:

PTL viewers could become a Lifetime Partner for a one-time gift of $1,000. The money would be used to build a first class hotel in a religious environment, and in return, each Lifetime Partner would be able to stay for free each year in the hotel for 4 days and 3 nights for life. . . . The government indictment charging Jim Bakker and Richard Dortch with wire and mail fraud states that PTL's solicitations from January, 1984 through April, 1987 resulted in the sale of approximately 152,903 fully paid lodging partnerships, producing at least $158 million in revenue for PTL.[17]

The relevant accounting problem is when to recognize as revenue the $158 million cash received.[18] Technically, revenue should be recognized as the service is provided. In this case, the amount of service provided is dependent on the life expectancies of the partners, which are uncertain. Furthermore, to measure revenue on this basis, each of the 152,963 partners would have to be tracked to determine actual usage and life expectancies based on actuarial estimates. This would be an untenable and impractical accounting solution.

Therefore, revenue recognition was based on estimates by management. At first, the estimate was made on a straight-line basis, recognizing revenue "as the participating partners exercised their right to stay at the hotel."[19] Subsequently, PTL management changed auditors. The

---

[17] G. L. Tidwell, "A Case Study of PTL: Will the Real Culprits Please Stand Up?", presentation at American Business Law Association, August 1989.

[18] Note that the portion of the indictment quoted above uses the term *revenue* to represent the total inflow of cash that was generated from Lifetime Partner sales.

[19] Footnote disclosure in May 31, 1984, annual report of Heritage Village Church and Missionary Fellowship, Inc..

revenue-recognition approach was changed to an accelerated revenue recognition method, which provided increased revenue recognition over a shorter period:

> The effect of the change in the estimate of the future incremental costs of providing lodging to donors at the HGH [Heritage Grand Hotel], and the period over which costs will principally be incurred, is to increase the amortization of deferred revenue and net income by approximately $24,950,000...[20]

The result was to present financial statements that indicated higher revenues and net assets than would have been recorded for financial reporting purposes if the original approach to recognizing revenues had been retained.

The real question is, Which of the revenue-recognition methods best reflects the economic consequences of providing free lodging for life to PTL partners in exchange for $1,000 cash in advance? One approach is more conservative, the other results in a more favorable impact on revenues over a shorter period of time. Ultimately, the same total revenues would be recognized. So with identical facts, the answer to the question What is net income? changed, depending on the group makeup (auditor and management) that decided the answer.[21]

Unlike the PTL situation, it is more typical for the receipt of cash, the delivery of the product or service, and the earning process to be completed simultaneously. In these cases, the cash basis of accounting and the accrual basis of accounting would recognize revenue at the same point. Therefore, revenue is recognized as cash is received.

In other situations, revenue is recorded as cash is received because the revenue is not objectively measurable at the point of sale. This approach to revenue recognition is often used in the retail industry to account for installment sales and in the franchise and real estate industries to account for revenue that is deferred until the cost of the product is recovered. When an installment sale is made, the total amount of cash to be received is dependent on the customers' integrity and ability to pay, which introduces an element of subjectivity regarding the amount of future cash collections. In certain circumstances in the real estate industry, the likelihood of receiving full sales price is diminished and often unpredictable. Therefore, revenue recognition is deferred until after the sale and after the cost is recovered.

---

[20]Footnote disclosure May 31, 1986 annual report of Heritage Village Church and Missionary Fellowship, Inc..

[21]The author wishes to thank Professor Gary Tidwell of the College of Charleston for his contribution of the PTL research.

Obviously, deferring revenue until after delivery of the product is a conservative approach to revenue recognition. Management usually does not wish to defer recognition of revenue. As with long-term construction contracts, management and auditors for one particular company can interpret a fact situation to allow immediate revenue recognition, while another group in another company can decide to defer the revenue when faced with similar facts. Thus, once again the answer to the question, What is net income? may be different, depending on which group answers the question.

The contribution that revenue recognition is making to the mystery of net income is based on the interpretations that often need to be given to particular sales transactions. Many of these sales transactions have evolved with the purpose of meeting revenue definition-and-recognition criteria while also accomplishing objectives associated with financing. Recall the example of a contract that provides for the "sale" of a product with the provision that the seller repurchase the product under certain conditions. This is more of a financing arrangement than a sale. Because the document evidencing the transaction contains elements associated with both revenue and debt, which are mutually exclusive, an interpretation has to be made. Since the income statement and balance sheet articulate, decisions affecting revenue recognition will impact balance sheet valuations. As the following section indicates, balance sheet valuations will also affect net income.

In summary, revenue is generally recognized when the earnings process has been completed. This normally happens at the point of sale. However, this approach can be justifiably modified under circumstances indicating that another approach will more fairly reflect the economic consequences. Revenue can, therefore, be recognized prior to or after the point of sale. Finally, sales transactions must be scrutinized to ensure that the transaction represents a sale in substance rather than a type of financing arrangement.

ASSET VALUATION PRINCIPLES

Chapter 3 defined assets as: "probable future economic benefits obtained or controlled by a particular entity as a result of past transactions or events."[22]

The question to be answered is, What is the appropriate valuation of the probable future economic benefits? Some possible approaches to the valuation of assets follow.

---

[22]SFAC 3, par. 19.

Historical Cost

Historical cost is the amount of cash (or its equivalent) paid to acquire an asset. This is the traditional approach to asset valuation. Its use is based on its high degree of reliability. If rational buyers and sellers are exchanging assets, it is assumed that the exchange is made at a fair rate. Subsequently, historical cost can be adjusted for depreciation or for other recognized declines in the utility of the asset. However, financial accounting takes the conservative view that the pure application of historical cost prohibits the recognition of increases in the utility or value of an asset.

The primary disadvantage associated with the use of historical cost for valuation purposes is that, over time, value changes in the asset take place at a rate different from that recognized through adjustments such as depreciation. Value changes can take place in an asset for a variety of reasons, but changes due to general inflation or specific market factors are the most common. For example, consider the purchase of an oil tanker in 1980 for $10 million. Assuming that the tanker has been well maintained, because of the decline in purchasing power of the dollar associated with general inflation, it may take $20 million in today's dollars to acquire the tanker now. Furthermore, assuming that there is a shortage of oil and tankers, the value of the tanker may have increased well beyond $20 million. Historical cost valuations require depreciation adjustments to recognize an assumed decline in utility of the tanker simply because of age and use. Therefore, the valuation of the tanker using historical cost will be substantially below the replacement cost. The usefulness of historical cost has been questioned for this reason.

Because stockholders' equity is defined as the residual interest in net assets (assets less liabilities), valuation changes in assets that do not affect liabilities will affect stockholders' equity. The historical cost approach has been criticized because it is too conservative and not relevant to users. The preceding example of the tanker indicates that, subsequent to the purchase of the tanker, the net assets of the entity will decline through recognition of depreciation of the tanker, an expense that will cause net income and stockholders' equity to decline. However, in the previous example, inflationary and/or market factors combined to indicate that the true economic consequences of the purchase should reflect an increase in net assets, which should have caused net income and stockholders' equity to increase.

The historical cost approach is a cost-allocation approach for assets that benefit more than one fiscal period. It is not intended to approximate market values. In part, the rationale for this approach is based on the going-concern assumption which would imply consumption of long lived assets rather than a sale of assets.

Current Cost (Input)

To compensate for the disadvantages of historical cost valuations, other approaches have been suggested for asset valuations that will make the balance sheet more useful. One suggestion has been to use current costs; that is, to value assets at the amount required to replace the asset (current acquisition cost) in its current condition. Any increase (or decrease) above (or below) the existing recorded value would require an adjustment to net income and stockholders' equity. The disadvantage to this approach is that it is difficult to objectively determine the current cost of an identical asset. While this approach can be more relevant to users, it lacks a degree of reliability.

Constant Dollar

Another approach to asset valuation is to use constant dollars. This variation of historical cost values assets using a cost index that reflects the decline in purchasing power of the dollar. The disadvantage of this approach is that cost indexes, such as the Consumer Price Index, are determined by cost changes in a "basket of goods", (e.g., eggs, meat, cars, and so forth) that may have no relevance to the specific assets being valued.

Prior to 1984, current cost and constant dollar valuation concepts were required as supplementary disclosures to the primary financial statements on the basis of providing useful information to users. However, such disclosures are now voluntary.

Current Exit Value

Another possible valuation approach is to use current exit values, which is the amount of cash that could be obtained upon the sale of the asset at the balance sheet date. Although this is a market valuation, it differs from input current cost because the focus is on the sale rather than the purchase. This method, which is in used in certain circumstances, is modified in a conservative manner to incorporate only decreases in value below historical cost. One example of its application accounting for certain securities purchased as investments. Its use is promoted because there is objective evidence (daily market quotations) of the market value of securities.[23]

Net Realizable Value

Net realizable value represents the amount of cash (or its equivalent) into which the asset is expected to be converted during the ordinary operations of the entity. This approach is currently used in the accounting for accounts receivable. Accounts receivable are valued at their net realizable value, which is the historical cost less amounts estimated to be uncollectible.

Present Value

Perhaps the best approach to the valuation of assets is to use present-value concepts. The present value of an asset is the discounted amount of expected net cash inflows to be generated by the asset over its useful life. This approach incorporates both the substance of the definition of an asset and the time value of money. It is considered appropriate practice to value specific assets, capital leases, through the use of present-value techniques.[24]

However, there are two disadvantages to using present value as a valuation concept. First, one must be capable of determining future net cash inflows to be generated by a particular asset. This is a formidable task when only one asset is involved; normally, it is assumed that all assets of an entity collectively generate revenue. This would make present value valuation for each asset practically impossible. The second disadvantage concerns the appropriate discount rate to use in applying present value techniques. A very subjective judgment would have to be applied, as the appropriate rate for any specific entity can be different from other entities and can change over time.

---

[23]There are interesting arguments for and against this valuation technique. The reader should refer to any current intermediate accounting textbook or to *SFAS 12* (Stamford, Conn.: FASB, 1975), app.

[24]Capital leases are transactions that are called "leases" but the terms of the contract evidence a purchase-sale transaction in *substance*, rather than a lease. Capital leases are discussed in Chapter 8 in more detail.

Thus, there are several possible approaches to the valuation of assets. Historical cost is the most extensively used approach, although the other approaches discussed in this section are used in isolated contexts. The primary justification for the use of the historical cost approach is its high degree of objectivity and reliability. However, its primary disadvantage is that, in many instances, its application has little relevance to financial statement users. As more emphasis is placed on the balance sheet perspective, the following has been suggested:

> It is more likely that there will be an increased use of valuation methods other than historical cost on the balance sheets (or related footnotes) of business entities. The extent of the use of other valuation methods will depend on the trade off between relevance and reliability.[25]

EXPENSES AND LIABILITIES

In many cases, the amount of expenses reported on the income statement and the amount of liabilities reported on the balance sheet will depend on the valuation of assets and the recognition of revenues. For example, eventually all assets are consumed. The initial valuation can affect revenue recognition or vice versa, depending on the orientation. Subsequent valuations required to report the consumption (or partial consumption) of the asset will effect expenses that are reported on the income statement. Liability valuations may depend on revenue recognition principles or asset valuation decisions. (For further explanation, see the Reading List at the end of this chapter.)

SUMMARY

This chapter has emphasized that financial statements are a product of estimates, theoretical arguments, judgments, measurement assumptions, and measurement limitations. While accounting numbers appear to be precise tools of measurement they are not scientific measurements based on immutable laws of nature. They represent the practice of the "art of accounting." Primarily, this imprecision relates to the nature of business transactions. When certain transactions are initi-

---

[25] L. A., Nicolai, and J. D. Baxley, Intermediate *Accounting*, 4th ed. (Boston: PWS-Kent Pub. Co. 1988), 111.

ated, there is often a great deal of uncertainty associated with the ultimate economic consequences. Because financial statements are prepared on a periodic basis and because the ultimate consequences may not be known for a long time, impreciseness is an inherent part of the reporting process.

Also, because financial statements are prepared on a periodic basis, accountants have adopted numerous approaches to measure the eventual economic consequences during the interim between the initiation of the transaction and the known consequences. This is done because it is believed that users will benefit by the attempts to allocate revenues and costs to particular periods before the actual consequences are known.[26]

Therefore, the inescapable result of preparing financial statements on a periodic basis is to require accountants to solve the mysteries, What is net income? and What are the proper balance sheet valuations? Because of the articulation of the balance sheet and the income statement, a solution to these two mysteries will be arrived at simultaneously.

However, it is important to remember that there is not always a unique solution because there are alternative revenue-expense recognition and asset-liability valuation principles. Furthermore, because there are alternative interpretations to identical circumstances, there are also appropriate alternative solutions. A financial statement analyst should keep these alternative possibilities in mind. The following chapter illustrates the practical implications of these possibilities.

READING LIST

Andresky, J. "Setting the Date," *Forbes*, July 16, 1984, 90.

Arnett, H. E. "What Does 'Objectivity' Mean to Accountants?" *Journal of Accountancy*, (May 1961): 63–68.

Beaver, W. H., Kennelly, J. W., and Voss, W. M. "Predictive Ability as a Criterion for the Evaluation of Accounting Data." *The Accounting Review* (October 1968): 675–683.

---

[26]It has been theorized that attempts at allocations may actually lead users to misleading inferences concerning some transactions. See A. L. Thomas, "The FASB and the Allocation Fallacy", *The Journal of Accountancy*, (November 1975): 65–68.

Gombola, M. J., and J. E. Ketz. "A Note on Cash Flow and Classification Patterns of Financial Ratios." *The Accounting Review*, (January 1983): 105–114.

Horngren, C. T. "How Should We Interpret the Realization Concept?" *Accounting Review* (April 1965): 323–333.

Ijiri, Y. and Jaedicke, R. K. "Reliability and Objectivity of Accounting Measurements." *The Accounting Review* (July 1966): 474–483.

Jones, R. G. "You Can Call It Earnings . . . You Can Call It Income, Or . . ." *Management Accounting* (May 1982): 17–21, 38.

Kahn, N. and Schiff, A. "Tangible Equity Change and the Evolution of the FASB's Definition of Income. "*Journal of Accounting, Auditing, and Finance* (Fall 1985): 40–49.

Liao, S. S. "The Matching Concept and Cost Allocation." *Accounting and Business Research* (Summer 1979): 228-236.

Miller, P. B. W. and Mosso, D. "Financial Accounting Measurement: Why Things May Not Be What They Seem to Be." *Financial Executive* (December 1983): 28–35.

Most, K. "The Rise and Fall of the Matching Principle." *Accounting and Business Research* (Autumn 1977): 286–290.

Scott, R. A., and Scott, R. K. "Installment Accounting: Is It Inconsistent?" *Journal of Accountancy* (November 1979): 52–58.

Siegel, J. G. "The 'Quality of Earnings' Concept — A Survey." *Financial Analysts Journal* (March/April 1982): 60-68.

Solomons, D. "Economic and Accounting Concepts of Income." *The Accounting Review* (July 1961): 374–383.

Sprouse, R. T. "The Importance of Earnings in the Conceptual Framework." *Journal of Accountancy* (January 1978): 64–71.

Sterling, R. R. "On Theory Construction and Verification." *The Accounting Review* (July 1970): 444–457.

Thomas, A. L. "The FASB and the Allocation Fallacy." *The Journal of Accountancy* (November 1975): 65–68.

STUDY QUESTIONS

1. A hurricane destroyed all living quarters on the coast of Mississippi. A mobile home manufacturer has 20 mobile homes ready for sale as of its fiscal year end. Because of demand, they are all expected to be sold within two to three days. When should revenue be recognized?
2. Given the facts for PTL and its Lifetime Partners, how would you decide on when and on how much revenue to recognize for each year?
3. PTL is not a publicly traded corporation. Why do you think PTL had independent auditors?
4. In your opinion, what would be the appropriate method to recognize revenue for a timber company? Assume that timber prices are relatively unstable.
5. You are the independent auditor retained by an oil company. Management has recognized revenue as the oil is *discovered* (prior to sale and production). What arguments will management make to justify this approach? What will be your decision as to the appropriate approach?
6. You are contemplating investment in a company that has large plant facilities built in 1969 in the Silicon Valley. For your purposes, what is the appropriate valuation technique for the plant facilities?
7. Bo Peep Restaurants is a fast-food company that franchises exclusive rights to restaurants. One way that Bo Peep earns revenue is through the sale of area development rights which grants rights to a developer to open franchises in a particular territory. Each area development right requires the developer to open five restaurants within 10 years. Bo Peep provides training and advertising support services. Bo Peep recognizes revenue as the cash is received. Comment on this situation.
8. What is the definition of revenue? What is meant by revenue-recognition principles? Are these concepts the same?

Chapter 6

Financial Statement Analysis—Effects Of Alternative GAAP And Other Considerations

As far as the laws of mathematics refer to reality, they are not certain; and as far as they are certain, they do not refer to reality.[1]

*T*he previous chapter investigated the conceptual limitations inherent in measuring net income and valuing balance sheet items. This chapter illustrates the measurement and valuation problems in more concrete terms.

The inherent limitations of the financial reporting process are aggravated by the fact that alternative accounting methods can be employed. Generally accepted accounting principles (GAAP) are accounting methods that are promulgated by authoritative sources or have evolved as appropriate methods to account for specific transactions. Often, a given transaction can be accounted for by alternative methods considered to be GAAP. Management can choose which alternative accounting method to utilize. It is believed that, by making choices available in the financial reporting process, management will have more flexibility in reflecting the true economic consequences of

---

[1]Albert Einstein, quoted in *The Tao of Physics*, Capra, F., New Science Library, Boston, 1985, 41.

the results of operations and the economic realities of the corporation's financial condition.

As shown in Chapter 5, the implications of having an accounting choice are that two identical companies having identical fact situations may choose different accounting methods to reflect the economic consequences of identical transactions. Since the application of the different accounting methods yields different interpretations of economic consequences, the analyst is placed in a difficult situation. Entities not following the same accounting methods may not be directly comparable. However, the disclosure of the accounting policies used should enable financial statement users to effectively bridge the differences. Analysts should carefully study the notes to the financial statements to determine which accounting policies are being followed:

> ... The usefulness of financial statements for purposes of making economic decisions about the reporting entity depends significantly upon the user's understanding of the accounting policies followed by the entity.[2]

For this reason, companies are required to include supplementary information concerning the significant accounting policies (methods) that are employed by the entity in the measurement-and-valuation process.

The ability to choose from alternative accounting treatments can pressure management to choose the treatment that is most favorable rather than the one that is most fair. In the early 1950s, it was recognized that a number of benefits could be reaped by companies from "income-smoothing" techniques using alternative accounting methods.[3] This is because volatile changes in net income from year to year are associated with higher-risk companies. Investors and creditors want higher returns on their investment as their perceived risk increases. Therefore, companies often attempt to use smoothing techniques to accelerate revenue recognition in a year of slow sales or to defer revenue recognition in a year of higher than expected sales. The goal of smoothing techniques is to reflect a more even pattern of net income over time.

In recent years, a substantial body of research supports the hypothesis that management is motivated by self-interests rather than by fair and full disclosure. If management's bonus is linked to increased stock prices, management may adopt income-smoothing techniques to de-

---

[2]*APB Opinion No. 22*, Accounting Principles Board, 1972.
    [3]S. R. Hepworth, "Smoothing Periodic Income", *The Accounting Review*, Jan., 1953, 32-39.

crease the risk associated with the purchase of the stock. All things equal, a reduced perception of risk can cause stock prices to rise, thus increasing management's bonus.

The analyst must carefully examine the notes to the financial statements and must consider the implications of management's accounting policies. This should be done with the knowledge of the inherent limitations of accounting and financial reporting and with the understanding that management's interests may not parallel investor interests. Furthermore, there may be additional factors, such as the social, political, and economic environments, that should be considered.

In another context, it has been said; "What we observe is not nature itself but nature exposed to our method of questioning."[4] The corollary in financial statement analysis is that, in order to arrive at a valid conclusion, one must know the appropriate questions to ask. This chapter will provide the reader with the basis for determining the appropriate method of questioning.

EFFECTS ON FINANCIAL RATIOS

In Chapter 4, a number of financial ratios were presented. The calculation of these ratios is the beginning of the analytical process. Subsequent to the calculation, the analyst should consider other factors that may have distorted each of the ratios such as the effects of alternative GAAP and inherent limitations of accounting. The remainder of this section presents examples of these effects on the interpretations of financial ratios.

Inventory

Inventory is an item that has the potential for distorting several financial ratios. Several inventory costing methods are considered GAAP. Two of these inventory costing methods are discussed; namely, first-in-first-out (FIFO) and last-in-first-out (LIFO).

Both FIFO and LIFO *assume* a particular sequence of sales of particular items in inventory. An assumption about the sequence of sales, or cost flow, is made because it is often cost prohibitive to design a record-keeping system to determine actual costs of specific goods sold. Therefore, accountants make assumptions about which inventory costs should be matched with the physical flow of goods that are sold.

---

[4]Capra. *Tao of Physics*, 140.

Consider the following scenario. Company X begins the accounting year with an inventory of 100 widgets that have an established total cost of $1,000. During the year, Company X made the following purchases and sales:

Purchases		Sales
Number of Units	Cost per Unit	Number of Units
100	$11	75
150	$12	175
200	$13	200
450		450

Based on these facts, there are still 100 units in ending inventory (100 units beginning inventory plus 450 units purchased less 450 units sold). If it is too costly to identify each item bought and to track it until it's sold, then the questions are, What is the cost of the 100 remaining unsold units? and What is the cost of the 450 units sold?

The answers depend on the cost-flow assumption adopted. If FIFO is adopted, it is assumed that the first units purchased are the first units sold. Therefore, the remaining 100 units are assumed to be from the last group purchased, and the cost is $13 per unit, or $1,300. The cost of the 450 units sold is $5,200 [($1,000 beginning inventory) + (100 units x $11) + (150 units x $12) + (100 units x $13)].

On the other hand, if LIFO is adopted, it is assumed that the *last* units purchased are the first units sold. While this is illogical in terms of physical movement, it is only an assumption adopted to answer costing questions. Using LIFO, the cost of the remaining 100 units is assumed to be the cost of the beginning inventory, or $1,000. This is because the units purchased were the same as the units sold, and it is assumed that the last units purchased are the first units sold. Therefore, the cost of the units sold is assumed to be $5,500 [(200 units x $13) + (150 units x $12) + (100 units x $11)].

Revenue recognized on the 450 units sold is the same regardless of whether LIFO or FIFO is used. But net income will be lower by $300 ($5,500 as compared to $5,200) if LIFO is used, since the cost of the units sold represents an expense. Inventory will be reported at a higher amount on the balance sheet if FIFO is used ($1,300 compared to $1,000).

The LIFO assumption places a priority on the valuation of cost of goods sold by valuing these goods at the most recent costs. The result is to approximately match current costs with revenues (assuming rising prices). Because of articulation between the income statement and the balance sheet, the valuation of cost of goods sold, which is an income statement item, determines the valuation of the remaining inventory, which is a balance sheet item. However, the remaining inventory is valued, under LIFO, at old costs that understate assets in terms of current costs. On the other hand, the FIFO assumption places a priority on the valuation of the remaining inventory by valuing it at the most recent costs. The result is to match old costs with current revenues on the income statement, which artificially inflates net income. In other words, the reality that either assumption intends to capture necessarily causes the opposite effect on another financial statement.

Therefore, even with identical facts, there are different results, depending on which inventory-costing assumption is used. Therefore, conclusions and inferences drawn from the results of financial statement analysis can be misleading, especially if the two companies being compared use different inventory-costing methods.

Both net income and current assets are affected by the inventory-costing decision, which has an effect on the following ratios: current ratio, working capital, day's sales in inventory, inventory turnover, inventory turnover in days, the degree of leverage, debt/equity, debt ratio, times interest earned, earnings per share, return on investment, return on common equity, return on operating assets, return on total assets, gross profit, net profit margin, P/E ratio, percentage of earnings retained, dividend pay-out, and book value per share. Additionally, in an environment of rising prices, a decision to adopt LIFO will increase cash flow. This is because LIFO will produce lower taxable income that will result in lower taxes, thus a lower payout of cash to the Internal Revenue Service.

Depreciation

Another area that gives management a choice in accounting methods is depreciation.[5] Depreciation has a pervasive effect on financial ratios because it affects total assets and net income. Remember that depreciation is recorded on operational assets in order to recognize the decline in the utility of the asset. The cost of an asset represents the cost of a bundle of services or resources to be obtained from the use of the

---

[5]The term *depreciation* is often used interchangeably with *amortization*, although depreciation is most commonly used in discussing the decline in service utility of property, plant, and equipment. The term *amortization* is most often used in discussing the decline in service utility of other types of assets.

asset. All depreciation methods would *ultimately* recognize the same total service decline, since the cost of the asset is a finite amount. The question is, When will the costs be allocated to expense?

Without addressing the theory supporting the use of various depreciation methods, it is sufficient to point out that some depreciation methods recognize a faster decline in service utility than others. Namely, the depreciation charged in the earlier years of the asset's service life will be higher when certain methods are used. Nevertheless, total depreciation is the same, regardless of which method is used.

Furthermore, since the service life and any residual value of the asset must be estimated, a subjective opinion must be used in calculating depreciation. Different groups of management and auditors can arrive at significantly different conclusions, even when they are given the same basic facts. For example, Delta Airlines maintains a policy of depreciating its airplanes over 15 years with a 10 percent residual value, while Pan Am depreciates the same type of airplane over 25 years with a 15 percent residual value.[6]

Therefore, identical companies with identical facts can have significantly different financial ratios due to the choice of depreciation methods. Many different types of assets are depreciated or amortized. Another example involving amortization is the decision by Blockbuster Video to lengthen the amortization period of videotapes it holds for rental. The result of increasing the estimated service life of videotapes was to increase earnings by almost 20 percent.[7]

As discussed previously, estimates are an inherent part of the accounting process and involve subjective judgments. The management of one company can be more adept at estimating than another. It has been suggested by some authors that management can sometimes become inept at making estimates by design in order to increase net income. However, such manipulative approaches eventually are exposed.[8]

Asset-Expense Decisions

Chapter 5 had numerous approaches to asset valuation. Historical cost is the most commonly used approach. However, note that the decision to use historical cost as the appropriate valuation concept does not eliminate the subjectivity in the accounting process. This is

---

[6] D. Weschler, "Earnings Helper," *Forbes,* June 12, 1989, 150–153.
[7] Ibid.
[8] L. Jereski, "Mystery Profits." *Forbes,* April 20, 1987, 54.

because the accountant must decide whether the expenditure has resulted in an asset or an expense. An asset produces *future* economic benefits and an expense represents the cost of generating *current* revenues.

The unique nature of the oil and gas industry has resulted in accounting and reporting difficulties because of different views concerning whether an expenditure has resulted in an asset or an expense. Two GAAP accounting methods are appropriate for use by oil and gas producing companies. One approach, *successful efforts*, expenses all costs of unsuccessful drilling ventures, while the other approach, *full cost*, capitalizes costs (i. e., considers the expenditure an asset) of unsuccessful wells and amortizes the capitalized costs based on production from existing wells. Each approach can be justified, but the merits of either approach are not important to this discussion. However, it *is* important to understand that two identical companies may treat identical expenditures in drastically different ways. Consequently, the effects on financial ratios of two identical companies, with one employing successful efforts and with the other employing full cost, will be quite different. Initially, both total assets and net income should be significantly higher for a full cost company, given otherwise identical facts.[9] However, as a full cost company matures, the results will reverse.

The asset-expense decision will not make a difference in the long run, as all assets are consumed eventually. However, since financial statements are prepared periodically, asset-expense decisions require cost allocations that can distort financial statements. For example, Noble Affiliates, a company using successful efforts accounting, is approximately the same size as Pogo Producing, a company following full cost accounting rules. Noble Affiliates lost $1 million in 1985, compared to Pogo Producing's loss of $82 million. The difference is attributed to the increased amortization charges for Pogo's assets. That is, Pogo had capitalized past dry holes under full cost rules, while Noble had expensed them. "Pogo was overstating true earnings in the past and is now paying the penalty."[10] Because of the difficulty in comparing oil and gas companies using different GAAP accounting methods, additional disclosures based on present value of reserves are required.[11]

---

[9]See Klingstedt, J. P., "Effects of Full Costing in the Petroleum Industry," *Financial Analysts Journal*, September–October 1970, 79–86 for a concise explanation.

[10] L. Saunders,"Drilling for Information," *Forbes*, July 28, 1986, 111.

[11]*SFAS 69.*

Contingencies

Often corporations enter into transactions or experience situations that result in a contingency. A *contingency* is "an existing condition, situation, or set of circumstances involving uncertainty as to possible gain or loss to an enterprise that will ultimately be resolved when one or more future events occur or fail to occur."[12]

Without investigating the details of the accounting treatment prescribed by *SFAS 5*, it is sufficient to point out that contingencies may not be recorded in the accounting records and that they may only be disclosed in footnotes to the financial statements. Therefore, users should review footnotes closely to determine the possibility of a significant understatement of recorded liabilities.

One example of a contingency is a guarantee of another entity's loans. A more common example is a lawsuit that is pending when the entity is the defendant. An unfavorable settlement could cause a liability to originate that had not been recorded previously in the accounting records. There are some contingencies that do not meet the criteria for disclosure established in *SFAS 5*. For example, companies that self-insure, rather than pay insurance premiums to insurance companies for protection, have a contingent liability that could seriously underestimate liabilities, yet they are not generally required to disclose such information.[13]

No disclosure is required of the airlines for their frequent-flyer programs. These programs provide free trips to flyers after they have accumulated a certain amount of mileage. It is estimated that as much as $1 billion worth of free trips have been accumulated by flyers within the industry.[14] The accounting practices of the airlines have been criticized.

> "It's evident from an accounting standpoint, they [airlines] were undercovered.... The idea is when you owe something, you put it on the books when you make the sale. But the airlines didn't."[15]

Therefore, the analyst should consider problems that are specific to an industry or a company that are not required to be incorporated into the financial statements.

---

[12]*SFAS 5*, para. 1.

[13]See L. Jereski, "The Naked Truth," *Forbes*, May 18, 1987, 86–87.

[14]D. Knox, "Frequent Flier Deals Worry Airlines," *Denver Rocky Mountain News*, March 6, 1988, D11.

[15]Ibid.

Consolidations of Entities

When two corporations merge or consolidate, a set of accounting rules applies based on the structure of the agreement. The consolidation can be accounted for as either a *purchase* or a *pooling of interests*. The accounting rules are complex, and the result of applications are significantly different. Parties involved in the merger can purposely structure the deal to allow for the accounting to follow the pooling of interests approach. The significance to an analyst is that a pooling of interests will result in greater reported earnings and lower assets than if the other approach, the purchase method, is used. The result will be an increase in profitability measures.

Under the purchase method, an asset known as *goodwill* emerges. This asset represents the difference between the price paid for a company and its book value. Since market prices usually exceed book value, goodwill may emerge. It is an intangible asset that is required to be amortized over a period of no longer than 40 years on the records of the acquiring company.[16]

Recently, however, the recognition of goodwill has come under criticism, especially with regard to its use in the savings and loan industry:

> Goodwill is nothing more than a phantom asset. Accountants create goodwill to explain why one thrift pays a premium for another institution....Goodwill, like peace on earth, has been something valued as an ideal, but something rarely realized in any practical way in the real world.[17]

The creation of goodwill in the accounting records results in higher assets and stockholders' equity of the acquiring entity. However, in subsequent years, the amortization of goodwill reduces net income and stockholders' equity. The analyst should consider the effects of the manner in which a merger or a consolidation is accounted for, since the results can significantly alter the financial statements of the consolidated entity.

Furthermore, consolidated financial statements represent the sum of the assets, liabilities, and results of operations of component entities owned in whole or in part by the parent company. These component entities, called subsidiaries, may issue separate financial statements

---

[16]*APB No. 16*, Accounting Principles Board, 1970.
[17]D. LaGesse, "Dangerous Case of Little Knowledge," *Dallas Morning News*, May 14, 1989, 2H.

reflecting what purports to be the subsidiary's financial condition and results of operations. In these cases, the financial statements of the subsidiary appear to be representative of an autonomous unit. However, subsidiaries are not independent. This situation creates reporting difficulties that can be handled in a variety of ways and that can obscure economic realities. Therefore, financial statement users should use caution when analyzing the financial statements of subsidiary companies.[18]

Investments in Other Entities

Companies often purchase the stock of other companies, but do not acquire a controlling interest (50 percent or more) that requires the preparation of consolidated financial statements. Such an investment is accounted for by either the *cost* method or the *equity* method of accounting for long-term investments. The equity method is required when the investor has acquired enough stock to exercise "significant influence" over the investee, which is usually presumed when ownership is at least 20 percent.[19] The resulting differences in application of the two methods can be quite significant. It is likely that an investor company using the equity method will report higher earnings and assets than if the cost method was applied. However, if the investee company suffers substantial losses, the reverse may be true. For example, Columbia Pictures reported a net loss of $105 million in 1987, which caused Coca-Cola, the owner of 49 percent of Columbia to record a $51 million decrease in net income.[20]

In-Substance Defeasance

In-substance defeasance of debt illustrates the problems encountered when attempting to report the economic consequences of complex transactions.[21] It also illustrates the creativity of management in attempting to use accounting standards to their best interests. In 1982, Exxon Corporation was able to remove $515 million in debt from its balance sheet and to record a $132 million profit at the same time. This

---

[18]See T. E. Allison, and P. B. Thomas, "Unchartered Territory: Subsidiary Financial Reporting," *Journal of Accountancy* (October 1989), 76–85.

[19]*APB No. 18*, Accounting Principles Board, 1971

[20]"Columbia Pictures Expects Net Loss; Coke with 49% Stake Will Feel Effect," *The Wall Street Journal*, March 16, 1988, 6.

[21]Defeasance is a term that signifies legal release of a debtor from liability.

was accomplished by purchasing U.S. Treasury securities and placing them in a trust. The income from the securities was used to retire the original $515 million in debt. The interpretation, based on accounting standards existing at the time, provided for a reduction of $515 million in debt with a transfer of securities that had cost $383 million to a trust. The difference represented a "profit," which had favorable effects on numerous financial ratios.

Pro and con arguments exist for allowing an entity to report such a transaction as full payment of a debt when, in fact, the debt has not been paid. After the Exxon transaction, the FASB issued *SFAS 76*, which restricted the removal of debt for such "in-substance" defeasance to certain circumstances. This treatment is founded on the premise that, in those restricted circumstances where low-risk securities earning sufficient income to pay off a debt have been transferred to an irrevocable trust, the transaction culminates, in substance, in the retirement of the debt.

The creativity of management should never be underestimated. With restrictive accounting rules in place, other companies were able to use the language from other accounting pronouncements to exclude existing debt from their balance sheets. This was done by acquiring a controlling interest in a subsidiary in a nonrelated industry, which allows the parent company to exclude the subsidiary in consolidated financial statements. This has excluded billions of dollars of debt from the balance sheets of parent companies.[22] Consequently, *SFAS 94* was issued to prevent this practice.

SFAS 94 can have some adverse economic consequences on financial ratios, once the previously excluded debt of the subsidiary is consolidated with the parent company's financial statements. It has been shown that consolidation of finance subsidiaries will cause financial ratios to deteriorate.[23] Subsequent to consolidation, the parent will become more highly leveraged. Increased leverage can be viewed by the market as a negative indicator of future prospects.

However, there is some evidence that corporate restructuring can prevent the effects of *SFAS 94* from having as adverse effects on balance sheets as were initially contemplated.[24] Nevertheless, the

---

[22]J. B. Heian, and J. B. Thies "Consolidation of Finance Subsidiaries: $230 Billion in Off-Balance Sheet Financing Comes Home to Roost", *Accounting Horizons*, March, 1989, 1-9.

[23]Ibid.

[24]L. Barton, "FASB Issues Rule Making Firms Combine Data of All Their Majority-Owned Units," *The Wall Street Journal*, November 2, 1987, 10.

experience of the last few years is a lesson for financial statement users in the creativity of management in discovering ways to produce "off-balance-sheet financing."

Sources of Net Income

Many financial statement users focus on "bottom line" net income. Note that the bottom line is often composed of many different elements that affect net income. News announcements of earnings can be just as misleading as focusing on the bottom line. For example, Sears reported that net income for 1984 had risen 8.4 percent to a record $1.45 billion. Upon closer inspection of the components of net income, it became apparent that approximately one-half of the bottom line number was composed of "other" income or nonrecurring types of income.[25]

In order to assist users in analyzing the bottom line, companies are required to disclose the components of net income. Perhaps the most important component is income from continuing operations, as this should be a better predictor of future income. This is because it is not composed of nonrecurring type revenues. Some items that are required to be shown separately are extraordinary items[26] and gains or losses on disposal of major segments of a company.

Companies are also required to disclose in the notes to the financial statements the information concerning major customers, sales by geographic region, and other items. The analyst should pay special attention to these disclosures in order to properly evaluate the true economic consequences of past and future events.

In fact, the notes to the financial statements contain voluminous required disclosures, and they often represent a mountain of rather dry reading. However, these supplemental disclosures contain an abundance of information, and a serious analyst should pay close attention to what is revealed in them.[27]

An analyst must also look closely at cash flows and must integrate the findings with other ratios. Careful analysis of the origins and nature of cash flows can place an analyst at an advantage over the

---

[25]S. Weiss, "A Hunt for Artificial Sweeteners in Earnings Statements," *Business Week*, February 25, 1985, 86. Also see C. J. Loomis, "The Earnings Magic at American Express," *Fortune*, June 25, 1984, 58–61.

[26]These are items that are unusual and infrequent in occurrence.

[27]See J. St. Goar, "The Footnote Follies," *Forbes*, March 11, 1985 for examples of the types of information to look for.

market, as evidenced by the bankruptcy of W. T. Grant in the mid-1970s.[28]

W. T. Grant was the nations's largest retailer in 1973. Net income had remained relatively constant at about $30 million from 1966 through 1973. The P/E ratio in 1973 was approximately 20 times its earnings, which indicated that the market placed a premium on W. T. Grant stock. However, from 1970 until bankruptcy in 1974, cash flow from operations was negative, which required the company to borrow large sums of money. In 1972, cash flows bottomed out at a negative $100 million. The statement of cash flows was not a required financial statement at this time, but if an analyst had computed cash flows, he or she could have predicted that the market's valuation of W. T. Grant was wrong.

The preceding discussion does not contain a comprehensive discussion of the effects of alternative GAAP and the inherent limitations of accounting on financial statement ratios. Rather, it illustrates the importance of paying attention to financial statement disclosures and of understanding the consequences of accounting choices on financial statement ratios. Otherwise, when comparing two companies, the analyst may not be comparing "apples with apples."

Other Considerations

Statistical models and analyses have been developed to assist financial statement analysts and others in the analytical process. Linear regression may be used to predict revenues, cash flows, or individual account balances. Additional statistical techniques, which are essentially offshoots of regression, have been developed to forecast financial distress. (A more detailed discussion of some of these statistical techniques is included in Appendix B to this chapter.)

Analysts should consider characteristics and statistics unique to particular industries. For example, in the oil and gas industry, reserve quantities represent very important assets, yet they are not correlated to costs reflected in the balance sheet. However, as already mentioned, *SFAS 69* requires detailed disclosures of reserve quantities in the notes to the financial statements.

In other industries, statistics not disclosed in the financial statements could be very useful, and the analyst must search for them. For

---

[28] J. A. Largay and C. P. Stickney, "Cash Flows, Ratio Analysis, and the W. T. Grant Bankruptcy," *Financial Analysts Journal* (July/August 1980), 51–54.

example, in the airline industry, the following statistics could provide insight into industry and specific company prospects (e.g., available seat-miles, load factors, revenue passenger-miles, costs per mile flown, and so forth). This type of information can be discovered from a variety of sources, including the section of the annual report devoted to management's discussion of the financial statements.

Most libraries contain reference volumes that are quite helpful in gathering data on companies of interest. A sample of what one might expect to find is listed below:

Industry Norms and Key Business Ratios. New York: Dun and
     Bradstreet Credit Services.
This service lists over 800 different areas of businesses, publicly and privately owned, in all size ranges.

Troy, Leo. *Almanac of Business and Industrial Financial Ratios.*
     Englewood cliffs, NJ: Prentice-Hall.
This book profiles corporate performance for each industry listing financial and operating information. The source of all data used in the almanac is the U.S. Treasury and the Internal Revenue Service. Statistics used are approximately three-years old.

Annual Statement Studies. Philadelphia: Robert Morris Associates.
This contains financial data on manufacturing, wholesaling, retailing, service, and contracting lines of business. Statements are arranged by company size, and they include ratios.

Standard and Poor's Surveys. Standard and Poor's Corporation.
This reference book contains basic data on major industries and includes financial comparisons of the leading companies in each industry.

Moody's Manual. New York: Moody's Investors Service.

Each corporate manual is published annually and kept up-to-date with the *News Reports.* Information in these manuals includes a brief history of each company, its subsidiaries, location of plants, income statement and balance sheet, and selected financial and operating ratios. Approximately 20,000 corporations are included.

While the services listed above are helpful in gathering and comparing data, an analyst should not restrict his or her analysis to the data contained in these services. Errors and problems are known to exist in these services.[29] When analyzing financial statements, the analyst

---

[29] J. L. Roberts, "Dun's Credit Reports, Vital Tools of Business, Can Be Off the Mark," *The Wall Street Journal,* October 5, 1989, 1A.

should request the statements directly from the company. The SEC requires that companies furnish financial statements to interested parties free of charge. The analyst then is able to personally compute ratios and has access to all disclosures.

Errors or mishandled estimates by "professional" analysts take place more often than one might think. In May 1989, Bear Stearns, a large investment-banking firm, criticized the accounting policies of Blockbuster Video. This resulted in a decrease of $226 million in the company's market value.[30] However, on a *Moneyline* broadcast on October 4, 1989, an increase in the stock price of Blockbuster Video was attributed to analysts revaluing Blockbuster's assets upward. Nothing of substance had transpired between May and October with regard to Blockbuster. The original report had prompted the chief executive of Blockbuster to respond: "If five analysts from Bear Stearns can't find the time, or don't have the interest, to sit down with management (and) understand our business, then the report isn't worth the powder to blow it to hell."[31]

Thus, a relatively small group of professional analysts funnels its estimates and opinions to stockbrokers and to the financial news media. Their opinions and conclusions do affect market prices, but those conclusions can be wrong. If an enlightened analyst who understands accounting choices and economic realities had purchased Blockbuster Video in May 1989, after the critical report by Bear Stearns, he or she could have made a significant amount of money when the company was revaluated in October 1989.

News reports not originating with professional analysts or dealing with financial stories also affect stock market prices. For example, in the late 1970s the oil and gas industry, experienced "bad press" due to so-called obscene profits. More recently, the Alaskan oil spill by the ExxonValdez caused investor concerns. The concerns stem from apprehension that government policies might be instituted, as a result of high profits or as a result of oil spills, that would adversely affect the companies in that industry.

Another consideration deals with a recently evolved theory called *agency theory*. There is evidence that management chooses accounting methods based on the effect on earnings if there is a direct connection

---

[30]Weschler, D. "Earnings Helper." *Forbes,* June 12, 1989, 150.
[31]"Blockbuster Defends Accounting Practices, Affirms its Outlook." *The Wall Street Journal,* May 17, 1989, 138.

between earnings and bonus.[32] In Chapter 9 agency theory is discussed in greater detail.

Management can change to accounting methods that have a favorable impact on financial statements when the entity is experiencing financial distress.[33] Accounting methods must be applied consistently, but companies can elect to change methods under certain circumstances. However, the change and its effects are required to be disclosed. Chapter 9 contains a discussion of whether the market is "fooled" by these changes. For now, be alert for accounting changes that can have cosmetic effects on financial statements.

Appendix A to this chapter includes a portion of a professional analyst's report on RJR. The purpose of this analysis is to assist in the investment decision of whether to buy bonds issued by RJR. The report is reproduced in the appendix to provide the reader with an idea of the considerations involved. Note the emphasis on cash flows.

SUMMARY

Numbers are used in accounting to reflect the economic consequences of transactions. The financial statements purport to represent the cumulative effect of economic consequences on elements of financial statements, and numbers are used to measure the effect. However, the reader should understand the full import of the quote at the beginning of the chapter.

Since many of the problems associated with accounting numbers stem from the use of alternative GAAP, the reader might ask, Why allow alternatives? The SEC has agreed with many members of the accounting profession that the use of alternatives allows for justifiable flexibility when differences in circumstances exist. Undoubtedly, this provides potential for abuse, and some of the research cited in this chapter has suggested that abuses have occurred. In theory, the independent auditor prevents abuses by fulfilling his or her role as prescribed by the SEC. Regrettably, in practice, this role has not always been fulfilled with due diligence. Nevertheless, the times that auditors have been negligent in their role are relatively few. Furthermore, the burden of understanding financial statements must fall on users:

---

[32]F. S. Worthy, "Manipulating Profits: How Is It Done." *Fortune*, June 25, 1984, 51.

[33]K. B. Schwartz, "Accounting Changes by Corporations Facing Possible Insolvency," *Journal of Accounting, Auditing, and Finance* (Fall 1982), 32–43.

Financial information is a tool and, like most tools, cannot be of much direct help to those who are unable or unwilling to use it or who misuse it. Its use can be learned, however, and financial reporting should provide information that can be used by all—nonprofessionals as well as professionals who are willing to learn to use it properly.[34]

An enlightened financial statement analyst will consider the problems inherent in the accounting process. With regard to any specific company, this may be done by assessing the quality of earnings and valuations through extensive study of the financial statement disclosures. The disclosures, combined with an analyst's understanding of the importance and consequences in accounting terms, should provide the analyst with a better insight into the entity's financial condition and profitability. It should be remembered that these results are useless in absolute terms, and that they can only be meaningful in relative terms when measured against similar entities.

Additional information that should be incorporated into the analytical process includes political and general economic conditions. As previously mentioned, political and economic factors have been important in the analysis of oil and gas companies. Recently, these factors have also been important concerns in the analysis of the savings and loan industry.

READING LIST

Altman, E. I. "Accounting Implications of Failure Prediction Models." *Journal of Accounting, Auditing, and Finance* (Fall 1982): 4-19.

Altman, E. I. "Financial Ratios, Discriminant Analysis and the Prediction of Corporate Bankruptcy." *The Journal of Finance* (September 1968): 589–603.

Altman, E. I., and McGough, T. P. "Evaluation of a Company as a Going Concern." *Journal of Accountancy* (December 1974): 50-57.

Beaver, W. H. "Financial Ratios as Predictors of Failure." Empirical Research in Accounting: Selected Studies (1966), *Journal of Accounting Research*: 71–103.

Berton, L. "Loose Ledgers." *The Wall Street Journal*, December 13, 1983.

---

[34]*SFAC 1*, Financial Accounting Standards Board, 1978, para. 36.

Biddle, G. C. "Paying FIFO Taxes: Your Favorite Charity?" *The Wall Street Journal*, January 19, 1981.

Biddle, G. C. "Taking Stock of Inventory Accounting Choices." *The Wall Street Journal*, September 15, 1982.

Coe, T. L., and Merino, B. D. "Uniformity in Accounting: A Historical Perspective." *Journal of Accountancy* (August 1978): 48–54.

Dhaliwal, D. S. "The Effect of the Firm's Capital Structure on the Choice of Accounting Methods." *The Accounting Review* (January 1980): 78–84.

Granof, M. H., and Short, D. G. "For Some Companies, FIFO Accounting Makes Sense." *The Wall Street Journal*, August 30, 1982.

Jaenicke, H. R., and Rascoff, J. "Segment Disposition: Implementing APB Opinion No. 30, *Journal of Accountancy* (April 1974): 63–69.

Loomis, C. J. "Behind the Profits Glow at Aetna." *Fortune,* November 15, 1982, 54–58.

Managan, Jr., J. "The Use of Bankruptcy Prediction Models and Microcomputers." *Journal of Commercial Bank Lending* (July 1986): 31–37.

Meyers, H. B. "A Bit of Rouge for Allis-Chalmers." *Fortune,* May 15, 1969, 234–240.

Ohlson, J. A. "Financial Ratios and the Probabilistic Prediction of Bankruptcy." *Journal of Accounting Research* (Spring 1980): 101–130.

Revsine, L. "The Preferability Dilemma." *Journal of Accountancy* (September 1977): 80–89.

Schwartz, K. B. "Accounting Changes by Corporations Facing Possible Insolvency." *Journal of Accounting, Auditing, and Finance* (Fall 1982): 32–43.

Scott, R. A. and Scott, R. K., "Retroactive Changes—A Practitioner's Checklist." *Journal of Accountancy* (May 1978): 42–48.

St. Goar, J. "The Footnote Follies." *Forbes*, March 11, 1985, 155–156.

Weiss, S. "A Hunt for Artificial Sweeteners in Earnings Statements." *Business Week*, February 25, 1985, 86.

Weiss, S. "How Inventories Could Bury 1985 Computer Profits." *Business Week*, April 8, 1985, 82–83.

Watts, R. L., and Zimmermann, J. L. "Toward a Positive Theory of the Determination of Accounting Standards." *The Accounting Review* (January 1978): 112–134.

Weil, R. L. "Managing Earnings Using an Insurance Subsidiary: A Case of Restraint by Sears/Allstate." *The Accounting Review*, (October 1980): 680–684.

Worthy, F. S. "Manipulating Profits: How It's Done." *Fortune*, June 25, 1984, 50-54.

APPENDIX A

ANALYSIS FOR RJR NABISCO

FOUNTAIN CAPITAL MANAGEMENT, INC. CREDIT REPORT RJR NABISCO

Portions of this report have been deleted at the request of Fountain Capital Management, Inc.

RECOMMENDATION

RJR Nabisco securities are recommended for the high-yield approved list. Though controversial due to the size of the deal, RJR is one of the most attractive LBO's we have seen. Each of the securities listed above has been issued at an attractive price considering the excellent quality of the credit and the company's prospects for improvement with asset sales. At recent prices of $21.50 and $88.00, the two "cramdown" securities—the PIK Preferred Stock and the Senior Converting Debentures, respectively—are especially attractive, even though the conversion feature has little value. They are rated lower than the subordinated issues because of their lower standing in the capital structure.

CONTENTS

NATURE OF BUSINESS

RJR Nabisco is among the world's largest and most profitable consumer products companies. RJR was created in 1985 when the R.J. Reynolds Tobacco Company acquired Nabisco Brands, Inc. The company, based in Atlanta, Georgia, has over 275 well-known brand names and holds leading positions in both the food and tobacco industries. In October 1988, the company's President and CEO, Ross Johnson, put RJR "in play" with an offer to take the company private in a leveraged buyout. After a well-publicized bidding contest, Kohlberg Kravis Roberts & Co. (KKR) was able to win control of the company, and the result was the largest LBO ever. KKR plans to sell pieces of the company to raise approximately $6 billion over the next 12 to 18 months in order to reduce bank debt. The following is a description of the company as it exists prior to any asset sales.

Food

The company operates its food business through three separate entities: Nabisco Brands, Inc., Planters Lifesavers Company, and Del Monte Foods.

Nabisco is a leading worldwide producer of a variety of packaged goods. Nabisco's business is conducted through four operating units: Biscuit, Foods, Nabisco Brands Ltd. (Canada), and International Nabisco Brands. Within the Biscuit group are the well-known cookie and cracker brands such as *Oreo, Chips Ahoy!, Fig Newton, Nilla, Wheat Thins, Triscuit, Ritz, Premium,* and *Honey Maid.* Major brands in the Foods group are *Shredded Wheat, Fleischmann's, Blue Bonnet, Milk-Bone, A.1., Grey Poupon, Chun King, Ortega,* and *Cream of Wheat.* The Canadian and International groups market a mixture of these brands as well as brands sold only outside the U. S. Nabisco has historically been managed to increase market share at the expense of profitability. With the LBO, Nabisco's operating strategy will shift to one of maintaining market share and improving cash flow. Recent capital expenditure programs should aid in the improvement of profitability.

Planters Lifesavers is the leading producer of nuts in the U. S. and is also a major producer of candy and gum. Brands include *Planters, Life Savers, Breath Savers, Care*Free,* and *Bubble Yum.*

Del Monte is the largest canner of fruits and vegetables in the U. S. Del Monte Tropical Fruit produces, distributes and markets bananas, fresh pineapples, and other tropical fruit throughout the world.

Tobacco

RJR is the second largest producer of cigarettes in the U. S., with a market share of 31.8% The company's *Winston, Salem, Camel, Doral* and *Vantage* brands, which are all among the top ten selling brands domestically, represent 80% of U. S. sales. Only Philip Morris's *Marlboro* brand, which alone has a 24.7% share, outsells *Winston* and *Salem*. RJR's established brands have held stable to slightly declining market shares over the past several years. The company is concentrating on maximizing cash flow of older brands such as *Winston*, and more aggressively marketing brands such as *Salem* and *Doral*. Internationally, the company markets its domestic brand names plus certain brands targeted to specific countries.

In 1980, RJR began a 10-year, $2 billion manufacturing facilities modernization program. The company's Tobaccoville complex, completed in January 1988, is the largest and most technologically advanced cigarette manufacturing facility in the world. Renovations of existing plants will be complete in 1989. As a result, RJR will be the industry's low cost producer and capital expenditures will fall dramatically.

Increased manufacturing efficiency, combined with price increases, has improved domestic operating margins from 27.6% in 1984 to 35.0% in 1988.

Other

Although relatively minor in size, RJR also owns 20% of ESPN, a leading cable television network specializing in sports programming.

QUALITY OF MANAGEMENT

Louis Gerstner has assumed the duties of Chairman, President and CEO of RJR Nabisco. Although he has no previous experience in the food or tobacco businesses, Gerstner developed an excellent reputation for building businesses as president of American Express Co. He and other top executives have a substantial financial stake in RJR equity.

KKR will control a majority of the common equity in RJR (94.2% currently, 55.2% fully diluted). KKR's experience with large LBO's, the food business, and the selling of assets should be considered positives for the credit. Past deals include Beatrice, SCI Holdings, Safeway, Stop & Shop, Owens-Illinois, Duracell, and Jim Walter. Other shareholders include Drexel and Merrill Lynch as underwriters.

INDUSTRY OUTLOOK/PROSPECTS

Food

As a whole, the food industry is very stable and over the long-term grows with the population. The industry should be considered recession-resistant.

The industry itself is highly fragmented, with varying fundamentals depending on product category. Some product categories, such as snacks, fresh produce, ethnic foods, and ready-to-eat cereals, are experiencing above-average growth. Other categories, such as pet food, are more mature.

Brand names and market share play a key role in participants' abilities to expand sales and improve profits. Brand loyalty is strong for many products, which protects margins from being squeezed by new competitors. Once a brand name is established, product line extensions provide a way to grow faster than the overall industry rate of growth.

Due to economies of scale and opportunities to brand internationally, there has been a trend toward consolidation across most categories.

Tobacco

Tobacco is a mature industry in which the key success factors are brand recognition, quality products, and manufacturing and distribution efficiencies. Large capital investment and marketing expenditures present formidable barriers for any new entrants. The industry should be considered recession-resistant.

Domestic cigarette unit volume is in a gradual decline. Consumption peaked in 1981, and since 1983 volume has declined by approximately 2% per year. It is expected that this trend will continue. With fewer smokers, competition between brands—especially for new smokers—has at times become intense in terms of advertising and promotions.

Foreign cigarette unit volume is growing at about 1% per annum. However, "American Blend" cigarettes (vs. local varieties) are growing in terms of market share. International sales, therefore, represent a growth opportunity for U. S. tobacco companies.

Historically, the industry has enjoyed significant pricing flexibility that has allowed industry participants to achieve profit growth on declining unit volume. Since 1977, cigarette prices have increased approximately 11% per annum. With the exception of 1983's excise tax doubling, price seems to have little impact on sales volume. Low-price brands, such as RJR's *Doral*, have been growing in market share, however. In sum, the industry should enjoy cash flow growth despite unit sales declines.

The detrimental effects of smoking on health ("alleged" according to management) and the increasingly negative social implications of smoking have made an impact on tobacco industry sales. Of long-term concern to the industry is litigation against tobacco companies. Although lawsuits have been brought since the 1950's, only one has resulted in liability for the industry, and in that case it was for a modest award and it has not led to other liabilities. Industry participants believe that future litigation will not have a material financial impact.

The larger industry participants, most notably RJR, have been attempting to create new products that would address some of the concerns discussed above. However, RJR's *Premier* "smokeless" cigarette proved to be a costly failure in test markets during 1988, and has since been shelved. No other competitors have tried to market such a product, although several have been trying to develop one. It is not yet clear whether these products will have a significant impact on the industry in the future.

INVESTMENT CONSIDERATIONS

Positives

RJR has numerous well-known brand names with leading market positions in stable industries.

RJR is made up of many independent operating companies which are saleable as separate entities. There are a number of companies, both domestic and foreign, that have a great interest in these entities. As asset sales are made to satisfy bank amortization requirements, bond prices should reflect credit quality improvement.

Operating cash flow coverage of interest is extremely strong for an LBO with such stable businesses.

Approximately 26.6%, or $8.3 billion, of the capital structure is below the subordinated securities.

Recent capital improvements along with a new strategy focused on cash flow generation should greatly improve profitability.

KKR is experienced in handling large leveraged buyouts involving food companies and asset sales.

The cramdown securities are trading at substantial discounts to par value. In one to two years, the coupons will be set to cause the securities to trade at par. Therefore in addition to an attractive floating coupons before the reset date, there is a high probability of realizing capital gains.

The warrants issued along with the Subordinated PIK and Discount Debentures appear to have significant value. Although not tradeable for one year and not exercisable for nine, the warrants have an exercise price of $0.07 to receive a share of stock for which KKR paid $5 in cash.

Negatives

Although it is highly unlikely, a change in the courts' view on the issue of tobacco liability could have a material financial impact on the company.

The magnitude of the RJR securities available may cause short-term price fluctuations as the high-yield and preferred stock markets absorb the new issues. the cramdown issues may have particular volatility as arbitrators who received the paper upon tendering their RJR common shares unwind their positions. There is also uncertainty as to the initial trading range of the Subordinated PIK and Discount Debentures. Some large buyers may have purchased the bonds only to receive the warrants and cash fees, and may not be long-term holders of the bonds.

An unforeseen event or sharp rise in interest rates could impair the value of assets that the company plans to sell.

With the replacement of the CEO and other top executives, a rough transition period could affect early results.

The declining nature of the tobacco industry could result in a more competitive environment over the the long term.

ASSET MARKET VALUES/CAPITALIZATION

CAPITALIZATION

	$	%
Assumed Short-term Debt	$ 423	1.4%
Assumed Senior Debt	5,312	17.0
Senior Bank Debt	12,175	39.0
Bridge IRN's	1,000	3.2
Subordinated Debts & FRN's	4,000	12.8
KKR Jr. Sub PIK Bridge	500	1.6
RJR Hldgs. Capital Corp.	23,410	75.0
PIK Exch. Pfd.	4,036	12.9
PIK Sr. Conv. Debts	1,807	5.8
Common Equity	1,992	6.4
Total Capital	$31,245	100.0%

Capitalization Structure

The following is a representation of the structure of RJR's parent companies and the location of debt and equity within those companies. The lower the company, the more senior the capital.

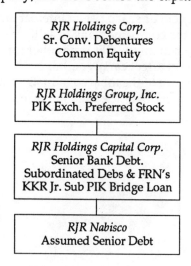

FINANCIAL DATE — RATIOS ($ IN MILLIONS)

	1986	1987	1988	1989	1990	1991
					estimates	
Coverage:						
Oper Cash Flow/Cash Int	5.50x	7.15x	6.63x	1.52x	2.22x	2.67x
Oper Cash Flow/Capital Int**	5.21x	6.71x	6.29x	1.37x	1.76x	2.04x
Oper Cash Flow/Group Int	na	na	na	1.19x	1.31x	1.42x
Oper Cash Flow/Holding Int+Pfd	na	na	na	1.13x	1.17x	1.25x
Oper Cash Flow/CI+CE+WC*	2.04x	2.25x	1.85x	0.98x	1.62x	1.86x
Leverage:						
LT Debt/Total Capital	48.4%	39.4%	50.7%	92.6%	92.4%	92.7%
Profitability:						
Oper Profit/Total Assets	14.6%	15.6%	16.0%	8.2%	10.9%	12.5%
Oper Profit/Revenue	15.5%	16.7%	16.8%	13.5%	19.7%	20.9%
Liquidity and Efficiency:						
Revenue/Fixed Assets	2.38x	2.70x	2.76x	2.27x	2.22x	2.39x
LT Debt/Oper Cash Flow	1.78x	1.23x	1.57x	6.30x	6.42x	6.09x

*Cash Interest + Capital Expenditures + Working Capital Requirements
**Capital Int = total interest for RJR Holdings Capital Corp. and subsidiaries.
Group Int = total interest for RJR Holdings Group, Inc. and subsidiaries.
Holding Int + Pfd = total interest and preferred dividends for RJR Holdings Corp. and subsidiaries.

FINANCIAL DATE — CASH FLOW ($ IN MILLIONS)

	1986	1987	1988	1989	estimates	
					1990	1991
Revenues	$15,102	$15,766	$16,956	$18,136	$13,309	$14,359
Operating Expenses	12,762	13,136	14,108	15,685	10,688	11,353
Operating Profit	2,340	2,630	2,848	2,451	2,621	3,006
Depreciation & Amort.	605	652	794	1,491	1,173	1,126
Operating Cash Flow	2,945	3,282	3,642	3,942	3,794	4,132
Cash Interest Expense	535	459	579	2,588	1,708	1,549
Capital Expenditures	1,022	936	1,179	1,179	561	486
Working Capital Reg.	(116)	62	281	254	79	184
Cash Taxes	533	682	678	(48)	73	(37)
Cash Dividends	480	470	494	0	0	0
Other	(182)	98	78	319	282	201
Asset Sales	(942)	(1,409)	(48)	(5,750)	(750)	0
Net LBO Debt Repayment	na	na	na	5,337	1,983	964
Net Stock Transactions	1,428	293	1,358	0	0	0
Net change in Pre-LBO Debt	(95)	1,413	(1,227)	na	na	na
Excess Cash	$282	$278	$337	$63	$(142)	$785

Financial Data Assumptions

1. Excludes results of operations sold prior to the leveraged buyout. On October 1, 1986, the company sold Kentucky Fried Chicken, and on March 6, 1987, the company sold its spirits and wine business (primarily Heublin, Inc.). These business represented sales of $1,896 in 1986.

2. Estimates are based on the sale of assets (identified above) on December 31, 1989.

3. Both actual results and estimates ignore costs associated with the development of the Premier "smokeless" cigarette. Premier has been shelved indefinitely.

4. Debt ratios include both cramdown securities as debt.

DESCRIPTION OF SECURITIES

Security:	Sub FRN's	Sub Reset Debs	Sub Debs	Sub PIK Debs	Sub Disc Debs
Coupon:	3-Month LIBOR + 400bp adjusted/ paid quarterly	13.125%, Reset 5/15/91 & each year thereafter at 101%. Cap rate of 15.625%, Floor of 13.125%.	13.5%	15.0%, PIK to 5/15/94	0% to 5/15/94, 15.0% thereafter.
Maturity:	5/15/99	5/15/01	5/15/01	5/15/01	5/15/01
Ranking:	Pari passu with other subordinated issues	same	same	same	same
Call Schedule:	callable at 100% at any interest payment date	101% at reset dates (earlier if change of control)	106.75% 5/15/94, to par 5/15/99 (earlier if change of control)	107.5% 5/15/94 to par 5/15/99 (earlier if change of control)	107.5% *accreted* 5/15/94 to par 5/15/99 (earlier if change of control)
Put Option: (Upon Change Of Control)	100%	101%	101%	101%	101% accreted value
Issue Size:	$250 million	$225 million	$525 million	$1.0 billion	$2.0 billion
Quality Rating:	I-B B1/B+	I-B B1/B+	I-B B1/B+	I-B B1/B+	I-B B1/B+
Sinking Fund:	none	none	5/15/99, 5/15/00 Each 25% of issue	5/15/99, 5/15/00 Each 25% of issue	5/15/99, 5/15/00 Each 25% of issue
Other:				Issued with warrants	Issued with warrants

Use of
Proceeds:

Proceeds of all five issues were used as permanent financing for KKR's leveraged buyout of RJR Nabisco. The securities replaced the Increasing Rate Notes issued in February 1989 as bridge financing.

Covenants:
(same for
all issues)

Limitation on Indebtedness: Except for $2.5 billion + $1.5 billion subordinated to these issues, any new debt must pass a coverage test. Except for the $500 million KKR Jr Sub PIK debt, debt subordinated to these issues cannot be refinanced with more senior debt.

Limitation on Dividends: Strong restricted payment test based on debt and asset coverage, but $2.0 billion may be dividended to holding companies to retire cramdown securities.

Asset Sale Proceeds: Large asset sale proceeds must first be used to retire senior debt, then an offer to purchase these securities must be made at par (or accreted value).

Merger Limitations: Debt, net worth, and coverage tests must be met.

	Cumulative Exchangeable PIK Preferred Stock	Senior Converting PIK Debentures
Security:		
Issue Size:	$4.036 billion	$1.807 billion
Stated value:	$25	100%
Maturity:	2/9/07	2/9/09
Rating:	II - B	II-B
Ranking:	Issued by RJR Holdings Group, Inc. Senior only to common stock and the Senior Converting Debentures, and subordinated to all other debt.	Issued by RJR Holdings Corporation (the parent company). The Debentures are senior only to common stock.
Coupon:	Dividends are PIK on a cumulative, semiannual basis for the first six years, and pay cash thereafter. Initially, the dividend rate will float at 550 basis points over the highest of 1) 3-month Treasury bills, 2)10-year Treasury bonds, or 3) 30-year Treasury bonds, with a floor of 12.65% and a ceiling of 16.625%. Within one year of refinancing the Increasing Rate Notes, or if earlier, two years from the date of the merger (April 28, 1989), the dividend rate will be set at a level that will cause the stock to trade at $25.	Interest will be PIK for ten years, and will pay cash thereafter. The initial interest rate will be the same as the Preferred Stock. At the same reset date, the interest rate will be fixed to make the bonds trade at par (ignoring any conversion option value). No interest will be paid (although it will accrue and compound semi-annually) until four years after issuance. Holders who allow the company to convert their shares into common stock will not receive any interest.
Call Features:	Callable anytime at $25	Callable at par after four years.
Exchange Option:	The company may exchange the Preferred for subordinated debentures with the same terms anytime. (It is expected that the exchange will take place when advantageous for tax purposes.)	The Debentures will automatically convert into common stock of RJR Holdings Corp. at the end of four years unless the holder elects not to convert. The Debentures represent approximately 25% of the common stock on a fully diluted basis.
Sinking Fund:	25%, 25%, and 50% will be retired at $25 plus accrued and unpaid dividends on the 16th, 17th, and 18th anniversaries.	None

Security:	Warrants
Stock:	When exercised, the warrants entitle the holder to one share of RJR Holdings Corp. common stock. On a fully diluted basis, the Warrants will represent approximately 7.9% of the common stock.
Stock Price:	Although RJR Holdings Corp. common stock is privately held, KKR and the other equity holders paid $5.00 per share based on their $1.5 billion cash equity contribution.
Issue Price:	$0.01
Exercise Price:	$0.07
Exercise Date:	Earliest of: (1) May 15, 1998; (2) date the stock becomes publicly traded; or (3) date of any merger or consolidation in which common shareholders receive cash or publicly traded securities.
Holders:	Only holders of the Second Subordinated Increasing Rate Notes who "rolled" into the Subordinated PIK or Discount Debentures were entitled to receive Warrants. The number of Warrants received depended on the dollar amount of the IRN's held.
Trading:	The Warrants are not attached to any other security. They may not be traded until May 22, 1990.

APPENDIX B

STATISTICAL MODELS

A statistical model that accurately predicts financial distress is beneficial to investors, as well as to creditors, management, and, auditors. Many models have been deployed in practice. These models generally use financial ratios in some combination as predictors of financial problems.

While the development of financial distress models requires a relatively sophisticated knowledge of statistics, the use of the model is a simple matter; one need only insert the computed values for financial ratios into the coefficients given for the model. For example, the early research on bankruptcy prediction used a technique known as discriminant analysis.[35]

Discriminant analysis is a statistical technique appropriate for identifying variables that discriminate between groups. In this case, the two groups are financially healthy companies and financially distressed companies. The discriminant model developed by E. I. Altman produces a score (i.e., Z-score) and takes the following form:

$$Z = 0.012X_1 + 0.14X_2 + 0.033X_3 + 0.006X_4 + 0.010X_5$$

where X_1 = Working Capital ÷ Total Assets
X_2 = Retained Earnings ÷ Total Assets
X_3 = Earnings Before Interest and Taxes ÷ Total Assets
X_4 = Market Value of Equity[36] ÷ Total Debt
X_5 = Sales ÷ Total Assets

A user of the model simply calculates each variable and plugs those amounts into the model. The 1987 Z-score for RJR is as follows:

$$Z = 0.012(0.102) + 0.14(0.329) + 0.033(0.137) + 0.006(2.33) + 0.010(0.94) = 0.001 + 0.046 + 0.005 + 0.014 + 0.009 = 0.075.$$

The higher the Z-score, the better the financial condition of the company. In Altman's model, a score below 2.675 indicates that a company is in financial distress.

---

[35]Altman, E. I. "Financial Ratios, Discriminant Analysis, and the Prediction of Corporate Bankruptcy," *The Journal of Finance*, September, 1968, 589–609.

[36]This is calculated by multiplying the market value per share times the number of shares outstanding (both common and preferred).

Note that Altman's model was developed from firms across numerous industries. A model developed specifically for an industry can be more relevant to a company in that industry. In addition, if more than one financial accounting method is acceptable under GAAP, a model developed for a given method in that industry would be even more relevant. For example, in the oil and gas industry, a model utilizing financial ratios and reserve variables for the successful efforts and full cost methods is probably necessary to capture the effects of different accounting methods.[37]

Discriminant analysis requires certain statistical assumptions concerning the financial data used. While an in-depth discussion of the assumptions is beyond the scope of this book, it is sufficient to indicate that, in most cases, the financial data used does not fit the statistical assumptions required. When the statistical assumptions are violated, the conclusions drawn from the model may not be valid.[38] Therefore, another statistical technique that does not have the statistical limitations of discriminant analysis has been developed. This technique is commonly used and is called *logit*, or *logistic regression*, and it provides a probability of financial distress that's based on the logarithm of the likelihood of specific outcomes. Again, the application of logit, once the model is developed, is a simple matter.

Logit is a technique that not only overcomes the statistical limitations associated with discriminant analysis, but that also provides an additional important advantage. Discriminant analysis provides dichotomous results. The Z-score determines whether the firm is predicted to be distressed or nondistressed. Many investment decisions do not lend themselves to such yes-no answers.

Logit overcomes this disadvantage by providing an estimate of probability of failure or success. A probability estimate allows for the formulation of risk premiums to associate with specific firms in making investment decisions.[39]

The preceding discussion has addressed a rather specific question the probability that a firm will experience financial distress. Other

---

[37]Gordon, G., Shaver, J., Posey, C., and Wibker, E., "Using Discriminant Analysis to Detect Future Going Concern Problems of Oil and Gas Companies", *Proceedings of the Southwest Decision Sciences Institute*, 1990.

[38]Ohlson, J. A., "Financial Ratios and the Probabilistic Prediction of Bankruptcy", *Journal of Accounting Research*, Spring 1980, 109-131.

[39]For a technical discussion of discriminant analysis and logit, see: Zavgren, C. V., "The prediction of Corporate Failure: The State of the Art," *Journal of Accounting Literature*, Vol. 2, 1983, 1–35.

statistical models have been developed to address the general question of market valuation. Market valuation is related directly to expected future returns associated with securities. The capital asset pricing model, one market valuation model, is used to specify a theoretical security price. *Beta,* a statistic introduced by the Capital Asset Pricing Model, is a theoretical effort to define the relation of risk to return for any particular security investment. The higher the beta, the greater the risk; and the greater the risk accepted, the higher the expected return.[40]

Beta can be estimated by using past security returns.[41] Or, it can be estimated by using financial statement data, such as financial ratios.[42] The estimate of beta will have a direct effect on security valuation. In general, the higher the beta, the lower the security valuation in order to earn higher expected returns.

The discussion in this appendix has been intended as a brief overview of statistical techniques being used. The information obtained by using these statistics is an invaluable aid to analysts in gaining additional insight. The reader can refer to the references or to investment textbooks for more detailed information.

---

[40]Sharpe, W. F., "Capital Asset Prices: A Theory of Market Equilibrium Under Conditions of Risk," The *Journal of Finance*, September 1964, 452–442.

[41]Scholes, M., and Williams, J., "Estimating Betas from Nonsynchronous Data," *Journal of Financial Economics*, December 1977, 309–327.

[42]Bildersee, J. S., "The Association Between a Marker-Determined Measure of Risk and Alternative Measures of Risk," *The Accounting Review*, January, 1975, 81–98.

STUDY QUESTIONS

1. You are considering investing in a company with stable income that has a ROTA of 20 percent. The industry average is 7 percent. What could cause this difference in ROTAs?
2. Sturdy Furniture, Inc., is a newly formed corporation. At the end of its first year of operations, management is deciding on appropriate accounting policies. The controller has provided information on net income, given two possible alternatives:

	Alternative A	Alternative B
Net Income (loss)	125,000	<75,000>
Accounting Policies:		
Inventory Costing	FIFO	LIFO
Depreciation Method	Straight-line	Declining-balance

   A. Which alternative do you believe provides the most fair presentation?
   B. Which alternative would you expect management to choose?
   C. If management chooses Alternative A, can the auditor issue an unqualified audit report?
3. What inventory-costing method does RJR use? Would you expect net income to be increased or decreased if RJR changed to another inventory-costing method?
4. Which inventory-costing method is best?
5. Alpha Oil and Gas is a 50 percent partner in every project with Omega Oil and Gas. They both use the successful efforts method of accounting and have identical revenues and expenses. Alpha uses LIFO and Omega uses FIFO. War breaks out in the Middle East, and oil prices rise to $100 per barrel from $23 per barrel. Would you prefer to be president of Alpha or Omega?
6. Joe's Used Cars has had average annual income of $40,000 per year. Joe learns that a 1959 pink Cadillac that he had paid $500 for once belonged to Elvis Presley. Sotheby's auctions it for $1 million. How is the $999,500 gain accounted for, and where does it show up on the income statement?
7. Does the use of GAAP produce reliable financial statements?
8. Should accounting alternatives be allowed?

Chapter 7

Politics and Its
Effect On GAAP

Man is by nature a political animal.[1]

Very often different groups (management and auditors) see the economic reality of transactions differently. Recall that the central theme in Chapter 5 concerned disclosing the economic realities underlying the effects of transactions on measuring net income and valuing assets and liabilities. It has been suggested that the different "views" of reality may be more a result of convenience or self-interest of particular parties affected by the disclosure than of actual differences. The possibility of interpretations motivated by self-interest is real, and it undoubtedly occurs. This possibility raises the question, Will uniformity, or a strict rule-book approach to accounting, result in a more fair presentation than the current practice of permitting alternatives in recording transactions?

Chapter 6 illustrated that the existence of accounting alternatives increases the complexity of the analytical process because alternatives allow companies the possibility to interpret seemingly identical facts in different ways. It has been shown that, when confronted with a relatively small set of possible events, management has a choice of 30 million accounting alternatives to disclose the combined effects of the set of events.[2] That is, because of alternative GAAP and alternative revenue and expense recognition criteria, an exponentially larger choice set grows out of a small set of events.

---

[1] Aristotle, *Politics* (Chicago: University of Chicago Press, 1984).

[2] R. J. Chambers, "Financial Information and the Securities Market," *Abacus* vol. 1 (1965), 3–30.

Therefore, at least on the surface, one may infer that accounting choices decrease comparability and consistency. One may logically conclude, then, that uniformity will enhance comparability and consistency.

Comparability and consistency have been identified as important characteristics of accounting data.[3] Once you understand the complicating effects of alternative GAAP and accounting choices on financial statement analysis, it is natural to question why authoritative bodies allow accounting alternatives. The FASB and SEC have the authority to impose uniformity in accounting and financial reporting. It has been suggested that, if uniformity is applied in accounting and financial reporting, then the result will be financial statements that are more comparable and consistent.

The uniformity question has been addressed before.[4] In recent years, Congress has become concerned with the question of uniformity. Several different congressional committees have suggested that Congress or some other governmental agency establish uniform accounting rules and regulate the accounting profession. However, this may not result in interpretations void of self-interests, because congressional representatives also are human and subject to influence.

Many accountants have consistently maintained that the flexibility afforded by nonuniformity is important because they believe, paradoxically, that alternatives in accounting produce greater comparability between companies. Namely, they believe that with the knowledge of all facts concerning the transaction and the management operating philosophy, an accounting alternative can honestly reflect the substance of the economic reality in a particular circumstance.[5] Furthermore, the "assumption that uniformity would result in better financial reporting may not be warranted" when judged by previous experiments with uniformity.[6] Uniformity cannot be substituted for judgment. This is particularly true when considering the differences in industries and when considering the uncertainty that characterizes business in general.

The ultimate goal, everyone seems to agree, is "truth," "fairness," "justice" or perhaps, more simply that financial statements not be misleading.

---

[3]*SFAC 2*, par. 111, 120.

[4]Merino, B. D. and Coe, T. L., "Uniformity in Accounting: A Historical Perspective," *The Journal of Accountancy*, (August 1978), 48–54.

[5]Refer to the oil and gas discussion later in this chapter.

[6]Ibid. 49.

But these concepts are essentially ethical—and not absolute—terms requiring that someone make a determination of what is fair.[7]

If someone (or some group) is required to determine what is fair, then subjectivity is necessarily introduced. With the introduction of subjectivity comes honest disagreements about what is the "truth" or reality.

To date, the SEC has agreed that accounting alternatives are important in order to accommodate the differences in circumstances from one entity to another. Moreover, the SEC recognizes that circumstances can change, which would require an entity to change to an alternative GAAP accounting method that more closely reflects the economic realities. Management and the independent auditor must state that the new method adopted is preferable to the previous approach in presenting fair disclosure.[8]

The argument that nonuniformity will provide the best framework for presenting the economic realities of financial condition and the results of operations is appealing. From a practical standpoint, it is in the stockholders' best interests if management may choose from alternatives:

> Management's choice of accounting methods can affect a firm's cash flows because the firm's reported accounting numbers influence its negotiations with government regulatory bodies, wage and price control agencies, unions, civil rights groups, politicians, environmentalists and consumer groups. If measurement rules are flexible, managers can choose rules which maximize the value of the firm, given the effect of those rules on negotiations with various parties. For example, if there is a world sugar "shortage", managers of sugar-refining firms can select rules which reduce reported income so that congressional committees find it more costly to accuse the firm of exploiting consumers.[9]

Unfortunately, the opportunity to select from accounting alternatives has resulted in abuses. The issue is described succinctly as follows: if two accounting methods are used by two groups of companies, and "if the two groups of companies are different in aspects other than choice of accounting methods, then the focus of accounting principles formulation may be better centered on the legitimacy of those

---

[7]Ibid. 54.

[8]See the explanation given for the change in revenue recognition for PTL in Chapter 5.

[9]R. Leftwich, "Market Failure Fallacies and Accounting Information," Journal of Accounting and Economics (December 1980), 207.

differences as a justification for alternative accounting method[s]. However, if companies used one method of accounting to mitigate the effect of adverse economic events, accounting principle formulation might be directed toward eliminating the abuses."[10]

The entire standard-setting process is at risk to subversion by individuals (or groups) who may intervene with a hidden agenda. It is natural for individuals or groups to act in their own self-interests, while disguising their motivation as altruistic or theoretical (e.g., fair presentation). In fact, it may be more realistic to consider that the economic consequences on the affected individuals (or groups) of accounting standards or choices of accounting methods is the motivation behind lobbying for certain standards or for particular choices of accounting methods.[11]

Because there can be more than one group of affected parties and their interests can conflict, accounting is *not* apolitical:

> My hypothesis is that the setting of accounting standards is as much a product of political action as of flawless logic or empirical findings. Why? Because the setting of standards is a social decision. Standards place restrictions on behavior; therefore, they must be accepted by the affected parties. Acceptance may be forced or voluntary or some of both. In a democratic society, getting acceptance is an exceedingly complicated process that requires skillful marketing in a political arena.[12]

As illustrated in the next section, the FASB has adopted a "due-process" approach to setting standards that naturally introduces political action. An implicit assumption in a democratic society is that political action will work to society's benefit as competing elements argue their points and assimilate other views. It is assumed that the collective wisdom of society will make the choice that has the greatest net benefit to society.

However, there are a number of considerations that impede the purported benefits of political action:

> One factor is that effective political action is not independent of the distribution of wealth in society... . A second factor is that political

---

[10] E. B. Deakin, "Auditor Selection, Organization Control, Adverse Events, and the Selection of Accounting Method for Oil Exploration," *Quarterly Review of Economics and Business* (Autumn 1980), 78.

[11] S. A. Zeff, "The Rise of 'Economic Consequences'" *Financial Accounting Theory*, 3rd ed., Zeff, S. A. and Keller, T. F. eds. (New York: McGraw-Hill 1985), 19–33.

[12] C. T. Horngren, "The Marketing of Accounting Standards," *Journal of Accountancy* (October 1973), 61.

agendas can be structured, and political processes can tend to operate, so as to severely delimit the possibility for reallocation of wealth, opportunities and power from the few to the many...[and] to render substantial wealth reallocations to less well-off groups largely impossible.[13]

Accounting standards are not set and chosen in a vacuum. The next section provides a brief description of the financial accounting environment and standard-setting process.

FINANCIAL ACCOUNTING ENVIRONMENT

The FASB is responsible for setting accounting standards and resolving controversial issues. The FASB board has seven members who preserve their independence by severing their relationships with previous employers. These members receive salaries as full-time employees of the FASB in excess of $200,000. The members come from different backgrounds, with experience in public accounting, industry, and education.[14]

The FASB has adopted a due-process attitude that encourages input and participation by a large number of interested parties. This process involves the following stages:

1. An accounting issue is identified and preliminarily evaluated. There are several different sources for identification of controversial accounting issues.

   One source is the Emerging Issues Task Force (EITF), which was created by the FASB for the purpose of identifying controversial issues. Another source is the Financial Accounting Standards Advisory Committee (FASAC), which is composed of approximately 30 prominent individuals. As the name implies, the purpose of the FASAC is to advise the members of the FASB. Additional sources of issues are the financial press, the technical inquiries from auditors, the professional groups (such as the AICPA), and the SEC.
2. The admission of an accounting issue to the agenda of the FASB is as follows. If, after preliminary evaluation, the FASB decides that the issue deserves further attention, it is admitted to the

---

[13]T. O'Leary, "Observations on Corporate Financial Reporting in the Name of Politics," *Accounting, Organizations and Society, vol.* 10, no. 1 (1985), 88.

[14]P. B. W. Miller, and R. J. Redding, *The FASB: the People, the Process and the Politics,* 2nd ed. (Homewood, IL: Irwin, 1988), 36.

agenda. After admission to the agenda, the issue is discussed in a series of public meetings. If further attention is deemed necessary and the FASB believes that the question warrants the issuance of a *Statement of Accounting Standards*, the issue enters the next stage.

3. The next stage involves a deeper analysis by the FASB staff and the holding of public hearings. The FASB staff conducts research and a review of the authoritative and professional literature to identify underlying concepts and alternative resolutions. This analysis culminates in the issuance of a Discussion Memorandum or an Invitation to Comment, after which the FASB conducts public hearings and additional board meetings in order to receive input from interested parties.

4. A tentative resolution is determined. After the FASB receives the results of research and public comments, a formal description of the issue and a proposed solution is outlined in an Exposure Draft.

5. The issue receives additional public discussion. The issuance of the Exposure Draft Statement will stimulate additional input from interested parties. The issue is formally discussed by the FASB again to determine whether any new evidence may change the collective position of the FASB subsequent to issuance of the Exposure Draft.

6. A final resolution is determined. The FASB votes on the final resolution and issues a *Statement of Financial Accounting Standards*, or *SFAS, which* describes the question under consideration and the resolution in terms of accounting application. The statement can also contain an appendix, which explains the FASB's basis for its conclusions. Additionally, if there are dissenting votes, the dissenting members can explain the reason for their dissent.

Because of the due-process approach adopted by the FASB, which encourages participation by interested parties, it should be quite obvious that the process is inevitably subject to political pressures. The interested parties (and their interests) can be divided into five groups.

First, as previously discussed, management of corporations have a direct interest in the manner in which transactions are accounted for and reported. This is because management's compensation is often either directly affected or indirectly affected by financial reporting through the calculation of net income. Therefore, it is hypothesized that management will support accounting methods that tend to accelerate the recognition of revenue or positively affect net income.[15] Consequently, management's participation in the standard-setting process is easily understood.

Management can also be expected to choose an alternative or to lobby for accounting standards that initially result in higher assets and/or lower debt. However, note that, if elements of management are evaluated on return on investment, management may lobby for alternatives that manipulate recorded asset values downward in order to increase the calculated return on investment.

The second group of affected parties is comprised of investors, potential investors and creditors, whose participation in standard-setting policy is easily understood. These financial statement users are seeking reported accounting information that enables them to make investment decisions based on reliable and factual data. Such information should reflect the "truth" of the economic realities of the entity that is reporting the information. It is easy to contemplate a scenario where the interests of management conflicts with that of investors, of potential investors and creditors (who are providers of capital resources).

Remember, management is the steward of investor and creditor funds. A fiduciary relationship exists between management and investors and creditors. This relationship and its expected consequences have resulted in a hypothesis described as *agency theory*. The name is derived from the relationship between management (as agents) and investors and creditors (as principals).

Because there is a separation of control (management) and suppliers of capital (investors and creditors), a natural conflict of interests emerges. Therefore, an incentive to monitor the agent exists. However, there are agency costs associated with monitoring the agent. A trade-off between costs and self-interests occurs. Agency theory examines when and how this trade-off takes place. Further discussion of agency theory is deferred to Chapter 9.

---

[15]It has been suggested that this may not be true in certain limited circumstances. When political costs outweigh the advantage of increased reported revenues, management may, in fact, lobby for an accounting method that slows the recognition of revenue or negatively affects net income. This may be true in the case of large regulated companies or when there is a threat of regulation. See R. L. Watts, and J. L. Zimmermann, "Toward a Positive Theory of the Determination of Accounting Standards," *The Accounting Review*, (January, 1978), 112–134.

The conflict between management and resource providers is described from two perspectives in terms of the standard-setting environment:

> In general, financial managers want to keep their options among accounting alternatives open to select the best one for a given situation. If accounting standards setters reduce the number of alternatives available—in an attempt to curb a potential for manipulation—they are assuming a serious responsibility. When it can be shown that the public benefit from curbs outweighs the economic advantages of flexibility, responsible business will support the change. But business will and should vigorously oppose straightjacket accounting standards predicated on an assumption that business cannot be trusted to act responsibly in its reporting.[16]

Contrast the preceding statement with the following sentiments:

> If you think that managements' defense of historical cost is based on the belief that it more fairly or accurately presents, you have a livelier imagination than I. It seems to me to be quite clear that managements desire "flexibility" to be able to realize and report the amount of income that suits their purposes. Thus some, if not most, accepted practices spring from managements' desire to serve their own ends.[17]

There is also an inherent conflict between groups of resource providers (investors and creditors). Investors are residual owners who theoretically direct the expenditure of funds and who can be expected to favor themselves in choices of when or how to expend available cash and other assets. On the other hand, creditors expect to receive a return on their loans, usually in the form of interest. Hence, there is an inherent conflict between investors and creditors when available cash is limited, because each resource provider desires a return on investment. Because of this inherent conflict, creditors often insert restrictive covenants into loan agreements to prevent management and/or investors from reducing assets otherwise available to satisfy creditor claims. Further discussion of this conflict is deferred until Chapter 9.

The government recognized this potential for conflict between management and resource providers and established the SEC. The overall objective of the SEC, which comprises the third group of interested parties, is to protect investors and creditors. It is assumed that investors and creditors are protected when the capital markets operate

---

[16]"New Directions for Financial Reporting: FASB Prospects Assessed by Financial Conference Speakers," *Journal of Accountancy* (April 1973): 10.

[17]R. R. Sterling, "Accounting Research, Education and Practice," *Journal of Accountancy* (September 1973), 52.

efficiently. A necessary condition for efficient capital-market operation is that financial statements must not contain misleading or false
information. Obviously, the SEC has a vested interest in the standard-
setting process.

The SEC requires that publicly traded companies be audited by
independent auditors. Independent auditors—the fourth group—are
charged with adding credibility to the financial statements and with
protecting investor and creditor interests by expressing an opinion
about the fairness of the financial statements. When auditors have
been negligent in their duties, they have been subject to litigation by
investors and creditors. Auditor participation in the standard-setting
process is often based on reducing audit risk through promoting policies that produce accounting information that is more auditable.

Furthermore, auditors can recommend an accounting alternative
to management that decreases recorded asset values or increases recorded debt, because this will reduce the risk of litigation. This is
because lawsuits are not usually filed in cases of undervalued or
conservatively valued assets.[18]

Finally, the fifth group, sometimes called "free riders," participates
in the standard-setting process. This group is composed of investment
advisors and counselors who are employed by investors and creditors.
In order to ensure that their clients receive a fair price for investments
and to provide more information in newsletters, investment advisors
often lobby for increased disclosure in financial reporting. Investment
advisors can cloak their lobbying efforts in a "public interest" theme by
claiming that more information will produce a more competitive and
efficient market.[19]

The process that culminates in the issuance of accounting standards is depicted in a flow chart in Figure 7.1. Various groups are
presented with opportunities to influence the ultimate pronouncement
at various times. The objective of the process is to develop accounting
standards requiring accounting treatments that enhance the usefulness of financial statements.[20] This necessitates the question, Useful to
whom?

---

[18]W. B. Meigs, et al. *Principles of Auditing*, 9th ed. (Homewood, Il: Irwin, 1989),
375.

[19]The assumption that more information will necessarily produce more efficient
markets depends on many factors. See J. G. Birnberg, "Human Information Processing and Financial Disclosure," *Corporate Financial Reporting: The Benefits and Problems
of Disclosure*, American Institute of Certified Public Accountants, 1976): 251–261.

[20]*SFAC 1*, par. 32 .

FIGURE 7-1

FASB DUE PROCESS

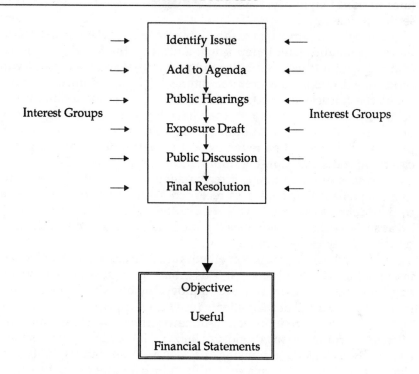

Identify Issue

Add to Agenda

Public Hearings

Interest Groups   Exposure Draft   Interest Groups

Public Discussion

Final Resolution

Objective:

Useful

Financial Statements

FIGURE 7-2

INTEREST GROUP INTERACTION

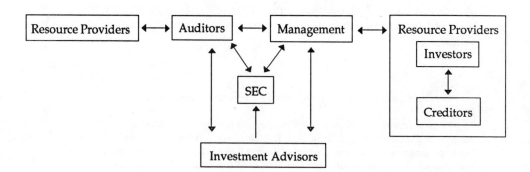

Resource Providers ← → Auditors ← → Management ← → Resource Providers

Investors

Creditors

SEC

Investment Advisors

Since there are a number of recognized user groups, the FASB has assumed that the primary user group for general-purpose financial statements is the resource providers (investors and creditors).[21]

Figure 7.2 reflects the interaction among user groups, which was described earlier. At the center of the interaction are auditors and management, who arrive at a group consensus concerning the fairness of the financial statements. Hence, there is two-way interaction among auditors and management.

The SEC's pervasive concern is the protection of resource providers. Therefore, the SEC mandates certain requirements of auditors and management, to assist in the production of useful and fair financial statements. Auditors and management are allowed input into SEC decisions, which causes a two-way interaction between the auditors and management and the SEC.

Resource providers interact with management in various ways. Theoretically, stockholders control management by voting at stockholder meetings; they make voting and investment decisions based on an evaluation of management's stewardship. Because management is in control of corporate assets that belong to resource providers, there is an inherent conflict between management and resource providers, which produces another two-way interaction. Management decides how to spend available cash; it can be paid to management as a bonus, to stockholders as dividends, to creditors as payment for principal and or interest, or it can be retained by the corporation.

Furthermore, there can often be an internal conflict between resource providers. As described earlier, there are basically two groups of resource providers, each with different types of claims. As previously discussed, investors and creditors can have conflicting views on when and to whom corporate assets should be distributed, simply because each group wants to increase their own return on investment.

Auditors are engaged to issue an opinion about the overall fairness of the financial statements. Because an auditor is an independent party who represents the resource providers' interests, but who is retained and paid by management, there is a potential conflict between the auditor and the resource providers. As discussed in Chapter 3, the fact that management selects the auditor could cause the auditor to favor management rather than to act as an independent party.

The FASB's due-process approach provides the opportunity to various groups to present arguments concerning the advantages and

---

[21]*SFAC 1*, par. 32.

disadvantages of proposed resolutions for specific issues. As mentioned, numerous groups are expected to participate in the standard-setting process, and many of these groups will have competing interests. Therefore, the potential exists for some groups to form coalitions and/or to develop the ability to use the standard-setting process to accomplish self-interested goals.

This potential for subversion naturally leads to an ideological question; Should there be more regulation of financial reporting and capital markets by government agencies? This question is considered in the next section.

ARGUMENTS FOR AND AGAINST REGULATION

A democracy and a capitalist economy are founded on the premise that self-interests are balanced against one another and that they produce results that are more beneficial to society as a whole than do any other approach. However, short-run inefficiencies or inequities can exist. In order to alleviate inequities, it has been suggested that increased regulation is necessary. Ideology, plays an important role in determining whether more or less regulation is beneficial.

It is sometimes argued that increased regulation of capital markets is necessary because of a perceived low quality of financial reporting and auditing. One of the common reasons advanced for the low quality of financial reporting is the potential for manipulation afforded to management through accounting choice. Audit failures, either through negligence or through fraud, are also presented as evidence that increased regulation is needed. The faults of the standard-setting process itself are implicit in the foregoing arguments. A possible conclusion that can be drawn from this evidence is that increased regulation of all parties will resolve the problems inherent in the existing structure of standard-setting and financial reporting.

One argument always advanced in favor of regulation is the promotion of social goals. In the context of the capital markets, the public-interest goal is the efficient allocation of resources, which presupposes free and fair access to information. Those with one particular ideological view argue that a free market will necessarily result in the most efficient allocation of resources. However, others believe that regulation is necessary in order to prevent segments of society from gaining at the expense of others through unfair advantage. In this context, an unfair advantage can be gained through access to accounting and financial information that is not available to all interested parties, a condition sometimes referred to as *information asymmetry*.[22]

Missing from the arguments discussed above is the concept of *cost-benefit*. There always is a cost to the production and dissemination of information. An enormous amount of information is available for production and dissemination. Not all of this information can be beneficial to the market, especially when it is considered in the light of production costs. Therefore, the perceived benefits from regulating increased disclosure must be considered in the light of costs incurred to produce the information.

Furthermore, human information processing is limited. Research has shown that a person's use of information increases until overload is reached and use of information begins to decline.[23] The point of information overload differs, depending on individual information-processing capabilities. Determining this point becomes problematic, given different user groups and different user information processing capabilities. The salient point from a financial reporting perspective is to determine the *relevant* information that users desire, rather than to assume that increased disclosure through regulation will necessarily be beneficial.

Ideologically, there are those who oppose regulation. While there have been, and presumably will be, market failures due to low quality financial reporting and auditing, it has also been shown that regulatory policies cannot knowingly maximize social goals.[24] Furthermore, existing evidence suggests that regulatory agencies eventually become "captured" by the group being regulated and begin to enact rules designed to protect the regulated industry rather than the consumer. Once the regulatory agency is captured, it is at cross-purposes with the original motivation behind establishing that agency.[25]

As previously mentioned, those who favor increased regulation of financial markets base their arguments on so-called market failures. However, they assume on an *a prior* basis that regulation will produce

---

[22]See Chapter 9 for more discussion of information asymmetry.

[23] J. G. Birnberg "Human Information Processing and Financial Disclosure," *Financial Accounting Theory*, 3rd ed., Zeff. S. A. and Keller, T. F., eds. (New York: McGraw-Hill, 1985), 211–220.

[24]This was shown through the so-called Impossibility Theorem. K. Arrow, *Social Choice and Individual Values* (New York: Wiley, 1963).

[25]G. J. Stigler, "The Theory of Economic Regulation" *Bell Journal of Economics and Management Science* (Fall 1971): 3–21.

greater benefits to society; the possibility of "government failure" is omitted:

> In summary, market failure theories are devoid of policy implications because those theories do not identify an attainable optimum. Despite the pejorative connotation of inefficiency associated with the term "market failure," the presence of those so-called failures has no implications for economic efficiency. At best the theories are empty, at worst they involve a seductive use of language.[26]

Also, there is evidence that regulation is often imposed by politicians who view it as a method of increasing their own political capital at the expense of society. "Political entrepreneurs" often create crises and then present convenient and simple "solutions" to solve the crisis, thus increasing respect for politicians. Deeper analysis of the crisis can provide evidence that the "solution" has no bearing on the real crisis.[27] While there is a potential for political entrepreneurs to intervene with simple solutions, this situation is not typical; it is only a consideration when arguing the benefits of regulation.

Thus, capital markets in this country are not purely "free," nor are they purely regulated. Based on the previous discussion, it is logical to conclude that neither extreme will result in the most efficient allocation of resources possible, given an imperfect world. Certainly, interest groups exist that desire to control the accounting information system for their own benefits.

The implications of the foregoing discussion are that regulation should not be attempted without considering those parties effected by the regulation process and their motivations for influencing the process. Furthermore, policymakers should consider the effects of regulation on society as a whole.[28]

This section has briefly addressed the issue of whether regulation of financial reporting and capital markets should be increased. The answer is necessarily rooted in political ideology and in the existing financial accounting environment. The next section provides a specific example of how groups have interacted in this environment to produce an accounting standard.

---

[26]R. Leftwich, "Market Failure Fallacies and Accounting Information," *Journal of Accounting and Economics*, (December 1980), 197.

[27]R. L. Watts, "Corporate Financial Statements, A Product of the Market and Political Process," *Australian Journal of Management* (April 1977), 53–75.

[28]C. W. Chow, "Empirical Studies of the Economic Impacts of Accounting Regulation: Findings, Problems and Prospects," *Journal of Accounting Literature* (Spring 1983), 73–109.

SETTING STANDARDS IN
THE OIL AND GAS INDUSTRY

The setting of accounting standards in the oil and gas industry provides a prime example of the due-process approach for establishing accounting principles.[29] Two accounting alternatives in the oil and gas industry have existed since the mid-1950s. The basic distinction between the accounting methods revolves around the treatment of unsuccessful drilling and exploration costs in the search for oil and gas reserves. These costs represent huge dollar amounts, and, therefore, the accounting treatments will have significant consequences on the financial statements of oil and gas companies. These expenditures totaled $56.5 billion at their peak in 1981.[30]

The *successful efforts* method of accounting considers the costs of unsuccessful exploration efforts as expenses. This treatment is justified on the basis of definitions of expenses and assets. Expenses are assumed to be the costs incurred in attempting to generate revenue in the current accounting period. Assets represent the costs of items from which revenue will be generated in subsequent accounting periods. If an oil well is drilled and it results in no oil or gas reserve discoveries, the reasoning is that the costs of the well are by definition an expense and not an asset. If oil reserves are discovered in commercial quantities, then the cost of the well represents an asset, since the reserves will generate revenues as they are produced and sold. Thus, the successful efforts view assumes a causal link between specific expenditures and future revenues.

On the other hand, the *full cost* method of accounting is founded on the premise that the oil and gas industry is very unique and that the full cost method incorporates the economic realities of this industry. Given current technology, the only way to determine with certainty the presence of oil and gas is through drilling and incurring the costs associated with drilling and exploration. The full cost method considers these costs to represent assets regardless of results, since drilling is necessary to discover the presence of oil and gas. In other words, full cost theorists take a global view when defining assets in the oil and gas

---

[29]The reader should understand that not all accounting controversies stimulate as much interest as this issue. It is used here to illustrate the possible effects of the process. However, it is uncommon for a controversy to involve such pervasive interest.

[30]*Basic Petroleum Data Book,* American Petroleum Institue (District of Columbia 1986), Sec 5 Table 9a.

industry and assume that *all* drilling costs, whether resulting in reserve discoveries or not, represent the cost of reserves that are ultimately discovered.

The consequences of application of either method should be obvious. All things equal, the initial consequences of using the full cost method will result in more favorable effects on the financial statements. This is because of the different views of unsuccessful drilling efforts. The full cost approach considers these costs as assets, and the successful efforts approach considers them expenses. Therefore, a full cost company, when compared to a successful efforts company, will necessarily have greater recorded assets and net income during the initial years of operation, even if both companies discover and produce the same amount of reserves. Eventually these consequences will reverse, as the full cost assets will be amortized to expenses. In the long run, both approaches will result in the same net income.

Accounting alternatives in the oil and gas industry also provide an example of the uniformity versus alternatives controversy. Those in favor of an accounting choice, when there are differences in circumstances, point to this industry as an example where flexibility is important to reflect underlying differences.

As discussed later in this section, proponents of the full cost approach argue that companies that have adopted the full cost method are different from successful efforts companies. The differences in companies primarily concern the aggressive philosophy of full cost companies' management. For instance, it is argued that full cost companies are more aggressive in exploration efforts and have a greater need for external funds raised in the capital markets.[31] If there is a greater need for external funds, management often argues that it is easier to generate external funds if the company is able to represent economic consequences in the most favorable terms. Hence, the full cost method will be used.

However, this presumes that investors and creditors are not able to recognize the value of oil and gas reserves, irrespective of capitalized drilling costs. This idea is discussed in more detail in Chapter 9. But suffice it to say at this point, that many accountants and financial analysts who do not believe that capital markets are fooled by artificial manipulations through the use of accounting alternatives.

---

[31]This assumption has been tested. See E. B. Deakin, "An Analysis of Differences Between Non-major Oil Firms Using Successful Efforts and Full Cost Methods," *The Accounting Review* (October 1979), 722–734. Deakin concluded that full cost firms were not more aggressive in their exploration efforts. However, full cost firms did have relatively greater amounts of debt than did successful efforts firms.

Those in favor of uniformity believe that, within the oil and gas industry, there cannot possibly be differences in circumstances. That is, all oil and gas producing companies are in business to explore for and to produce oil and gas reserves. The entire process is characterized by high risk, and there are no fundamental differences among companies that justify accounting alternatives.

The following discussion illustrates that the due-process approach to standard-setting is not limited to accounting theory.[32]

The initial attempt to produce uniformity in the oil and gas industry was promoted by *Accounting Research Study No. 11 (ARS 11)* commissioned by the AICPA and published in 1969. The author, Robert Field, recommended that the successful efforts method of accounting be adopted as the uniform approach.

In 1971, the Accounting Principles Board (APB) issued a draft opinion and an invitation to comment on the draft opinion. The draft opinion followed the logic of *ARS 11* and recommended that the successful efforts method be adopted as the uniform approach.

Oil companies that were using the full cost method commissioned a study to investigate the propriety of both accounting methods. Not surprisingly, the results of this study supported the use of the full cost.

Before the APB could finalize an *opinion* concerning accounting for oil and gas companies, the Federal Power Commission (FPC), which maintains regulatory powers for the transmission of natural gas, mandated that companies under its jurisdiction employ the full cost method. The reasoning was as follows:

> Companies engaged in exploration for and production of oil and gas must measure their performance by comparing their costs of finding oil and gas reserves with the value of oil and gas reserves discovered. The costs include costs incurred in nonproductive efforts as well as costs which result in productive wells.[33]

The FPC order related only to regulatory accounting, not for financial reporting. However, it clouded the issue to the extent that the APB dropped the issue from its agenda. The APB was soon superseded by the FASB, which placed oil and gas company accounting on its agenda.

In the interim, the oil embargo brought the practices of the oil industry under widespread public scrutiny. During this period, oil companies reported increased profits, which led to further scrutiny. In

---

[32]Much of the following discussion is a synthesis of A. M. Sedaghat, "The Interaction Process of Accounting: An Analysis of the Development of Financial Accounting and Reporting Standards for Oil and Gas Producing Activities," unpublished dissertation 1986.

[33]Federal Register, November 18, 1971, 36F.R.21963 (46FPC1150).

December 1975, Congress passed the Energy Policy and Conservation Act (EPCA), which mandated that the SEC or FASB develop within two years accounting practices to be followed by the oil and gas industry. Many interpreted the law as requiring a uniform method.

The FASB formed a task force in January 1976 to assist in drafting a Discussion Memorandum on the subject of oil and gas accounting. The Discussion Memorandum was issued on December 23, 1976, but it did not contain a recommendation as to which method was preferred. Public hearings were held on March 30 and 31 and on April 1 through 4, 1977, and 39 presentations were made by interested parties.

On July 15, 1977, an Exposure Draft was issued by the FASB which recommended the use of successful efforts accounting. Many who favored the use of full cost accounting petitioned to their representatives in Congress to intercede on their behalf. As a result, the EPCA was amended as follows:

> This Section 503 is intended to apply only to the development of accounting practices required for the preparation of the reports to be filed with the Department of Energy for use in compiling a reliable energy data base; nothing contained in this Section 503 shall be construed to establish or to affect the establishment of generally accepted accounting principles for financial reporting purposes.[34]

Quite naturally, the FASB was concerned that its efforts could be undermined and that requests for intercession by Congress and by affected parties could "encourage complaints against FASB pronouncements to petition congress to act as the ultimate accounting standards setter."[35]

Congressional interest was stimulated by constituents who were affected parties. The senator sponsoring the EPCA amendment made comments in the Congressional Record that appeared "to be extensive excerpts from a memorandum prepared by" a large company with an investment in an oil and gas producing company.[36]

Finally, on December 5, 1977, barely within the two-year limit established by the EPCA, the FASB issued *SFAS 19*, which recommended successful efforts accounting. The decision was based on the idea that the successful efforts method more closely followed traditional accounting concepts regarding assets and expenses: "In the Board's judgement, successful efforts costing is consistent with that

---

[34]FASB, *Status Report No. 55*, October 14, 1977.
[35]Ibid.
[36]Ibid.

[conceptual] accounting framework, and full costing is not."[37] Successful efforts accounting better reflected the risks involved in the oil and gas industry.[38] Furthermore, the FASB did not find the full cost argument concerning ability to raise capital a persuasive one.[39]

Passage of SFAS 19 did not end the controversy. The Department of Justice (Antitrust Division) was concerned about the competitive effect of *SFAS 19*. Furthermore, the SEC and Department of Energy began a series of hearings in early 1978. The effective date of *SFAS 19* was December 1978, and these hearings were devoted to determining whether or not *SFAS 19* should be adopted. While the SEC has statutory rights to prescribe accounting rules, it had previously relied on the FASB to establish those rules. Therefore, the implication of this series of hearings was a source of concern for the future of FASB.

Subsequent to the public hearings, the SEC issued *Accounting Series Release No. 253 (ASR 253)*, which effectively nullified *SFAS 19*. The SEC had concluded that neither successful efforts nor full cost adequately reflected the economic consequences of transactions in the oil and gas industry. Therefore, the SEC intended to develop an accounting method that was based on the value of reserves discovered, or *reserve recognition accounting* (RRA). While RRA was being developed, oil companies could continue to use either successful efforts or full cost. The FASB was left with no alternative other than to rescind *SFAS 19*. This was done with the issuance of *SFAS 25*, allowing the use of either successful efforts or full cost.

RRA is a revolutionary approach to accounting that recognizes revenue upon *discovery* of reserves, rather than upon their sale. Oil and gas reserves are akin to inventory of a manufacturing firm. However, reserve quantities must be estimated. Reserve estimates are notoriously unreliable. One study has indicated that reserve estimate corrections in any year are substantial. Another study has shown that initial reserve estimates are subsequently adjusted by an average of 50 percent. Under RRA, these adjustments would result in large income effects in the year of the adjustment. For this reason, the SEC ultimately recognized the impracticality of RRA, and in 1981, it issued *ASR 289* indicating an intention not to implement RRA.

However, the SEC wanted supplemental reserve disclosures based

---

[37]*SFAS 19*, par. 144.
[38]Ibid. par. 151.
[39]Ibid. par. 158.

on discounted dollar values. Therefore, in August 1981, the FASB began to consider requiring reserve disclosures. Accounting methods were not going to be reconsidered; both full cost and successful efforts were acceptable. Appendix C of *SFAS 69* explains the reasons for the requirement of reserve disclosures:

> The underlying causes of the problem leading to this Statement relate to some significant and unusual economic characteristics of oil and gas producing activities:
> (a.) The principal assets are oil and gas reserves.
> (b.) There is no necessary correlation between the costs and the values of oil and gas reserves.
> (c.) The costs of finding specific reserves are unique.
> ... An important quality of information that is useful in making rational investment, credit and similar decisions is its predictive value—specifically, its usefulness in assessing the amounts, timing and uncertainty of prospective net cash inflows to the enterprise. Historical cost based financial statements [successful efforts and full cost] for oil and gas producing enterprises have limited predictive value. Their usefulness is further reduced because a uniform accounting method is not required to be used for costs incurred in oil and gas producing activities.[40]

For 20 years, the accounting profession has attempted to set uniform standards in the oil and gas industry. After the FASB due process, *ARS 11* and *SFAS 19* (a result of the FASB due process) recommended adoption of successful efforts. However, the affected parties appealed to the government because of perceived adverse effects. The SEC, FPC, Justice Department, Department of Energy, and both houses of Congress intervened.[41] As a result, the accounting profession was forced back to square one—both successful efforts and full cost were acceptable. This result points out that affected parties are motivated to act with all of their resources when there are perceived adverse consequences to their own well-being.

---

[40]*SFAS 69*, par. 55–56.

[41]A reason often given for congressional intervention and the passage and amendment of EPCA was national policy. Congress was fearful of dependence on foreign oil for economic and national defense reasons and, therefore, did not wish to unfavorably affect exploration efforts. Interestingly, at about the same time, Congress passed a series of tax acts, including so-called windfall profits, which would have been expected to decrease exploration efforts and increase dependence on foreign oil. G. Gordon, and C. L. Posey , "The Case for a Windfall Loss Tax Credit," *Oil and Gas Tax Quarterly* (December 1986), 224–237. On the surface, these actions appear to be at cross-purposes.

To understand that individuals act, within certain parameters, in their own self-interests is, perhaps, a truth of nature. Often, however, this truth may be overlooked in the context of financial statement analysis and in the standard-setting process. The implications of this truth require users of financial statements to conduct an analysis with a heightened awareness of managements' interpretations of events and accounting choices.

SUMMARY

Accounting choice exists on the premise that the flexibility afforded by choice is important in reflecting economic realities. Unfortunately, accounting choice does provide potential for choosing the alternative that favors an affected group, as opposed to choosing the alternative that results in the most fair presentation.

The independent auditor's role and its importance should now be clearly understood. The independent auditor is fulfilling a societal need by providing an *independent* opinion concerning management's interpretations and reporting.[42]

Financial reporting has been likened to cartography:

> Information cannot be neutral—it cannot therefore be reliable—if it is selected or presented for the purpose of producing some chosen effect on human behavior. It is this quality of neutrality which makes a map reliable; and the essential nature of accounting, I believe, is cartographic. Accounting is financial mapmaking. The better the map, the more completely it represents the complex phenomena that are being mapped. We do not judge a map by the behavioral effects it produces. The distribution of natural wealth or rainfall shown on a map may lead to population shifts or changes in industrial location, which the government may like or dislike. That should be of no concern of the cartographer. We judge his map by how well it represents the facts. People can then react to it as they will.[43]

It is the auditor who has access to internal records and documents and who judges if the map represents the facts fairly.

---

[42]Note that the independent auditor is subject to certain human pressures as well. Refer to Chapter 2.

[43]D. Solomons, "The Politicization of Accounting," *Journal of Accountancy* (November 1978), 70.

The map analogy can also be used to represent the fundamental problem faced by accountants even if economic consequences and motivations of affected parties can be assumed away:

> A three dimensional space cannot be represented by two dimensions without some loss of accuracy....Accounting reports are inherently distortions of reality as are any other abstractions. Degree of accuracy depends on how much cost users are willing to bear to obtain information they consider useful in order to reduce the distortion.[44]

Most would agree that accounting is a search for "truth": "unfortunately, truth from an accounting perspective is not an empirical fact to be discovered; it is a subjective understanding to be manufactured and agreed upon."[45]

This discussion has gone full circle. The map analogy indicates that accounting reports *ought* to reflect reality. But, there may be different views of what reality is. This is true not only in financial reports themselves, but also in the process of setting standards from which to derive the reports.

In the financial accounting environment, implications and consequences can be summarized as follows:

> ... Any accounting contains a representation of a specific social and political context. Not only is accounting policy essentially political in that it derives from the political struggle in society as a whole but also the outcomes of accounting policy are essentially political in that they operate for the benefit of some groups in society and to the detriment of others.[46]

Very few solutions to problems in accounting or anything else are unambiguous. Economic reality is an elusive concept and accounting concepts are unable to measure all of the dimensions of reality. Furthermore, human intervention and interpretation is required. The results of human intervention are problematic. While a perfect solution is desirable, it is not always obtainable.

This chapter has illustrated that accounting standards are not set in a vacuum and that affected parties will lobby for their interests. The

---

[44]R. W. Ingram, and F. R. Rayburn, "Representational Faithfulness and Economic Consequences: Their Roles in Accounting Policy," *Journal of Accounting and Public Policy*, (Spring 1989), 58.

[45]Ibid, 59.

[46]D. J. Cooper, and M. J. Sherer "The Value of Corporate Accounting Reports: Arguments for a Political Economy of Accounting," *Accounting, Organizations and Society* (September 1984), 208.

next chapter illustrates the thought process and accounting *theory* that is involved in deriving accounting standards, assuming little or no deflection through political interaction.

READING LIST

Arrow, K. *Social Choice and Individual Values*. (New York: Wiley, 1963).

Birnberg, J. G., "Human Information Processing and Financial Disclosure." In *Corporate Financial Reporting: The Benefits and Problems of Disclosure*. (AICPA 1976): 251–261.

Chambers, R. J. "Financial Information and the Securities Market." *Abacus*, Vol. 1, (1965): 3–30.

Chow, C. W., "Empirical Studies of the Economic Impacts of Accounting Regulations: Findings, Problems and Prospects", *Journal of Accounting Literature* (Spring 1983): 73–109.

Cooper, D. J., and Sherer, M. J. "The Value of Corporate Accounting Reports: Arguments for a Political Economy of Accounting." *Accounting, Organizations and Society* (September 1984): 208.

Deakin, E. B. "An Analysis of Differences Between Non-major Oil Firms Using Successful Efforts and Full Cost Methods." *The Accounting Review* (October 1979): 722–734.

Deakin, E. B. "Auditor Selection, Organization Control, Adverse Events, and the Selection of Accounting Method for Oil Exploration." *Quarterly Review of Economics and Business*, (Autumn, 1980): 78.

Horngren, C. T. "The marketing of Accounting Standards." The *Journal of Accountancy* (October 1973): 61.

Ingram, R. W., and Rayburn, F. R. "Representational Faithfulness and Economic Consequences: Their Roles in Accounting Policy." *Journal of Accounting and Public Policy*, (Spring 1989): 58.

Leftwich, R.W. "Market Failure Fallacies and Accounting Information" *Journal of Accounting and Economics* (December 1980): 207.

Meigs, W. B., et al. *Principles of Auditing*, 9th ed. Homewood, IL: Irwin, 1989.

Miller, P. B. W., and Redding, R. J., *The FASB: the People, the Process and the Politics*, 2nd ed. Homewood, IL: Irwin,1988.

"New Directions for Financial Reporting: FASB Prospects Assessed by Financial Conference Speakers." *Journal of Accountancy* (April 1973): 10.

O'Leary, T. "Observations on Corporate Financial Reporting in the Name of Politics." *Accounting, Organizations and Society*, vol. 10, no. 1, (1985): 88.

Sedaghat, A. M. *The Interactive Process of Accounting: An Analysis of the Development of Financial Accounting and Reporting Standards for Oil and Gas Producing Activities.* Ph. D. diss., University Microfilms International, 1986.

Solomons, D. "The Politicization of Accounting." *Journal of Accountancy* (November 1978): 70.

Sterling, R. R. "Accounting Research, Education and Practice." *Journal of Accountancy* (September 1973): 52.

Stigler, G. J. "The Theory of Economic Regulation." *Bell Journal of Economics & Management Science* (Fall 1971): 3–21.

Watts, R. L. "Corporate Financial Statements, A Product of the Market and Political Process." Australian *Journal of Management* (April 1977): 53–75.

Watts, R. L. and Zimmermann, J.. L. "Toward a Positive Theory of the Determination of Accounting Standards." *The Accounting Review* (January 1978): 112-134.

Zeff, S. A. "The Rise of 'Economic Consequences'." *Financial Accounting Theory*, 3rd ed., Zeff, S. A. and Keller, T. F. eds..(New York: McGraw-Hill, 1985): 19–33.

STUDY QUESTIONS

1. Outline the FASB due-process approach to setting standards. What groups are likely to participate in the standard-setting process? Would you have any preconceived notions about a particular group's stance on any specific issue?
2. QQQ Corp. is on the verge of bankruptcy. The company has $10 million in 10 percent bonds outstanding and $100,000 in cash. Interest is due in three months and there are no restrictive covenants in the bonds. Management owns 37 percent of outstanding stock in QQQ. Bankruptcy is inevitable within the next six months. As a bondholder, what is your concern?
3. What are the advantages and disadvantages of the FASB due-process approach? What are some implications to financial statement analysis of this approach?

Chapter 8

Selected Issues And Decided Questions

Nothing is constant but change.[1]

The previous chapter discussed the mechanics of the standard-setting process and demonstrated that the mechanics are often influenced by numerous factors that may be characterized as "political." Therefore, it is evident that accounting standards are a product of politics. However, theory is not ignored in producing accounting standards. The purpose of this chapter is to discuss the application of accounting theory as it is used in the standard-setting process.

To accomplish this purpose, several controversial issues and the merits of their resolution are discussed briefly. The discussion will focus on normative accounting theory: What should be the standard when considered strictly in the light of practical theory?[2] However, since accounting standards are not set in a vacuum, understand that the resolution is always accomplished against the backdrop of politics. Figure 8.1 illustrates the political and theoretical influences on the process of standard-setting.

An additional purpose of this chapter is to establish that accounting is not static. Instead, the accounting profession is dynamic and

---

[1]Anonymous

[2]The reader should remember that normative therory is not always a black-and-white issue. There are many individual devoid of self-interested motivations who will honestly disagree on what should be the proper resolution, whether dealing with accounting or any other issue. With regard to accounting, the conceptual framework was established on which to construct a normative theory to apply to specific issues. It is hoped that the result of the conceptual framework will be to diminish the subjectivity involved in applying theory to specific issues so that a consistent, underlying theory emerges across all issues.

FIGURE 8-1

POLITICAL & THEORETICAL INFLUENCES ON STANDARD SETTING

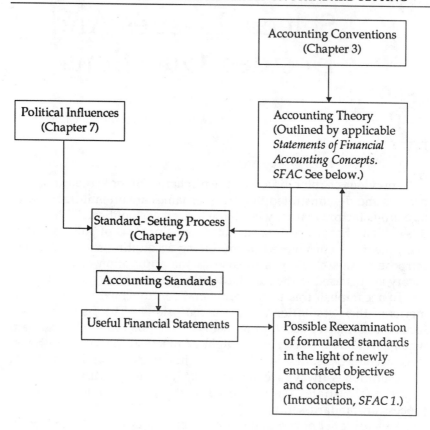

SFAC 1: Primary objective of financial statements is to provide information useful in investment and credit decisions.

SFAC 2: Qualitative characteristics of accounting data and constraints to providing information that is useful: relevance, reliability, comparability and consistency, materiality, costs and benefits

SFAC 6: Defines elements of financial statements. (See Chapter 3)

SFAC 5: Sets forth guidance and recognition criteria on what information is incorporated into financial statements and when it should be incorporated.

evolving. This was demonstrated by the oil and gas industry controversy discussed in the last chapter. Other specific examples used in this chapter demonstrate that standards are changed from time to time as theory evolves.

The specific examples used are not a comprehensive set of issues.[3] Moreover, the discussion is intended to be an overview and not a complete description of the issue and the merits of the resolution.

ACCOUNTING FOR INCOME TAXES

Accounting for income taxes has been a controversial issue for many years. It was resolved initially in 1967 with the issuance of *APB 11*. However, the profession eventually concluded that the resolution *APB 11* was inappropriate. Hence, *SFAS 96* was issued, which prescribed a different approach. However, the FASB has delayed the effective date of *SFAS 96* in order to resolve a number of technical problems.

The basic issue is how to determine and when to record income tax expense on the financial statements in order to best match the income tax expense with the transactions that caused the tax consequences. It may appear that accounting for income taxes is not a serious problem. Why not calculate taxes on the income tax return and present the same amount as income tax expense on the financial statements, as suggested by the "flow-through" method? However, there are two concepts of income involved in the process; namely, taxable income as defined by statutes and passed by Congress and financial income as defined by GAAP. Consequently, there are differences in definitions and in timing of revenues and expenses for tax purposes and differences for financial reporting purposes. Therefore, using the flow-through approach would not provide for the matching of financial revenues and expenses.

Temporary, or timing, differences cause the major problems. Tax statutes can be utilized to defer revenue recognition and accelerate expense recognition for tax purposes or vice versa. For example, a company can choose to use the *completed contract* method of recognizing revenue for tax purposes and use the *percentage of completion* method for financial purposes. The result is that no *taxable* revenue is recorded until the project is completed, while recording *financial* revenue during the years that the project is in progress. Ultimately, the same amount of taxable and financial revenue is recorded over time.

---

[3]As of this writing, approximately 100 *SFAS*s and 30 *APBO*s have been issued.

Another example of a timing difference relates to depreciation. A company can choose the *straight-line* method of depreciation for financial purposes and an acceptable *accelerated-depreciation* method for tax purposes. The result is to increase financial income relative to taxable income in the early years of the asset's use. Ultimately, the same total expense is recorded for tax and financial purposes, because straight-line depreciation charges increase relative to accelerated depreciation charges in later years. An example is provided in Table 8.1.[4]

Timing differences can cause significant differences between taxable income and financial income in any one year. Most accountants believe that recording actual tax payments, calculated on tax rules for financial expense, can render the financial statements misleading. This idea conforms to the matching concept discussed in Chapter 3; financial expenses should be matched to financial revenue on the assumption that expenses are incurred with the objective of earning revenue. Therefore, the recognition of tax expense on the financial statements should be tied to the recognition of financial revenue reported on the financial statements, rather than to tax payments, which are based on tax statutes.

Linkage of tax expense reported on financial statements to financial revenue recorded in the current year, irrespective of taxes actually due, is accomplished through a process called *interperiod tax allocation*. Interperiod tax allocation applied by *APBO 11* requires a calculation of differences in taxes actually paid that are based on taxable income for the current tax period and income tax expense recorded that is based on financial income for the current accounting period. The difference represents an asset or a liability, depending on whether the actual amounts paid are more or less than the amounts recorded based on financial income.

On the other hand, there are arguments for no interperiod tax allocations or attempts to match financial tax expense with financial income. First, income tax expense emerges only when income is earned, as defined by tax regulations, and the income taxes become a legal liability in the period when *taxable* income emerges. Second,

---

[4]Both examples illustrate the use of tax statutes and alternative GAAP to initially increase recorded financial income above taxable income. Opposite results could be attained. One example is the receipt of rent paid by a tenant in advance. Tax statutes require the rent to be included in taxable income as received. However, GAAP requires rent income to be recognized as earned. Rent is earned as time passes, regardless of when the cash is actually received. Therefore, taxable income exceeds financial income.

TABLE 8.1

EFFECTS OF INTERPERIOD TAX ALLOCATION

NO INTERPERIOD TAX ALLOCATION

Year	1		2		3		4		Total	
Company	A	B	A	B	A	B	A	B	A	B
IBT	100	100	100.0	100	100.0	100	100	100	400	400
ITE	25	50	37.5	50	62.5	50	75	50	200	200
NI	75	50	62.5	50	37.5	50	25	50	200	200

INTERPERIOD TAX ALLOCATION

Year	1		2		3		4		Total	
Company	A	B	A	B	A	B	A	B	A	B
IBT	100	100	100	100	100	100	100	100	400	400
ITE										
Payable	25	50	37.5	50	62.5	50	75	50	200	200
*Deferred	25		12.5		<12.5>		<25>		0	
NI	50	50	50.	50	50.	50	50	50	200	200

IBT = Income before taxes
ITE = Income tax expense
NI = Financial net income
Total depreciable asset cost = $300,000

ANNUAL DEPRECIATION

Year	1	2	3	4	Total
Accelerated	125	100	50	25	300,000
Straight Line	75	75	75	75	300,000
Difference	50	25	<25>	<50>	0
x Tax Rate	0.50	0.50	0.50	0.50	0.50
*Deferred Tax	25	12.5	<12.5>	<25.0>	0

corporate management that takes advantage of favorable tax treatment by deferring taxable revenue and accelerating expenses in accordance with statutory definitions is effectively receiving an interest-free loan from Uncle Sam. By not recording tax expense until it is a legal liability, management is able to report the company's economic gain by deferring taxes and distinguishing itself from corporate management that is not taking full advantage of tax laws.[5] By deferring taxes and not making interperiod tax allocations, the economic gain will be reflected through higher net income than if a tax allocation is made. This is because a tax allocation will accrue tax expense to match financial income, which is higher than taxable income.

However, those in favor of interperiod tax allocation point out that no allocation will create volatility in reported financial income because of the frequency of timing differences and because it violates the principle of matching. Furthermore, the timing differences that create the interperiod tax allocation problem are only temporary, and they eventually reverse. That is, the same amount of income and expense is ultimately reported under tax and financial rules.[6] Therefore, assets or liabilities created under interperiod tax allocation are assets that will ultimately be consumed or liabilities that will be met; no allocation only postpones the recognition of assets or liabilities that are created by interperiod allocation.

For example, assume that two identical companies have identical revenues and expenses, except that Company A computes taxable income under an accelerated depreciation method and that Company B uses the straight-line method for computing taxable income. Further, assume that both companies have adopted the straight line method for computing financial income. This will cause timing differences for depreciation expense on Company A's books. Taxable income will be lower initially because depreciation expense for tax purposes will be higher.

Table 8.1 presents the effects of the assumed data with and without interperiod tax allocations. Without interperiod tax allocations, the economic gain from using accelerated-depreciation for calculating taxes directly impacts net income in the first two years.

---

[5]An economic gain is experienced because taxes are deferred which allows the corporation to retain more cash than if taxes had not been deferred.

[6]Some differences are permanent. By definition, certain types of income and expense are excluded from taxation, but they are still considered income and expense for financial purposes. Such permanent differences do not cause interperiod tax allocation problems.

Since the two depreciation methods ultimately expense the same total over the assets' life, the calculated differences reverse in the last two years. However, note that a growing company will be continually acquiring new assets and that the reversal of timing differences can be offset by using accelerated depreciation methods on the newly acquired assets. This indefinitely postpones the net reversals of timing differences.

Since Company B calculates depreciation in the same manner for tax and financial purposes, there is no difference in financial net income whether or not interperiod tax allocation is applied. Furthermore, since interperiod tax allocation matches total taxes to be paid with financial accounting income, there is no reported difference in financial net income between Company A and Company B. However, if no interperiod tax allocation is made, reported net income in the first two years for Company A is higher than Company B. This reflects the economic gain that Company A has experienced by deferring taxes to be paid to future years.

The accounting profession has decided on allocation because it is believed to make financial statements more useful by matching expense to financial net income. Recall that matching, which was discussed in Chapter 3, is considered an important principle in the accounting model. Once allocation was decided as appropriate because of the matching principle, the next question was to determine the amount of the allocation. Three different approaches to determine the amount of allocation were considered: the deferred, liability, and net-of-tax methods.[7]

The *deferred method* of interperiod tax allocation is an income statement approach. Essentially, income tax expense is recorded based on financial income and the tax liability is based on taxable income. Any timing difference between the two is considered an asset (i.e., if taxable income is greater than financial income) or a liability (i.e., if financial income is greater than taxable income as in years 1 and 2 in Table 8.1). No adjustments are made to the asset or liability if subsequent tax rates change. The APB adopted the deferred approach: "the deferred method of tax allocation should be followed since it provides the most useful and practical approach to interperiod tax allocation and the presentation of income taxes in financial statements."[8]

---

[7]For a concise argument against allocation and a deeper explanation of the methods of allocation see: P. Rosenfeld and W. C. Dent, "No More Deferred Taxes," *Journal of Accountancy* (February 1983), 44–55.

[8]*APBO 11*, par. 35.

The net-of-tax method of allocation associates the effects of timing differences with specific assets and liabilities. The tax effects reduce specific assets or liabilities. This approach is considered a valuation concept. Instead of affecting an income tax asset or liability, as in the deferred method, the tax effects are allocated to the specific asset or liability that initially created the timing difference. For example, in Year 1, rather than assuming that the $25 timing difference on Company A's books is a liability, the timing difference is recorded as a contra asset, further reducing the book value of the depreciable asset.

The liability method is a balance sheet approach that attempts to accurately measure the deferred tax liability or asset. After the development of the conceptual framework, it became clear that the assets and liabilities that were created as a result of timing differences under the deferred method, which is required by *APBO 11*, did not truly meet the definitions of assets and liabilities. Therefore, a project was undertaken in 1982 to reexamine the appropriate method of allocating income taxes.

In 1987, *SFAS 96* was issued that promulgated the liability method, which is a balance sheet approach. The objective of accounting for income taxes is:

> ...to recognize the amount of current and deferred taxes payable or refundable at the date of the financial statements (*a*) as a result of all events that have been recognized in the financial statements and (*b*) as measured by the provisions of enacted tax laws.[9]

Therefore, the liability method is now considered the superior method of recording interperiod tax allocation. In the example in Table 8.1, there is no difference in reported amounts between the deferred method and the liability method. However, as tax rates change and other assets are acquired, the two methods will provide different results.

CAPITAL LEASES

A *lease* is a contract that outlines an agreement where the owner (lessor) of an asset allows another party (lessee) to use the asset for a rental fee. Leasing is an alternative to purchasing an asset that is needed in the operation of a corporation.

There are several advantages to leasing an asset over purchasing it. A primary advantage is that leasing normally requires no down payment. Therefore, initial cash requirements are lower. Also, leasing

---

[9]*SFAS 96*, par. 7.

represents a 100 percent financing arrangement without many of the restrictions often associated with conventional debt agreements. Furthermore, leasing is a hedge against obsolescence because many lease agreements are structured for short terms, enabling the lessee to return the asset if it has become outdated. All of these advantages combine to provide the lessee with greater flexibility in designing an operating strategy.

Finally, there is an additional strategy to leasing; namely, it is a form of off-balance-sheet financing. As already mentioned, leasing is essentially a 100 percent financing arrangement. However, future rental fees are not recorded as a liability of the lessee. Contrast the accounting treatment for leases with the purchase of an asset that is financed with loan proceeds. The liability for future payments for a purchased asset is recorded. Also, a leased asset is not recorded as an asset on the books of the lessee, since it is not owned by the lessee.

The management of some corporations has recognized that the favorable treatment of operating leases has produced an opportunity to acquire assets in financing arrangements without creating liabilities that appeared directly in the balance sheet. For example, suppose Fast Freddy, a new fast-food chain, wants to expand nationwide, but does not have sufficient capital to buy each location. Fast Freddy can commit to lease the locations on a long-term basis by entering into a contract that transfers the risks and benefits of ownership to the lessee, Fast Freddy.[10] Because the contract is a lease, Fast Freddy does not record the liability. While no asset is recorded either, Fast Freddy can report a large expansion of facilities without the accompanying debt recorded directly on the balance sheet. To an uninformed prospective investor, Fast Freddy looks great.

Assume Fast Freddy is considering the addition of 100 locations during the next year, and the expansion is expected to increase net income by 50 percent. Fast Freddy's management has the option of buying the locations for $50,000 each by paying $5,000 ($500,000 total) and issuing a $45,000 mortgage debt for each location. This would cause a net increase in assets and liabilities of $4.5 million ($45,000 times 100). Alternatively, Fast Freddy can lease the properties on a long-term basis with a total initial payment of $500,000 and future rental payments that are equal to the mortgage payments. Table 8.2

---

[10]One example of such a provision is a clause that provides Fast Freddy with an option to acquire title to the property for a nominal price, such as $1, at the end of the lease term. Such a provision is called a *bargain purchase option*. The lease payments outlined in the contract are actually more akin to mortgage payments, since Fast Freddy may become the legal owner at the end of the lease term with payment of $1.

TABLE 8-2

	Prior to Acquisition	Subsequent to Purchase	Subsequent to Lease
Current Assets	$2,000,000	$1,500,000	$1,500,000
Total Assets	5,000,000	9,500,000	4,500,000
Current Liabilities	1,000,000	1,000,000	1,000,000
Total Liabilities	3,000,000	7,500,000	3,000,000
Stockholders Equity	1,000,000	1,000,000	500,000
Net Income	500,000	750,000	750,000
Financial Ratios:			
Current Ratio	2:1	1.5:1	1.5:1
Debit to Equity	3:1	8.5:1	5.3:1
Return on Assets	10.0%	7.9%	16.7%
Return on Equity	50.0%	75.0%	150.0%

presents relevant data and reflects assumed data and the projected effects of the alternatives on several financial ratios.

Financial ratios are very favorably influenced if the property is leased, which is really a form of off-balance-sheet financing. Recognizing the potential for abuse, the FASB created criteria for determining whether such a transaction is really a lease or, in substance, a purchase.

The appropriate manner in which to account for leases has been addressed in *ARB 38* (1949), *ARS 4* (1962) and in *APBO 5, 7, 27* and *31*. The SEC addressed the topic in *ARS 132, 141,* and *147*. Most of the reporting requirements in these pronouncements dealt with the disclosure in the notes to the financial statements. There were no requirements mandating recognition of a liability directly on the balance sheet until *SFAS 13* was issued in 1976.

SFAS 13 made a distinction between an *operating lease* and a *capital lease*. An operating lease is an agreement between a lessee and a lessor that does not effectively convey ownership of the leased asset. If the document describing the transaction is called a lease, but meets FASB criteria for a purchase in substance, the transaction is considered a *capital* lease. Since a capital lease is in substance a purchase, the lessee (buyer) must record an asset and related obligation so that the debt is disclosed on the balance sheet.[11]

---

[11]*SFAS 13*, 1976.

The provisions of this Statement derive from the view that a lease that transfers substantially all of the benefits and risks incident to the ownership of property should be accounted for as the acquisition of an asset and the incurrence of an obligation by the lessee and as a sale or financing by the lessor.... In a lease that transfers substantially all of the benefits and risks of ownership, the economic effect on the parties is similar, in many respects, to that of an installment purchase.[12]

If the transaction in the Fast Freddy example meets capital lease criteria, then the transaction should be recorded as a purchase and the effects on the financial ratios are the same as the purchase alternative in Table 8.2. Obviously, this requirement was established with the intent of making financial statements more useful for decision making by external users of financial statements.

PENSIONS

Pensions represent an important retirement benefit for employees and a significant cost for employers. For example, in 1995, it is estimated that private pensions will cover 44.5 million individuals, pay benefits of $106 billion, and have assets of $2.5 trillion.[13]

Pension expense and the associated obligation for future benefit payments are difficult to determine and, therefore, are difficult to account for.[14] The pension benefit payments are usually contingent upon factors presently unknown, such as life expectancy and future compensation levels of individual employees. Furthermore, the growth in pension assets is dependent on such uncertain factors as the level of future interest rates.

APBO 8 addressed the issue from a revenue-expense orientation. While this issue is complex, it is sufficient to say that the recorded expense was essentially determined by a set of rather flexible criteria, which allowed considerable latitude in determining recorded pension expense. Funding of the pension by the employer was to some extent discretionary. Therefore, actual cash payments to pension funds could be different amounts than recorded expense. If funding was greater

---

[12]*SFAS 13*, par. 60.

[13]D. E. Kieso, and J. J. Weygandt, *Intermediate Accounting*, 6th ed. (New York: Wiley, 1989), 983.

[14]In this section, pension refers to a *defined benefit plan*, as opposed to a *defined contribution plan* for which the accounting is straight forward.

than recorded expense, an asset was recorded. If funding was less than expense, a liability was recorded.[15]

APBO 8 did not require companies that had pension plans for which future benefit payments exceeded the fair value of plan assets to record an additional liability. This unrecorded liability had the potential for misleading investors. For example, as of 1980, the amount of unfunded vested benefits for General Motors was $6.1 billion, an amount equalling approximately 32 percent of net worth.[16] Unfunded vested benefits are the present value, based on actuarial estimates, of future benefit payments that are in excess of current pension plan assets. GM was not atypical. Other companies, such as Lockheed, have had unfunded obligations that exceeded net worth. Consequently, there was concern that users of financial statements were unaware of these obligations since no liability was recorded under *APBO 8* rules.

However, some accountants claimed that the liability that was missing from the balance sheet was too difficult to measure with any degree of accuracy because of the uncertainties associated with length of life, future interest, and other contingencies.[17] Others argued that estimates were acceptable and that the disclosure of unrecorded liabilities would make financial statements more useful.

Accordingly, *SFAS 87* was issued in 1985. The objectives were to provide a more representationally faithful measure of pension expense, make financial statements more understandable with regard to pensions, provide better disclosure, and improve the reporting of financial position. *SFAS 87* adopted a balance sheet orientation, which results in recognition of a liability earlier than was required by *APBO 8*, and which requires the recording of an additional liability when the estimated future pension obligation exceeds the fair value of the pension assets.

RESEARCH AND DEVELOPMENT

Research and Development (R&D) costs are incurred for the purpose of developing new products or processes. Sometimes these expenditures result in new products that ultimately generate revenues. However,

---

[15]In 1974, the *Employers' Retirement Income Security Act* (ERISA) was passed, which held employers to stricter funding standards.

[16]"Pension Survey: Unfunded Liabilities Continue to Grow," *Business Week*, August 14, 1978, 60–64.

[17]R. Greene, "Can you Measure the Unknowable?" *Forbes*, March 17, 1980, 160.

sometimes the efforts to develop new products are unsuccessful. So what is the nature of these costs? Do they represent an asset or an expense? Prior to *SFAS 2* issued in 1974, companies were free to interpret the nature of these costs in different ways so that there was little consistency. This situation made the comparing of companies difficult.

In theory, it is a simple proposition to support the notion that R&D costs represent the costs of assets. Assets are rights or properties from which future revenues will be generated. Ultimately, new products are developed as a result of R&D costs, and in turn revenues are generated from the new products. However, some R&D costs never result in new products. Furthermore, the R&D process usually takes place over a relatively long period of time. Because there is a long time lag between the expenditures and the subsequent revenues, the causal link between the expenditures and revenues becomes tenuous.[18] Therefore, all R&D costs (with certain exceptions) are expensed when incurred.

Expensing R&D costs as incurred violates the matching principle, since revenues probably will be generated in the future as a result of some current R&D expenditures. Hence, in theory, R&D costs should be capitalized and allocated to expense in future years when revenue is earned from the sale of products developed through R&D. The FASB, however, believes that the theory of matching expenses and revenues is impractical because of the tenuous link between R&D expenditures and subsequent revenues.

It is interesting to note, however, that it had been hypothesized that a requirement to expense R&D costs, rather than to capitalize them, would not be in the national interest. That is, lower earnings caused by the requirement to expense R&D costs would cause companies to decrease R&D efforts and would make them less competitive in international markets. At least one study confirms these suspicions.[19]

INTEREST CAPITALIZATION

There have always been advocates for considering the cost of borrowed funds to be a part of the cost of assets purchased with borrowed funds. In theory, this argument has merit. Without the borrowed

---

[18]*SFAS 2*, par. 41.

[19]B. Horwitz, and R. Kolodny, "The FASB, the SEC, and R & D," *Bell Journal of Economics* (Spring 1981), 249–262.

funds, the asset could not have been acquired and the interest costs associated with the borrowed funds could have been avoided. Therefore, the interest costs logically represent an additional cost of assets acquired.

Nevertheless, the traditional approach has been to expense all interest costs as a cost of operations, regardless of how the borrowed funds were used. One argument against interest capitalization is that identical assets could have different costs if interest was capitalized as part of an asset's cost. For example, assume Company A borrows funds to acquire or construct a machine and capitalizes interest costs. Further, assume that Company B uses internally generated (or nonborrowed) funds to acquire or construct an identical machine at the same cash price. Since Company A capitalized interest costs, the recorded costs of an identical machine will be different because the cost of Company B's machine would not include interest costs since no interest costs would have been incurred.

One suggestion to overcome this discrepancy is to impute an interest cost for equity.[20] If a corporation has available cash, it has the option of using internally generated funds for acquisition of assets or for paying dividends to stockholders. By opting to purchase assets with internally generated funds, the corporation risks stockholder discontent that may translate into higher costs of equity capital. Many investors use dividend yield as a criterion for investment decisions. If dividends decrease because corporate management forgoes dividends in order to use available cash for other purposes, dividend yield will decrease. As a result, stock prices may fall to a point that restores dividend yield to its prior level. In effect, the corporation is "borrowing" from the stockholders by using funds that could be used to pay dividends. Therefore, the cost of equity capital is a substitute for an interest cost for internally generated funds. However, determining an appropriate interest rate for equity capital would require a number of subjective decisions because it would have to be imputed; it is not a market-determined rate like interest rate.

SFAS 34 addressed the interest capitalization question. The FASB concluded that interest should be capitalized on borrowed funds for assets that are *constructed* by a company for its own use or as a discrete project for sale or lease to another company. Interest is required to be capitalized only during the construction period:

---

[20]R. N. Anthony, "Equity Interest—Its Time Has Come," *Journal of Accountancy* (December 1982), 76–93.

The Board concluded that interest cost is a part of the cost of acquiring an asset if a period of time is required in which to carry out the activities necessary to get it ready for its intended use. In reaching this conclusion, the Board considered that the point in time at which an asset is ready for its intended use is critical in determining its acquisition cost. Assets are expected to provide future economic benefits, and the notion of expected future economic benefits implies fitness for a particular purpose.[21]

However, some members of the board believed:

> ...interest to be a cost of a different order from the cost of materials, labor and other services....Cash—the resource obtained by the payment of interest on debt has unique characteristics. It is fungible. It is obtained from a variety of sources..., only one of which (borrowings) gives rise to a cost that is recognized in the present accounting framework.... Because of those characteristics of cash, interest on debt cannot be assigned or allocated to noncash resources in the same way as material, labor, and overhead costs, and association of interest on debt with a particular category of noncash resources, such as assets undergoing a construction or production process, is inherently arbitrary.[22]

SFAS 34 does not apply to inventory or assets acquired from another entity.[23] Nevertheless, two companies may construct identical assets with identical costs for material, labor and overhead but arrive at different capitalized costs for the asset, depending on the method of financing. By borrowing the funds rather than financing with internally generated funds, the interest costs are added to the cost of the asset.

INFLATION

Accounting for the effects of changing price levels, or inflation, was discussed briefly in Chapter 5. The valuation principles of constant dollar and current cost attempt to incorporate the effects of inflation on the financial statements.

Inflation accounting has been a subject of controversy for many years.[24] When inflation was relatively low (2 to 4 percent), the argu-

---

[21]SFAS 34, par. 39.

[22]Dissent, SFAS 34.

[23]SFAS 34 does not apply to public utilities which capitalize interest costs as part of their rate base.

[24]Perhaps the first discussion was: L. Middleditch, "Should Accounts Reflect the Changing Value of the Dollar?", Journal of Accountancy (February 1918), 114–120. For a more contemporary discussion, see R. F. Vancil, "Inflation Accounting—The Great Controversy", Harvard Business Review (March-April 1976), 58–67.

ments in favor of adopting an accounting technique to incorporate inflationary effects into the financial statements were academic. However, as inflation began to rise to double digits in the mid, and late seventies, the effects of inflation became more significant.

Accordingly, the FASB addressed the problem and concluded in 1979 that disclosing price-level-adjusted financial statements as supplementary information would aid financial statement users in decision making.[25] As the level of inflation diminished, support for these disclosures eroded. Pronouncements were issued, in 1984 (SFAS 82) and in 1986 (SFAS 89), that modified these disclosures and made them voluntary. If inflation increases to double-digit levels, there could be increased support for price-level disclosures again. However, this may be difficult to accomplish without causing delays in implementation and without risking loss of credibility by the FASB:

> Although Statement 33 had obvious shortcomings, it was a base on which to build. It represented years of due process—research, debate, deliberations, decisions—and application experience. As last amended, it had made significant progress in eliminating alternative concepts and methodologies. Its recision means that much of that due process and application experience will have to be repeated in response to a future inflation crisis. That will entail great cost in terms of time, money, and creative talent, and, because due process does not permit quick reaction to crises, it risks loss of credibility for the Board and loss of initiative in private sector standard setting.[26]

EMERGING ISSUES

The foregoing discussion provides a brief overview of the thought process involved in developing theory in order to support accounting standards. When more is learned about investor behavior, theory naturally evolves over time that requires recognition and disclosure of financial statement items that enhance the overall usefulness of financial statements. As theory evolves, standards can change specific treatments, such as in the case of accounting for income taxes.

The ever-increasing complexity of the economy and the structure of transactions is another driving force behind the evolution of theory. For example, new and ingenious methods of financing asset acquisitions or facilitating sales are being developed for which no accounting

---

[25]SFAS 33.
[26]Dissent, SFAS 89.

standards exist. To address these problems, the FASB has organized the Emerging Issues Task Force (EITF).

Accounting theory, then, is in a constant state of flux. The development of theory is a dynamic process that incorporates what is learned about investor and management behavior so that useful financial statements result from the accounting process.

In recent years, the emphasis in the recognition-and-measurement process has shifted from the income statement to the balance sheet. Examples of this shift are seen in the new FASB statements on accounting for income taxes and pensions. This shift, coupled with the increased complexity of the economy, should cause financial statements to become longer, due to increased disclosure requirements.[27]

By focusing on the recognition and measurement of assets and liabilities, income statement elements become recognized and measured as a by-product.[28] One consequence is likely to be more volatility in reported earnings. Volatile earnings imply that valuations of companies based on their earnings stream will cause volatile security price swings, which can increase the risk of investment.

The remainder of this section is devoted to gaining an insight into a few of the emerging issues that are likely to impact financial statements. This is not a comprehensive coverage of the issues. Since 1984 (and the inception of the EITF) and through October 1988, almost two hundred separate issues have been identified by the EITF.[29] Some of these issues have been resolved; others are still unresolved.

Other Post-Employment Benefits[30]

One example of an unresolved and contentious issue is *other post-employment benefits* (OPEBs). OPEBs are benefits offered to retired employees, such as health benefits, that will be paid by the employer after the employee has retired. Currently, it is accounting practice to record these expenditures as they are paid. However, the FASB is considering requiring companies to accrue the liability associated with OPEBs as the employee earns them during employment, rather than

---

[27]M. V. Sever, and R. E. Boisclair, "Financial Reporting in the 1990s," *Journal of Accountancy* (January 1990), 36–41.

[28]See Chapter 5 and the discussion of articulation.

[29]*EITF Abstracts*, FASB, October 6, 1988.

[30]Soon after completion of this manuscript *SFAS 106*, which governs accounting and disclosure requirements for OPEBs, was issued. It requires recognition of OPEBs in the accounting records similar to the requirements for pension liabilities.

when the company actually pays the benefits. It has been estimated that the accrual of OPEBs would decrease the net worth of affected companies by as much as $1 trillion.[31]

The effect of this action on a particular company will depend on the demographics of the work force, since the accrual will be based on actuarial estimates. Field tests indicate that the effects of accruals on specific companies will increase income statement expense between two and seven times current levels.[32]

This is a material unrecorded liability that the FASB may require to be recognized. Not recognizing the liability and the associated expense violates the matching principle, since employees earn the right to post-employment benefits as they work. Namely, while employees are working, they are generating revenues that should be matched against their compensation; OPEBs are simply additional compensation to be paid at a future date.

Off-Balance-Sheet Financing

Another emerging problem is the use of innovative financial instruments to create off-balance-sheet financing. New financial instruments have been devised to accommodate the growing complexity and internationalization of the economy. One consequence of the increased complexity and internationalization of the economy has been interest and exchange rate volatility. Several examples of innovative financial instruments are financial futures and forward contracts, interest rate swaps, and various types of financial guarantees.

These financial instruments are extremely complex and often represent hedge positions (taken by either party to the transaction) that can have either favorable results or unfavorable results. Often these transactions are not recorded because the exchange of cash or other assets is contingent upon some future unknown event.

An option contract is a much simpler financial instrument. However, it demonstrates the basic accounting issues involved. Assume that an option is issued obligating the issuer to sell a commodity to the option holder at a specific price, which is known as the *strike price*. As long as the market price of the commodity remains below the strike price, the holder of the option will not exercise the option. However, if

---

[31]J. R. Norman, and S. Garland, "First Thing We Do Is Kill All the Accountants," *Business Week*, September 12, 1988, 94–95.

[32]Sever, M. V. and Boisclair, R. E. "Financial Reporting in the 1990s", *Journal of Accountancy* (January 1990), 36–41.

the market price rises above the strike price, the holder of the option will probably exercise the right to acquire the commodity. This transaction is contingent on the market price rising above the strike price.

The basic accounting issues are twofold. One issue is *when* to recognize the liability in order to provide the commodity. Is it a liability at the balance sheet date if the market price is below the strike price? If the liability is recognized, another issue concerns the *amount* at which to recognize the liability. Even if the market price is above the strike price at the balance sheet date, the market price could rise or fall prior to the exercise of the option.

The FASB has recently issued *SFAS 105*; it requires specific footnote disclosures for certain types of financial instruments that represent off-balance-sheet financing. Furthermore, the FASB is in the process of identifying various financial instruments that are being used and is considering the appropriate recognition and measurement criteria for recording these financial instruments in the accounting records. The decision concerning recognition and measurement could be based on market values.[33] A market value approach could add volatility to recorded amounts in financial statements because of the price swings associated with these financial instruments.

Employee Stock Option Plans and Other Issues

Another contentious issue that has reemerged is accounting for employee stock option plans. The current accounting treatment is governed by *APBO 25*. Criticism has surfaced in recent years because a number of new types of stock option plans have been developed that were not explicitly covered by *APBO 25*.

Furthermore, *APBO 25* was controversial when it was originally issued. Stock option plans are essentially a form of additional compensation that grant employees the option to purchase the employer-corporation's stock at a specified price. The basic accounting questions are how to determine the amount of compensation expense and over what accounting periods to allocate the expense.

These issues are difficult to resolve because of the structure of compensation plans. Some option plans set the option price above the market price, which means that the option will not be exercised unless the market price rises above the option price. Otherwise, the stock

---

[33]M. V. Sever, and R. E. Boisclair, "Financial Reporting in the 1990s," *Journal of Accountancy* (January 1990), 36–41.

could be purchased at a lower price on the open market. Also, the exercise period is usually restricted to a definite period of time, but the employee is being rewarded for past and future efforts on behalf of the corporation.

Accordingly, *APBO 25* set accounting guidelines that recognize expense over a defined "service period" and only if the exercise price is below the market price as of the measurement date, which is also specifically defined. These rules result in many stock option plans that require no recognition of expense or value. Theoretically, however, all stock option plans have some value.

Since *APBO 25*, several option-pricing models have been developed that estimate the future value of options.[34] Consequently, the FASB is working on a project to account for stock option plans that use a fair value approach, which should provide more useful financial statements and should require different accounting treatment from *APBO 25* requirements.

The FASB is also considering the use of a discounted present value approach for measuring financial statement elements. The conceptual merits of such a valuation approach was discussed in Chapter 5. However, there are numerous practical considerations involved in an across-the-board implementation.

Many other topics are also being considered by the FASB, and they are in various stages of resolution. Other topics will be considered as issues emerge. As issues are resolved, they may still be subject to reconsideration, as with stock option plans, income-tax accounting and pensions. Furthermore, as the FASB adopts a position for each issue, controversy may remain, as theorists continue to disagree and as interested parties continue to attempt to influence the resolution. While the due process approach has some shortcomings, it does appear to be working.[35]

SUMMARY

It is difficult to capture the essence of complex problems in the small amount of space allotted. The primary objective of this chapter was to provide an overview of selected issues and of the theories involved in their resolutions. Furthermore, the issues discussed are not a comprehensive set; but rather, a selected set of issues.

---

[34]B. P. Robbins, "FASB's Long Look at Stock Compensation Plans," *Journal of Accountancy* (August 1988): 60–68.

[35]D. R. Beresford, "What's Right With the FASB," *Journal of Accountancy* (January 1990): 81–84.

As shown, some issues are "resolved" more than once. As theory evolves over time, the accounting treatment for some issues changes or is refined to better meet the overall objectives of financial reporting. However, the evolution of theory *is* guided by the conceptual framework. Through the conceptual framework, normative accounting theory is applied in the hopes of resolving specific problems in a manner that reflects a consistent theory.

Prominent examples of issues that have been resolved more than once are accounting for income taxes and accounting for pensions. A new resolution for income taxes was deemed necessary once the conceptual framework defined the elements of financial statements. Accounting for income taxes under *APBO 11* created an asset or a liability that did not conform to the definition of assets and liabilities as established by the conceptual framework.

Also, in meeting the objectives of financial reporting as established by the conceptual framework, the focus for measurement and recognition of financial statement elements has shifted to the balance sheet from the income statement. This shift in focus is a primary reason for the FASB's reconsideration of accounting for pensions; the result has been additional disclosure and the potential for recording increased liabilities.

Moreover, the shift in focus to the balance sheet has the potential to make an enormous impact on recorded liabilities for accounting issues currently under consideration by the FASB. One example is the accounting for OPEBs.

As the economy changes and becomes more complex, other issues will emerge and, in general, transactions will become more complex. This, in turn, will present new challenges to the accounting profession to produce useful financial statements. Various groups will have self-interested motivations in adopting a particular view in reporting the economic consequences of transactions. On the other hand, the conceptual framework presents a normative theory to guide accountants in order to accomplish the objective of financial reporting.

While this chapter focused on the application of theory, the previous chapter focused on the politics of setting standards. The resulting standards are a product of both theory and politics. In practice, do financial statements make a difference to users? The next chapter investigates this question.

READING LIST

Anthony, R. N. "Equity Interest—Its Time Has Come." *Journal of Accountancy* (December 1982): 76–93.

Greene, R. "Can You Measure the Unknowable?" *Forbes*, March 17, 1980, 160.

Horwitz, B., and Kolodny, R. "The FASB, the SEC, and R&D." *Bell Journal of Economics* (Spring 1981): 249–262.

Kieso, D. E. and Weygandt, J. J. *Intermediate Accounting*, 6th ed. (New York: Wiley, 1989).

Middleditch, L. "Should Accounts Reflect the Changing Value of the Dollar?" *Journal of Accountancy* (February 1918): 114-120.

"Pension Survey: Unfunded Liabilities Continue to Grow." *Business Week*, August 14, 1978, 60–64.

Rosenfeld, P. and Dent, W. C. "No More Deferred Taxes." *Journal of Accountancy* (February 1983): 44–55.

Vancil, R. F. "Inflation Accounting—The Great Controversy." *Harvard Business Review* (March–April 1976): 58-67.

STUDY QUESTIONS

1. Payments from pension plans to retired employees are not considered expenses. However, the payment *to* the pension plan is an expense. Why?
2. A capital lease transfers the risks and benefits of ownership. In your opinion, what criteria could be used to determine whether the risks and benefits of ownership have been transferred?
3. You notice that a company in which you are considering investing has no assets for a pension plan on its balance sheet. Does this mean that the company has no pension plan?
4. Define the cost of equity capital.
5. Do you believe that financial statements are more useful with or without interperiod tax allocations?
6. How is the *deferred method* different from the *liability method* of accounting for income taxes?
7. What are the basic issues in accounting for leases for the lessee? For the lessor?
8. If an asset and a liability are to be recognized by the lessee, how should the asset and the liability be measured?
9. What is the difference between an operating lease and a capital lease? How does the classification of a lease affect the financial statements of both the lessor and the lessee?
10. What is a temporary difference? How do temporary differences affect the determination of income tax expense and tax liability?
11. The concept of interperiod tax allocation can be applied using the deferred method or the liability method. What is the basic difference between the two approaches?
12. What are the primary accounting issues faced by a company who has a pension plan for its employees?
13. Should the method of financing a self-constructed asset affect its cost?
14. In your opinion, what conditions should be present for interest capitalization?
15. What are the advantages and disadvantages of inflation-adjusted financial statements to the users?
16. Will certain accounting issues, such as the accounting for pensions or income taxes, ever be resolved, or will they always be in an evolutionary stage?
17. In your opinion, what will be some of the more important accounting issues in the year 2,000?

Chapter 9

Do Financial Statements Make A Difference?

...I'm surprised at the lack of sophistication by the investing public. There's got to be some education coming into the process. One thing I have proven to myself is that managements do believe that they own the companies...I think the lethargic attitude of stockholders has played into the hands of management...These are not fiefdoms that managements run.[1]

*T*he implicit assumption underlying the practice of financial statement analysis is that, by analyzing financial statements, a competent analyst is able to distinguish companies that represent good investments from companies that represent bad investments. The inference drawn from this assumption is that financial statements contain data useful in making investment decisions. In fact, *SFAC 1* has established that the broad objective of financial reporting is to provide useful information to external users in their decision-making process.[2]

However, Chapter 7 presented evidence that financial statements are a product of a political process. Have external influences of the standard-setting process corrupted the end product (i.e., financial statements) to the extent that financial statements are no longer useful to external users in their decision-making process? Furthermore, even if the political process has not corrupted the end product, do financial statements provide useful information to decision makers?

---

[1]Boone Pickens quoted in: K. M. Welling, "The World According to Boone Pickens," *Barrons*, September 23, 1985, 49.

[2]*SFAC 1*, par. 32, 34.

The ability to distinguish good from bad investments implies the ability to predict the general course of future events with respect to the investment being considered. Most agree that the *focus* of the prediction should be on cash flows.[3] Since financial statements are prepared based on accrual concepts rather than on a cash basis, and since they represent historical data, there can be some question concerning their usefulness to predict future cash flows. Therefore, the statement of cash flows should provide useful insight into future cash flows. Nevertheless, there is evidence that accrual data is a better predictor of future cash flows than is contemporary cash flow data.[4]

Do financial statements actually contain information that allows an analyst to make the distinction between good investments and bad investments? Are financial statements attaining the objectives of financial reporting established through the FASB's conceptual framework? One approach to test whether financial statements contain the data necessary for decision making is to observe the reactions of security prices to the introduction of financial statement data.

The securities markets reflect the current valuation of all companies that are publicly traded. The market price per share multiplied by the number of shares outstanding provides a market valuation of the company being considered. In theory, the securities markets are presumed to be efficient. The *efficient market hypothesis* states that a security price reflects all relevant information.

In fact, there are three forms of the efficient market hypothesis. The *strong form* assumes that market prices reflect all public and private information.[5] The *semistrong form* argues that securities prices reflect all information *publicly* available. The *weak form* assumes that market prices reflect information implied by historical-cost data. The efficient market hypothesis provides a framework for testing the usefulness of financial statements. Financial statements that present good news should result in favorable security price reactions, and financial statements that present bad news should produce negative security price reactions.

If prices do not react, one may infer that either the market is not efficient or that financial statements do not contain data useful for

---

[3]*SFAC 1*, par. 32, 37.

[4]R. M. Bowen, D. Burgstahler, and L. A. Daley "Evidence on the Relationships Between Various Earnings Measures of Cash Flow," *The Accounting Review* (October 1986): 713 –725. Also see *SFAC 1*, pars. 42 – 44.

[5]Some information can be private in the sense that it is only available to a select few, such as "insiders." This is referred to as *information asymmetry* and can have adverse social consequences. Information asymmetry is discussed later in this chapter.

decision making, or both. However, it has been suggested that, if markets are efficient, financial statement analysis does not benefit individual investors, and that financial statement analysis cannot yield information to a specific analyst that can be used to obtain a superior investment.

For example, assume that an analyst discovers an undervalued company through financial statement analysis. Then the analyst can realize investment profits by acquiring equity in the undervalued company and by waiting for other investors in the market to discover the undervaluation and to buy the stock, thereby driving up the stock price.

However, if markets are efficient (semistrong form), all publicly available information is immediately reflected in the stock price. Therefore, an analyst is unlikely to discover an undervalued company, since all stocks are correctly valued by the market once the information is available. The implications are that a portfolio of stocks randomly selected will perform as well as a portfolio of stocks selected on the basis of conscientious analysis.

Of course, some people can contend that some analysts assimilate data faster than others or that markets are not efficient. Furthermore, there are cases where financial statement analysis can be useful, even if information is assimilated immediately by all market participants and reflected in stock prices.[6]

The next section discusses some of the empirical evidence concerning the usefulness of accounting data, which is tested through the efficient market hypothesis and security price reactions.

SECURITIES PRICES AND ACCOUNTING DATA

It seems obvious that accounting data contained in financial statements would be useful to analysts. However, no direct evidence of that usefulness was available until 1968. At that time, two researchers tested the linkage between publication of financial statements and security price changes. The results provided evidence that a correlation does exist between reported earnings and stock price changes.[7]

---

[6] J. M. Patton, "Ratio Analysis and Efficient Markets in Introductory Financial Accounting," *The Accounting Review* (July 1982), 627 – 630. See also A. E. Serwer, "How to Profit in the Dicey World of Small Stocks," *Fortune*, January 15, 1990, 25 – 28.

[7] R. Ball, and P. Brown, "An Empirical Evaluation of Accounting Income Numbers," *Journal of Accounting Research* (Autumn 1968), 159 –177.

Subsequent to the seminal research, noted in the preceding paragraph additional research has been conducted to test the linkage between accounting data and securities prices in other ways. For example, alternative GAAP are available that provide management with the opportunity to choose the accounting method that presents facts in the most favorable light. Could the investing public be tricked by such choices?[8]

The idea that the market may be tricked by accounting choices has been tested in several ways. One study tested the market's valuation of companies that employed straight-line depreciation against those using an accelerated method of depreciation. All things equal, the company using straight-line depreciation will initially have higher net income than companies using accelerated depreciation. However, since depreciation is a noncash expense, there are no cash-flow consequences to using a depreciation method, assuming all companies use the same depreciation method for computing income taxes. The results of this study indicate that investors see through the superficial effects of the use of different depreciation methods.[9] When the income of the companies using an accelerated method was adjusted to earnings assuming straight-line depreciation, it was found that there was no significant difference between the P/E ratios of the two groups of companies. Prior to this adjustment, the companies using an accelerated method had lower reported earnings and higher P/E ratios. In other words, the market valued the two groups of companies by adjusting its collective perception to fit the substantive effect of reported earnings, rather than by focusing simply on the superficial effects of accounting methods on net income.

The sophistication of investors in interpretation of accounting data is further tested in studies that have been conducted to examine the security price reactions to a change from FIFO inventory costing to

---

[8]The fact that there may be naive participants in the market who might be fooled and exploited is an idea that has been advanced in order to increase regulation. However, naive investor presence in the market does not preclude these investors from purchasing investment advice (or books such as this one). Presumably, naive investors will act rationally and purchase investment advice. Naivete is present in most markets. For example, consider a consumer of stereo equipment who has little or no expertise in electronics. He or she relies on the expertise of the sales clerk. For a more complete discussion see R. Leftwich, "Market Failure Fallacies and Accounting Information," *Journal of Accounting and Economics* (December 1980), 202 – 203.

[9]W. H. Beaver, and R. E. Dukes "Tax Allocation and Depreciation Methods: Some Empirical Results," *The Accounting Review* (July 1973), 549 – 559.

LIFO. In periods of rising prices, LIFO, in most circumstances, will produce lower reported earnings than FIFO. However, Internal Revenue Service regulations require companies that use LIFO to use it for both financial and tax purposes. The implications of this requirement are that reported financial income will be lower but that there will be positive cash flow consequences, since taxable income also will be lower than if FIFO had been used. Therefore, a change from FIFO to LIFO will result in lower financial income, which is only a superficial adverse effect; the substantive effect is that cash flow increases because of deferred tax payments. Are investors sophisticated enough to see beyond the superficial effect of using LIFO inventory costing? Research results have not been entirely consistent on this point. Therefore, the evidence is not entirely clear.[10]

The superficial effects of changes in accounting methods have been examined in other areas. Often such superficial effects have produced security price reactions, which are contrary to the expectations concerning the efficient market hypothesis or which indicate that investors can be deceived by accounting data. However, a deeper analysis of these findings in specific areas suggests that the superficial effects can, in fact, have substantive consequences that the market impounds into security prices, thus confirming the efficient market hypothesis.

For example, because of the passage of *SFAS 19*, which prescribes successful efforts as the uniform method of accounting in the oil and gas industry, many companies immediately changed from full cost to successful efforts.[11] These companies reported lower assets and lower net income in the period of change from full cost to successful efforts, but this was only due to the difference in the accounting view of certain expenditures. Namely, the change in net income and assets was only superficial and not brought about by a substantive change in the results of operations. However, security prices reacted in a negative manner.[12]

The explanation suggested for negative price reaction involves the adverse consequences that the change in accounting numbers has on

---

[10]G. C. Biddle, and F. W. Lindahl, "Stock Price Reactions to LIFO Adoptions: The Association Between Excess Returns and LIFO Tax Savings," *Journal of Accounting Research* (Autumn 1982): 551 – 588; and W. E. Ricks, "The Market's Response to the 1974 LIFO Adoptions," *Journal of Accounting Research* (Autumn 1982), 367 – 387.

[11]*SFAS 19* was subsequently rescinded by *SFAS 25*. See Chapter 7.

[12]D. W. Collins, M. S. Rozeff, and D. S. Dhaliwal, "The Economic Determinants of the Market Reaction to Proposed Mandatory Accounting Changes in the Oil and Gas Industry." Journal *of Accounting and Economics* (March 1981), 37 – 71.

restrictive debt covenants. *Debt covenants* are clauses inserted in lending agreements (bonds or notes) that require the debtor to maintain minimum financial ratios and/or other measures that restrict the debtor's actions with regard to dissipation of assets. One example would be that the current ratio must be maintained at a minimum level of 1.85 to 1. If the current ratio drops below this minimum level, the debt is immediately callable at the option of the creditor.[13] The purpose of such clauses is to protect the creditor from actions by the debtor, regardless of whether those actions are either intentional or occur as a natural consequence of the deteriorating conditions that result from reducing cash or other assets to the point that the creditors' claims to remaining assets are diminished.[14]

A full cost company that changed to successful efforts more than likely would have superficial effects that had adverse consequences on financial ratios. Conceivably, this superficial effect could result in a substantive consequence, especially if it caused financial ratios to dip below minimum requirements in restrictive debt covenants, thereby triggering technical default on outstanding debt. While creditors might be expected to waive their rights for calling the debt under these circumstances, that decision remains entirely under the control of the creditors.

The adverse market reaction is based upon the perception that the debt "call" will disrupt the achievement of debtor company goals. This disruption is expected to reduce stockholder returns. Therefore, stock prices can react negatively. This is a response to the market's evaluation of the increased risk associated with full cost companies that changed to successful efforts. The risk is increased because creditors have the option of calling the outstanding debt, which may disrupt company goals.

There are also instances where empirical evidence does not support the efficient market hypothesis. One such study involved measuring security price reactions to the publication of articles by Abraham Briloff, an outspoken critic of financial reporting.

Briloff analyzes financial statements by using public information. He is critical of managements that appear to intentionally place a favorable "spin" on the interpretation of events and use accounting alternatives to produce favorable results that obscure the economic

---

[13]The debt is required to be paid immediately, regardless of the original payment schedule detailed by the debt instrument.

[14]Refer to the discussion of agency theory later in this chapter.

substance of events. If the market is not fooled by these manipulations, there should be no market reaction to the publication of Briloff articles. However, the market appears to react adversely to Briloff's articles.[15]

It can be argued that there are a number of reasons explaining why the market reacts to Briloff's criticisms. However, no more support exists for the other reasons than exists for arguing that the market is inefficient.[16]

In summary, it appears that accounting data has an impact on securities prices. While there may be evidence to the contrary in isolated instances, most of the evidence supports the efficient markets hypothesis. Furthermore, there is little evidence to conclude that accounting information does not contribute to an efficient market. While this may have been intuitively obvious, the empirical evidence serves as a formal proof.

NEWS ANNOUNCEMENTS AND SECURITY PRICES

Firms often release news concerning significant events prior to the issuance of financial statements. If markets are efficient, then securities prices should react favorably to good news and unfavorably to bad news. These reactions should diminish the effects of subsequently published accounting data on capital markets, since the effects would already have been impounded into security prices. One important factor to consider is that, if the announcement originates with management, then management has total discretion; that is, management decides when to issue the announcement or even if the announcement should be made.

The effects of announcements concerning earnings on trading volume and security prices has been studied. While controlling for other factors, it has been shown empirically that trading volume and security prices were correlated to these announcements.[17]

Managements' earnings *forecasts* also are often publicly disseminated. Research has been conducted on the effects of managements' forecasts compared to the forecasts of professional analysts. This

---

[15]G. Foster, "Briloff and the Capital Market," *Journal of Accounting Research* (Spring 1979), 262 – 274.

[16]G. Foster, *Financial Statement Analysis*, 2nd ed. (Englewood, Cliffs, NJ: Prentice-Hall, 1986), 399.

[17]W. H. Beaver "The Information Content of Annual Earnings Announcements," *Journal of Accounting Research Supplement* 1968, 67–92.

research has provided evidence that the market responds to deviations between managements' forecasts and professional analysts' forecasts.[18]

Another example of the effect of news on security prices was illustrated by *The Wall Street Journal's* "Investment Dartboard Column." This column featured well-known investment advisors who suggested specific stocks as good buys. The selected stocks' performance were compared to a random selection picked by *The Wall Street Journal* staffers, who threw darts at a page of stock listings to determine their portfolio.

Initially, the investment advisors' selections outperformed the randomly selected portfolio. However, an investigation of the performance over a longer period of time indicated that the initial surge in price of the advisor-selected stocks was offset by a subsequent price decline. It was hypothesized that the initial price surge was due to the "publicity effect" as readers rushed to buy the advisor-selected stocks.[19] The study concluded that, if the recommended stocks were bought the day after publication date, then the average gain would have been no greater than the market, in general, experienced.

News announcements are an example of the application of *signaling theory*. Signaling theory hypothesizes that individual firms and society can benefit if the capability exists for individual firms to signal higher quality relative to other competing firms. The theory is based on the idea that the market may not be aware of specific differences in quality due to a lack of information, which is a condition that is referred to as *information asymmetry*. Information asymmetry can be reduced through signaling specific differences to the market. One method used to accomplish this is news releases.

Another typical news release concerns the decision of a corporation to increase dividends. It is generally believed that increased dividends will create a favorable impression for investors. This is because dividends increase the return to investors, and provide information that suggests earnings are expected to increase in the future; otherwise, the entity would not have been able to increase dividends because this reduces the cash available to the entity for use in operations and investment. Therefore, an announcement of increased dividends should signal to investors a set of favorable information. Re-

---

[18] G. Waymire, "Additional Evidence on the Information Content of Management Earnings Forecasts," *Journal of Accounting Research*, (Autumn 1984), 703 – 718.

[19] J. R. Dorfman, "Publicity Effect Aided Stock Picks by Market Pros," *The Wall Street Journal*, July 9, 1990, C1, 16.

search has confirmed this assumption.[20] However, it should be noted that more esoteric research has questioned the validity of this assumption.[21]

It has been suggested that management can attempt to misrepresent corporate performance through Management's Discussion in annual reports. Management may attempt to signal high quality in narrative disclosures to offset otherwise negative signals presented in the audited financial statements. To test this hypothesis, research was conducted on narrative disclosures contained in annual reports.[22] The researchers concluded that distressed firms attempted to mimic nondistressed firms through their narrative disclosures. The study also discovered systematic differences in content of distressed and nondistressed narratives. Distressed firms tended to focus on externalities, rather than on internal points in an apparent effort to deflect blame for the entity's distressed condition. Interestingly, it also has been discovered that narrative disclosures can be more helpful in predicting distress than can accounting numbers.[23]

Finally, there appears to be a reaction of securities prices to nonfinancial information that is perceived to have financial consequences. For example, oil and gas reserves are usually expressed in quantities (barrels of oil or MCF of natural gas). The costs to discover the reserves are not always easily discernible from the financial statements.[24] However, future revenues are directly linked to existing reserve quantities. Therefore, announcements of reserve discoveries should have an effect on security prices. Research has confirmed this belief.[25]

---

[20]T. E. Dielman and R. H. Oppenheimer "An Examination of Investor Behavior During Periods of Large Dividend Changes," *Journal of Financial and Quantitative Analysis* (June 1984), 197–216.

[21]K. Avner "Corporate Dividend Policy," (Ph. D. diss., University Microfilms International, 1979).

[22]K. B. Frazier, R. W. Ingram and B. M. Tennyson, "A Methodology for the Analysis of Narrative Accounting Disclosures," *Journal of Accounting Research*, (Spring 1984): 318 – 331. See also: B. M. Tennyson, "The Usefulness of Narrative Disclosures in Predicting Bankruptcy". Ph. D. diss., University Microfilms International, 1982.

[23]B. M. Tennyson, "The Usefulness of Narrative Disclosures in Predicting Bankruptcy," unpublished dissertation, 1982.

[24]Refer to the discussion of oil and gas accounting in Chapter 7.

[25]C. Wright, "A Study of Effects of News Reports on Stock Prices: Implications for Reserve Quantity Disclosures," *Journal of Extractive Industries Accounting* (Fall/ Winter 1982), 109–115.

The implications of the research findings in this section are important to investors because the findings imply that investors should scan the financial press for announcements that can have security price consequences. However, investors should also be aware of the originating source of the announcement and any motivations of the source to intentionally direct a market response by the announcement. Also, an investor should be aware that unintentional distortions may exist. In the case of reserve quantity disclosures, it has been shown that initial estimates are incorrect by as much as 15 percent to 85 percent.[26]

Based on these findings, one can conclude that financial statements most likely contain data that does convey information to the market. However, financial statements are not the only source of data. News announcements also convey data that contains information that the market utilizes. Moreover, news announcements can contain more timely information than financial statements. The following section investigates the link between financial statements and motivations of different groups.

AGENCY THEORY AND FINANCIAL STATEMENTS

The question posed in this chapter's title is important to answer, not only from the standpoint of security prices, but also from the standpoint of the implications of agency theory. Agency theory provides the basis for explaining the behavior of the parties involved in an agent-principal relationship. The agent is represented by management of corporations, and the principal is represented either by stockholders or by creditors, depending upon the perspective taken.

Agency theory is based on the assumption that all individuals are self-interested and that self-interests provide the primary motivation for explaining actions, particularly in economic contexts. Furthermore, there is an inherent conflict between management and stockholders and creditors. This conflict derives from the fact that absentee investors (most stockholders) have entrusted their funds to management. It is assumed that management utilizes these investor funds in the pursuit of the investors' best interests. Therefore, a fiduciary relationship exists between management and stockholders. However, it should be understood that the corporate arrangement produces the

---

[26]J. E. Connor, "Reserve Recognition Accounting: Fact or Fiction?" *Journal of Accountancy* (September 1979), 92 –9 8.

potential for conflict, especially if managements' personal goals are not congruent with stockholders' goals.

For example, if the corporation unexpectedly has a great deal of cash, management can use these funds in several ways. The cash could be used to pay dividends to stockholders or to invest in a corporate project that is expected to yield future benefits beyond the present value of the existing cash. Presumably, either of those alternatives is in the best interests of stockholders. On the other hand, the cash could be used to pay bonuses or to provide perquisites to management. The latter alternatives would only be in the best interests of stockholders if the additional compensation would induce improved agent performance in the future.

The idea that individuals or groups act in their own self-interests is aptly demonstrated in hostile takeovers. Corporate "raiders" often use corporate mismanagement as a reason for targeting corporations for takeover. Raiders often allege that the management of a specific corporation is using the corporation to advance its own interests, rather than to advance the interests of all stockholders. Corporate raiders believe that the effect of this mismanagement is to reduce overall entity value, since resources are being transferred to management rather than being put to a productive use for the entity as a whole:

> ...One thing I have proven to myself is that managements do believe that they really own the companies. And they have done a magnificent job of divorcing stockholders from ownership; I think the lethargic attitude of stockholders has played into the hands of management, and that there's got to be an accountability brought back into corporate America that isn't there today. These are not fiefdoms that managements run; they are really companies; they're employees. ...[27]

Interestingly, management often refuses buy-out offers, even when they are above current market value, on the basis that to accept the offer is not in the best interests of stockholders. One example of such a rejected offer was explained as follows:

> ...[The offer] is not in the best interests of our stockholders at this time. ... [The buyer's] interests, which have been represented on our board for almost a year, are aware of CalMat's values and are attempting to appropriate them for themselves.[28]

---

[27]K. M. Welling, "The World According to Pickens," 41 – 50. This is an interview with Boone Pickens that provides an overview of purported reasons for many hostile takeovers and resistant management's strategies to prevent the takeover.

[28]B. J. Stein, "The CalMat Maneuver," *Barrons*, September 12, 1988, 13.

Even more interesting are the subsequent actions by CalMat's management. To reduce the attractiveness of the company, assets were sold to
a third party at a price reportedly below true market value.[29] One
reason provided for management's action was that the takeover group
would have replaced current management.[30] Thus, management may
have reduced company value in order to preserve its jobs. In addition,
a complicated agreement between the takeover group, which already
owned several million shares, and CalMat resulted in the purchase of
the takeover group's shares at a price of, reputedly, $100 million *above*
current market value.[31] This last transaction, sometimes called greenmail,
resulted in the buying group abandoning the takeover attempt.

Furthermore, management has become sensitive to charges of mismanagement, as leveled by raiders, and to the possibility of takeover
and displacement. To combat personal adverse effects of displacement
on management, the board of directors often adopts a policy of providing "golden parachutes" to top officers. Golden parachutes are provisions that require the corporations to provide corporate officers with
large amounts of cash and/or stock in the event that the company is
taken over and they are displaced. Various types of "parachutes" have
been developed over the years.[32]

The conflict between takeover artists and corporate management is
evidence that the foundation of agency theory is valid. Individuals do
act in their own self-interests, within certain parameters. Raiders often
allege that management have abdicated their fiduciary responsibilities
and that they are pursuing their own self-interests, rather than those of
the stockholders. Management, on the other hand, sometimes allege
that raiders have their own interests, and not stockholders' interests, at
heart.

A corporation's financial statements can serve as monitoring devices that allow stockholders to evaluate management's performance
and assess management's stewardship. However, financial statements
can also become a double-edged sword. Management is responsible
for the financial statements, and it is in a position to significantly
influence reported earnings and asset values, thus causing an inappropriate evaluation of performance and stewardship.

---

[29]Ibid. 37.
[30]Ibid. 37.
[31]Ibid. 38.
[32]T. J. Murray, "Here Comes the 'Tin' Parachute," *Dun's Business Month* (January
1987), 62 – 64.

Research has shown that management can and sometimes do elect accounting methods that are in their best interests. If management-bonus schemes are related to certain performance measures, management can select accounting and reporting methods that enhance their bonuses.[33] Because alternative GAAP exists and recognition-and-valuation techniques are often dependent on estimates, management is given an opportunity to manipulate performance measures. Agency theory supports the idea that such behavior might be expected.

Agency theory provides a framework for formalizing the nature of the inherent conflicts in the corporate form of ownership. Financial statements are a monitoring device that can be utilized by principals to determine whether agents are pursuing the principals' best interests. If it is perceived that management is not pursuing the best interests of stockholders, agency costs are represented by the decline in entity market value. There are also costs associated with monitoring of agents. It has been shown that there is an optimal trade-off in these costs.[34] Agency theory has important implications for the setting of accounting standards as well. This was briefly discussed in Chapter 6.[35]

This section has discussed the inherent conflicts between management and resource providers. Financial statements can make a difference in two ways not previously discussed. First, financial statements can be used by management to promote their own self interests. Second, financial statements also serve as a monitoring device that enables stockholders and creditors to make judgments about whether management is fulfilling their fiduciary responsibilities.

INFORMATIONAL CONTENT OF AUDIT REPORTS

Auditors are charged with expressing an independent opinion concerning the overall fairness of financial statements prepared by management. The audit report, which contains that opinion, is considered

---

[33] F. S. Worthy, "Manipulating Profits: How Is It Done", *Fortune* June 25, 1984, 51. See also L. T. Starks, "Performance Incentive Fees: An Agency Theoretic Approach," *Journal of Finance and Quantitative Analysis* (March 1987), 17 – 32.

[34] R. D. Morris, "Signalling, Agency Theory and Accounting Policy Choice," *Accounting and Business Research* (Winter 1987), 47 – 56.

[35] R. L. Watts, and J. L. Zimmermann, "Toward a Positive Theory of the Determination of Accounting Standards," The *Accounting Review* (January 1978), 112 – 134.

an integral part of the financial statements. In past years, auditing standards have required a qualified audit report if a major contingent liability existed or if there was evidence that the entity under audit had violated the going-concern assumption.[36]

Either of these reasons for qualifying audit reports have significant implications, since both imply significant uncertainties with respect to the future of the entity. Increased uncertainty is associated with increased risk, which would imply decreased security prices once the increased risk becomes apparent to the market.

When financial statements are issued with an accompanying audit report that is qualified for either of these two reasons, does the market react? This broad question leads to other questions: Is the market efficient? Is there a security price reaction? If so, when does the market react? The market may react at the time of the issuance of the financial statements, or it can have already impounded this information into security prices from other sources.

Another question is whether the auditor's report conveys any information. Recall that an independent audit fulfills a societal need by providing an objective opinion concerning the fairness of financial statements. In the case of audit reports that are qualified because of uncertainties, is the market previously aware of these uncertainties or does the audit report convey new information to the market?

All of the questions raised in this section are related. If the audit report conveys new information to the market, security prices should react once this new information is known. If the market does not react, it is presumed that the audit report does not convey new information. The results of the limited research that addresses these questions have been contradictory, which is often the case with empirical research.

One study directed at security price reaction to qualified audit reports found no significant response.[37] The implications are that audit reports produce no additional information. However, another study provided evidence that stock prices react to *media* disclosures of qualified audit reports.[38] The researchers were unable to discover a reason for the contradictory findings.

---

[36]Auditing standards have now been modified to provide for an unqualified opinion with explanatory language in these circumstances. See Chapter 2.

[37]P. Dodd, N. Dopuch, R. W. Holthausen, and R.W. Leftwich, "Qualified Audit Opinions and Stock Prices, Information Content, Accouncement Dates and Concurrent Disclosure," *Journal of Accounting and Economics*, vol. 6 (1984), 3–38.

[38] N. Dopuch, R. W. Holthausen, and R. W. Leftwich, "Abnormal Stock Returns Associated with Media Disclosures of 'Subject to' Qualified Audit Opinions," *Journal of Accounting and Economics*, vol. 8 (1986), 93–117.

Plausible reasons considered in regard to this finding were (1) that dissemination of information by the market is slow and (2) that information is contained in audit reports, but the information is too costly for all market participants to obtain. That is, the second study found that security prices reacted to disclosures in the media subsequent to the distribution or public availability of annual reports. This implies that information content exists, but that only a narrow market absorption of the information takes place; while the information might be publicly available, it is not effectively or completely disseminated until disclosed by the media.[39]

The notion of slow dissemination of information was rejected by the researchers because they found no statistically significant difference between price responses to initial media disclosures 5 days subsequent to public availability as compared to initial media disclosures 20 days subsequent to public availability. The conclusion was based on the fact that the researchers believed it was "inconceivable" that this information had not been disseminated for 20 days. However, this conclusion may be based on an invalid assumption by the researchers. In other words, is there any *a priori* reason to assume that a 5-day absorption period is different from a 20-day absorption period?

Regardless of whether there are existing deficiencies in research in this area, the implications are important. Financial statements are not the only source of information for analysts. When making investment decisions, be careful to scan the financial press for additional insight.

INSIDER TRADING

As previously discussed, information asymmetry is a condition that provides information to some groups at the expense of others. It can result in harmful effects to society. One consequence is the so-called *adverse selection process*.[40] The classic example of information asymmetry is insider trading. Insider trading occurs when people inside the corporation have access to information not yet publicly available and use it to gain an unfair advantage in security trading.

There are basically two types of insider trading. The first type involves corporate officers who trade in the stock of their company, using information that is not yet publicly available and the second type

---

[39] P. Lloyd-Davies, and M. Canes, "Stock Prices and the Publication of Second Hand Information," *Journal of Business* vol. 51(1978), 43–56.

[40] G. A. Akerlof, "The Market for 'Lemons': Quality Uncertainty and the Market Mechanism," *Quarterly Journal of Economics* (August 1970), 488–500 .

involves the use of nonpublic information by those who are not officers or employees of the corporation whose stock they are buying or selling on the basis of nonpublic information.

Insider trading by corporate insiders has been shown to yield excess profits for the insiders.[41] This implies that those who are without inside information are at a disadvantage and that, as the amount of inside information increases, the disadvantage increases. In fact, it has been shown that the greater the information asymmetry, the more often the noninsider is on the wrong side of the trade.[42]

Insider trading by individuals who are not officers or employees of the involved corporation has been well documented in the financial press. Enormous profits have been made by Michael Milken, Ivan Boesky, and others. One scandal involved a pressperson at *Business Week* who sold advance copies of the magazine to a stockbroker. The stockbroker then traded stocks mentioned in a weekly column one day prior to the distribution of the magazine. The result was that stocks mentioned in the column had very large percentage changes in price and volume one day prior to the distribution of the magazine.[43]

Insider trading is an ethical issue that can have a profound impact on efficient operation of markets. It shows that financial statements can make a difference. Unfortunately, financial statements can also make a greater difference to those who have advance information concerning the statements' content.

This type of problem triggers a demand for increased regulation of capital markets. The discussion of regulation in Chapter 7 points out that increased regulation does not necessarily lead to better results. Infrequent problems regarding insider trading should not prevent the market from operating to the net benefit of society.

---

[41]J. E. Finnerty, "Insiders and Market Efficiency," *The Journal of Finance* (September 1976): 1141–1148. See also J. F. Jaffe, "Special Information and Insider Trading," *Journal of Business* (July 1974), 410–428.

[42]R. Chiang, and P. C. Venkatesh, "Insider Holdings and Perception of Information Asymmetry: A Note," *Journal of Finance* (September 1988), 1041 – 1048.

[43]C. Welles, et al. "The Case of the Purloined Magazines," *Business Week*, August 15, 1988, 40 – 44.

INVESTOR PERCEPTIONS
OF FINANCIAL STATEMENTS

The degree to which investors rely on financial statements to make investment decisions is another question that deserves attention. There is evidence that individual investors use accounting data, but not to the extent that might be expected.[44] However, institutional investors appear to rely to a greater degree on financial statements.[45]

One explanation for relatively low reliance on financial statements by individual investors might be that individual investors rely on professional analysts to interpret the financial statements and then to sell their advice to the investors. (See Footnote 8). Undoubtedly, institutional investors and professional analysts as a group have more sophisticated interpretive abilities than do individual investors.

Because some investors do not have sophisticated interpretive abilities, it has been suggested that those investors have a tendency to rely on specific accounting measures only. This has been referred to as the phenomena of *anchoring* and *functional fixation*. For example, rather than attempt to absorb and interpret a large amount of data, investors may anchor on earnings per share on the assumption that earnings per share impounds all or most of the information needed for investment decisions. If investors attach the same meaning to earnings per share regardless of the accounting methods employed to derive the statistic, they are said to be functionally fixated.[46]

The implicit assumption contained in analyzing the effects of anchoring and/or functional fixation is that it will result in incorrect investment decisions. However, to assume these ill effects does not question the accuracy and integrity of accounting numbers or financial statements; rather, it assumes a limitation of individual decision makers.

---

[44]R. D. Hines, "The Usefulness of Annual Reports: The Anomaly Between the Efficient Markets Hypothesis and Shareholder Surveys," *Accounting and Business Research* (Autumn 1982), 296–309.

[45]R. Anderson, "The Usefulness of Accounting and Other Information Disclosures in Corporate Annual Reports to Institutional Investors in Australia," *Accounting and Business Research* (Autumn 1981), 259 – 265.

[46]A. R. Abdel-khalik, and T. F. Keller, "Earnings or Cash Flows: An Experiment on Functional Fixation and the Valuation of the Firm," (*Studies in Accounting Research No. 16*, American Accounting Association, 1979), 50.

SUMMARY

The purpose of this chapter was to investigate the usefulness of financial statements. To accomplish that purpose, empirical research was reviewed. The efficiency of capital markets was also investigated, because market efficiency and usefulness of accounting data are complementary concepts.

While it might have been obvious that financial statements do make a difference, no formal proof was available until the idea was subjected to empirical tests. Occasionally, contradictory or inexplicable results were obtained. However, on the whole, the idea that financial statements do make a difference in decision making has been empirically validated. The introduction of accounting data through financial statements does cause security prices to react. Moreover, announcements of information that has financial consequences also cause security price reaction.

Financial statements can also make a difference from the standpoint that they can serve as a monitoring device for investors and creditors to determine whether management is pursuing corporate goals established by stockholders. Without proper monitoring, financial statements can be used by management to further their interests by manipulating financial statement elements to produce greater bonuses or other such compensation.

Finally, stocks are bought and sold by the investing public under the assumption that markets are efficient and that they reflect all publicly available information. Unfortunately, instances have occurred in which specific investors have profited from inside information at the expense of others in the market. Given human nature, this will happen again. However, these infrequent occurrences should not prevent the market from operating to the net benefit of society.

READING LIST

Abdel-khalik, A. R., and Keller, T. F. "Earnings or Cash Flows: An Experiment on Functional Fixation and the Valuation of the Firm." In *Studies in Accounting Research No. 16,* American Accounting Association, 1979.

Acharya, S. "A Generalized Econometric Model and Tests of a Signalling Hypothesis with Two Discrete Signals." *The Journal of Finance* (June 1988): 413–429.

Akerlof, G. A. "The Market for 'Lemons': Quality Uncertainty and the Market Mechanism." *Quarterly Journal of Economics* (August 1970), 488–500.

Anderson, R. "The Usefulness of Accounting & Other Information Disclosures in Corporate Annual Reports to Institutional Investors in Australia." *Accounting and Business Research* (Autumn 1981): 259–265.

Araskog, R. "How I Fought Off the Raiders." *Fortune* (February 27, 1989): 110–112.

Avner, K. "Corporate Dividend Policy." Ph. D. diss., University Microfilms International, 1979.

Ball, R., and Brown, P. "An Empirical Evaluation of Accounting Income Numbers." *Journal of Accounting Research* (Autumn 1968): 159–177.

Beaver, W. H. "The Information Content of Annual Earnings Announcements." *Journal of Accounting Research Supplement* (1968): 67–92.

Beaver, W. H., and Dukes, R. E. "Tax Allocation and Depreciation Methods: Some Empirical Results." *The Accounting Review* (July 1973): 549–559.

Biddle, G. C., and Lindahl, F. W. "Stock Price Reactions to LIFO Adoptions: The Association Between Excess Returns & LIFO Tax Savings." *Journal of Accounting Research* (Autumn 1982): 551–588.

Bowen, R. M., Burgstahler, D., and Daley, L. A. "Evidence on the Relationships Between Various Earnings Measures of Cash Flow." *The Accounting Review* (October 1986): 713–725.

Chiang, R., and Venkatesh, P. C. "Insider Holdings and Perception of Information Asymmetry: A Note." *The Journal of Finance* (September 1988): 1041–1048.

Chow, C. W. "Empirical Studies of the Economic Impacts of Accounting Regulations: Findings, Problems and Prospects." *Journal of Accounting Literature* (Spring 1983): 73–109.

Collins, D. W., Rozeff, M. S., and Dhaliwal, D. S. "The Economic Determinants of the Market Reaction to Proposed Mandatory Accounting Changes in the Oil and Gas Industry." *Journal of Accounting and Economics* (March 1981): 37–71.

Connor, J. E. "Reserve Recognition Accounting: Fact or Fiction?" *Journal of Accountancy* (September 1979): 92–98.

Demski, J. S. "Choice Among Financial Reporting Alternatives." *The Accounting Review* (April 1974): 221–232.

Dielman, T. E., and Oppenheimer, H. R. "An Examination of Investor Behavior During Periods of Large Dividend Changes." *Journal of Financial and Quantitative Analysis* (June 1984): 197–216.

Dobrzynski, J. H., Schiller, Z., Miles, Gregory L., Norman, J. R., and King, R. W. "More Than Ever It's Management for the Short Term." *Business Week* (November 24, 1986): 92–93.

Dodd, P., Dopuch, N., Holthausen, R., and Leftwich, R. W. "Qualified Audit Opinions and Stock Prices, Information Content, Announcement Dates and Concurrent Disclosure." *Journal of Accounting and Economics*, vol 6 (1984): 3–38.

Dopuch, N., Holthausen, R. W., and Leftwich, R. W. "Abnormal Stock Returns Associated with Media Disclosures of 'Subject to' Qualified Audit Opinions." *Journal of Accounting and Economics* vol 8 (1986): 93–117.

Finnerty, J. E. "Insiders and Market Efficiency." *The Journal of Finance* (September 1976): 1141–1148.

Foster, G. "Briloff and the Capital Market." *Journal of Accounting Research* (Spring 1979): 262–274.

Foster, G. *Financial Statement Analysis*, 2nd ed. (Englewood Cliffs, NJ: Prentice-Hall, 1986).

Frazier, K. B., Ingram, R. W., and Tennyson, B. M. "A Methodology for the Analysis of Narrative Accounting Disclosures." *Journal of Accounting Research* (Spring 1984): 318–331.

Frost, C. A. and Bernard, V. L. "The Role of Debt Covenants in Assessing the Economic Consequences of Limiting Capitalization of Exploration Costs." *The Accounting Review* (October 1989): 788–808.

Haugen, R. A. and Senbet, L. W. "On the Resolution of Agency Problems by Complex Financial Instruments: A Reply." *The Journal of Finance* (September 1987): 1091–1095.

Hines, R. D. "The Usefulness of Annual Reports: The Anomaly Between the Efficient Markets Hypothesis and Shareholder Surveys." *Accounting & Business Research.* (Autumn 1982): 296–309.

Holthausen, R. W. and Leftwich, R. W. "The Economic Consequences of Accounting Choice." *Journal of Accounting and Economics* (August 1983): 77–117.

Jaffe, J. F. "Special Information and Insider Trading." *Journal of Business* (July 1974): 410–428.

John, K. "Risk-Shifting Incentives and Signalling Through Corporate Capital Structure." *The Journal of Finance* (July 1987): 123–141.

Johnson, W. B.,and Ramanan, R. "Discretionary Accounting Changes from 'Successful Efforts' to 'Full Cost' Methods: 1970–76." *The Accounting Review*, (January 1988): 96–110.

Kosnik, R. D. "Greenmail: A Study of Board Performance in Corporate Governance." *Administrative Science Quarterly* (June 1987): 163–185.

Lewellen, W. G., Loderer, C., and Martin, K. "Executive Compensation and Executive Incentive Problems." *Journal of Accounting and Economics* (December 1987): 287–310.

Leftwich, R. W. "Market Failure Fallacies and Accounting Information." *Journal of Accounting and Economics* (December 1980): 202–203.

Lloyd-Davies, P., and Canes, M. "Stock Prices & the Publication of Second Hand Information." *Journal of Business*, vol.51 (1978) 43–56.

Morris, R. D. "Signalling, Agency Theory and Accounting Policy Choice." *Accounting and Business Research* (Winter 1987): 47–56.

Murray, T. J. "Here Comes the 'Tin' Parachute." *Dun's Business Month* (January 1987): 62–64.

Naryanan, M. P. "On the Resolution of Agency Problems by Complex Financial Instruments: A Comment." *The Journal of Finance* (September 1987): 1083–1090.

Ng, D. S. "An Information Economics Analysis of Financial Reporting and External Auditing." *The Accounting Review* (October 1978): 910–920.

Patton, J. M. "Ratio Analysis and Efficient Markets in Introductory Financial Accounting." *The Accounting Review* (July 1982): 627–630.

"Pickens's Last Laugh." *Fortune*, August 5, 1985, 10–11.

Ricks, W. E. "The Market's Response to the 1974 LIFO Adoptions." *Journal of Accounting Research* (Autumn 1982): 367–387.

Schwartz, K. B., "Accounting Changes By Corporations Facing Possible Insolvency." *Journal of Accounting, Auditing, and Finance* (Fall 1982): 32–43.

Serwer, A. E. "How to Profit in the Dicey World of Small Stocks." *Fortune*, January 15, 1990, 25–28.

Starks, L. T. "Performance Incentive Fees: An Agency Theoretic Approach." *Journal of Finance and Quantitative Analysis* (March 1987): 17–32.

Stein, B. J. "The CalMat Maneuver." *Barrons*, September 12, 1988, 13.

Tennyson, B. M. "The Usefulness of Narrative Disclosures in Predicting Bankruptcy." Ph. D. diss., University Microfilms International, 1982.

Watts, R. L., and Zimmermann, J. L. "Toward a Positive Theory of the Determination of Accounting Standards." *The Accounting Review* (January 1978): 112–134.

Waymire, G. "Additional Evidence on the Information Content of Management Earnings Forecasts." Journal *of Accounting Research* (Autumn 1984): 703–718.

Welles, C., et al. "The Case of the Purloined Magazines." *Business Week*, August 15, 1988, 40–44.

Welling, K. M. "The World According to Boone Pickens." *Barrons*, September 23, 1985, 41–50.

Williams, J. "Perquisites, Risk, and Capital Structure." *The Journal of Finance* (March 1987): 29–48.

Worthy, F. S. "Manipulating Profits: How Is It Done." *Fortune*, June 25, 1984, 51.

Wright, C. "A Study of Effects of News Reports on Stock Prices: Implications for Reserve Quantity Disclosures." *Journal of Extractive Industries Accounting* (Fall/Winter 1982): 109–115.

STUDY QUESTIONS

1. Assume that last year you invested in a large manufacturing company that had, five years previously, acquired another company in a different industry for approximately $2 billion. In the last quarter of this year, the manufacturing company wrote off half of its investment, causing net income to be reduced by $1 billion. A friend says that he is about to invest in the manufacturing company and thinks that you should buy more stock. What are the favorable implications of this write-down *after* it takes place?

2. You are on the board of directors of a manufacturing company that is just beginning operations. You have invested a large portion of your savings in the stock of the company. Management is deciding on an inventory-costing method for financial reporting. What are management incentives for choosing FIFO? For choosing LIFO? What method would you prefer as a stockholder?

3. What is the efficient market hypothesis? What are the implications of this hypothesis to financial statement users? To Preparers?

4. What characteristics should accounting information have in order to be useful for a decision maker?

Chapter 10

International
Financial Reporting

There are no distant points in the world any longer.[1]

---

*T*he world is becoming smaller in the sense that modern technology can provide instant access to individuals and markets. A well-developed system of telephone and satellite networks can produce instant communication from any point in the world. The time required to transport people and products between continents has decreased with the development of large airliners that are capable of supersonic speeds. Modern technology also allows instantaneous electronic transfer of funds across continents. These factors and others have combined to facilitate a global economy that operates across national boundaries.

Companies have several reasons to engage in international commerce. The two primary reasons are profit and labor. The ability to sell products in foreign markets expands the potential for profits through increased sales. Also, because labor represents a cost of products sold, countries with low-cost labor markets provide potential for increased profits. Therefore, one company can obtain a competitive advantage over another by manufacturing a product in a foreign country with inexpensive labor.

Increased commerce in a global economy has created additional demand for financial resources by companies engaged in international trade. In order to compete for capital on a global basis, companies list their securities on the stock exchanges of foreign countries; approxi-

---

[1]Radio broadcast in 1942 by Wendell Wilkie. Quoted in J. B. Hoyle, *Advanced Accounting*, 3rd ed. (Homewood, IL: Richard D. Irwin, 1991), 606.

mately five hundred companies have listed their stock in more than one country.[2] During the second quarter of 1989, U.S. investors purchased a net of $4.4 billion in foreign securities, and foreign investors purchased a net of $4.5 billion of U.S. securities.[3] In fact, the following well-known companies or products are now owned by foreign companies: Alka-Seltzer, Thermos, Smith-Corona, Brooks Brothers, Pillsbury, General Electric (television sets), Wilson Sporting Goods, and Carnation.[4]

Corporations compete for capital primarily through financial reporting. The previous nine chapters have been devoted to financial reporting within the United States. The same limitations that apply to financial reporting in the United States also apply to international financial reporting, except that the limitations are magnified due to lack of comparability between accounting principles in different countries; cultural differences; and transactions often being denominated in a foreign currency. Specific examples of how these problems are manifested in international financial reporting are provided later in this chapter.

Useful definitions contained in this chapter are as follows:

International financial reporting — Financial reporting designed for financial statement users in more than one country.

Multinational corporation — A corporation that operates or sells securities in more than one country.

Home country — The country in which a multinational corporation is headquartered or in which the parent corporation of a multinational corporation resides.

Foreign financial statement user — A financial statement user who resides in a country other than the home country of the multinational corporation.

CAUSES FOR INTERNATIONAL FINANCIAL REPORTING DIFFERENCES

Accounting is a social science. Therefore, cultural perspectives and business conventions influence accounting principles and reporting practices. GAAP in the United States has evolved in a somewhat

---

[2] D. J. Moulin, and M. B. Solomon, "Practical Means of Promoting Common International Standards," *The CPA Journal* (December 1989), 38–48.

[3] G. G. Mueller, H. Gernon, and G. Meek, *Accounting, an International Perspective*, 2nd ed. (Irwin, 1991), 3.

[4] W. McWhirter, "I Came, I Saw, I Blundered," *Time*, October 9, 1989, 72.

unique manner, based on such endemic factors as societal values, political and economic systems, and business conventions. Other countries with similar values and business systems have developed GAAP similar to those of the United States.

For example, the United States and the United Kingdom have similar accounting models that are influenced by their respective societal values. Other countries, such as Greece, Italy, and Spain, have a somewhat different model, sometimes called the *Continental model*. Still another model, the *South American model*, is somewhat different than the Continental and U.S. models due to South American political and societal influences.

Even though countries such as the United States and the United Kingdom have developed similar models, do not infer that the financial statements of companies from different countries that use the same model are directly comparable. One example of this is the difference in valuation of assets between companies in the United States and companies in the United Kingdom. As discussed in previous chapters, historical cost, with a few exceptions, is the primary asset valuation approach in the United States. However, in the United Kingdom, a reevaluation of some or all assets to current cost or market value is permitted, even though the United Kingdom model is similar to the United States model.

Useful insight can be gained by potential investors if they understand the *causes* for differences in the financial reporting between countries. This is because accounting is a social science, and the causes for differences can reflect cultural differences that are inherent to certain societies. This section contains a brief discussion of some of the primary causes for financial reporting differences.

Standard-Setting Philosophy

The philosophical approaches to standard-setting within countries can differ. The approach in the United States to standard-setting uses the due-process approach described in Chapter 7. After input from interested parties, accounting and reporting standards are established by the FASB, a private foundation. The SEC, a governmental regulatory agency, enforces standards set by the FASB.

In the United Kingdom, standard-setting is accomplished by private accountants, but no regulatory agency exists, and enforcement is provided through the courts. Intervention is possible only if a complaint is filed in court and a lengthy legal process ensues.

In Switzerland, financial reporting standards are a part of the Swiss Commercial Code of Obligations, a federal law. Accounting and reporting standards are seldom changed, and then only through the federal political process, which is quite slow. Under Swiss law, corporate managers have a much greater discretion in financial reporting than do managers in the United States.

While there are statutory requirements for audits under Swiss law, auditors are generally not required to be independent or professionally certified. Furthermore, Swiss auditors are rarely subject to litigation. A reason for such stark differences in United States and Swiss auditing and reporting standards is the cultural differences that produce more opportunistic behavior on the part of United States managers.[5] Consequently, there are more extensive efforts in the United States to produce unbiased financial statements.

For companies that operate in the *European Economic Community* (EC),[6] standards are set by EC *Directives*, which are designed to create more reporting uniformity. *Directives* are required to be incorporated into the law of all EC countries. The goal of increased uniformity is to enhance capital movement and capital formation across national borders within the EC.[7]

---

[5] J. Pratt and G. Behr, "Environmental Factors, Transaction Costs and External Reporting: A Cross National Comparison," *The International Journal of Accounting* (Spring 1987), 1 – 24.

[6] The EC, previously called the European Common Market, is a group of 12 countries that have banded together (through a treaty) to increase trade among the 12 member nations by reducing restrictions on the free flow of goods. The objective is to erase national borders for economic purposes. This objective is founded on economic theory that predicts most market participants are better served if there are fewer restrictions on the flow of labor, capital, and products. The EC is currently considering the adoption of a single currency and monetary authority for all 12 nations. (See R. Alm, "EC Tackles Money Barriers," *Dallas Morning News*, December 17, 1990, pp. 1D, 7D.)

[7] Recall the uniformity discussion in Chapter 7. Many accountants believe that strict uniformity disallowing accounting alternatives can cause financial statements to be misleading when circumstances differ. However, the context of this argument is within U.S. boundaries and capital markets. Since financial reporting practices can differ significantly across boundaries and because different cultures can interpret financial events differently, the advantages of imposition of uniformity across national borders may outweigh the disadvantages.

Needs of Resource Providers

An additional reason for differences in financial reporting concerns the difference in resource providers. Because of the manner in which the corporate form evolved in the United States (see Chapter 2), a variety of resource providers exists and ownership is not concentrated. As a result, there are well-developed stock exchange and bond markets that require relatively large amounts of financial disclosure.

Contrast the United States resource providers with those in Japan. The Japanese economy developed in a different manner from that of the United States. The result is concentrated ownership in Japanese companies with capital requirements satisfied through a relatively small number of large banks. Consequently, financial reporting in Japan does not require as much disclosure as United States investors expect from United States companies.

The Political System

The political system of a country can have an important influence on financial reporting as well. In some countries, such as Sweden, the government plays an active role in managing national resources. Financial reporting in these countries is uniform and directed toward facilitating data gathering for use by the government in formulating economic policy.

Inflation

Another factor affecting financial reporting is the level of inflation within the country. Recall from Chapter 5 that inflation can cause financial statement valuations based on historical cost to be less useful for decision-making purposes because assets and liabilities are acquired at different times with monetary units that have different purchasing power. This presents interpretational problems for financial statement users. The interpretational problem becomes greater as the level of inflation rises.

Countries with high levels of inflation, such as Brazil, are less likely to adhere to the historical cost principle. On the other hand, Japan has experienced low levels of inflation and, consequently, financial reporting in Japan generally conforms to historical cost. Recall that, in the United States, supplementary information on selected financial statement items was required for large companies. However, after inflation abated in the mid-1980s, disclosure of price-level-adjusted information became voluntary.

In summary, financial reporting varies between countries because the cultural, political, and economic environments vary. Because environments are different, the perspectives of financial statement users from different countries also vary. The result is that international financial reporting can cause interpretational problems for financial statement users from different countries.

EXAMPLES OF INTERPRETATIONAL PROBLEMS

Interpretational problems can be classified into three types of problems. The first type concerns differences in GAAP between countries. The implications of these problems to an analyst are similar to those discussed in Chapter 6. The second type of problem concerns differences in currency exchange rates. The third type of problem concerns interpretational difficulties that are rooted in cultural differences.

Differences in GAAP

Financial analysis is initiated with the calculation of financial ratios. Use of different accounting principles can cause significant differences in calculated financial ratios. An overview of selected differences in selected countries follows.

Inventory Costing. Inventory-costing methods can pervasively affect financial ratios. A wide choice of inventory-costing methods is considered GAAP in the United States. Two choices, first-in-first-out (FIFO) and last-in-first out (LIFO) are on either end of a continuum in terms of financial statement effects. In periods of rising prices, LIFO produces the lowest reported net income and inventory valuations on the balance sheet. LIFO either is not GAAP or is rarely used in the following industrialized nations: the United Kingdoms, France, Australia, and West Germany.

Consequently, U. S. companies using LIFO cannot be directly compared with companies from any of the above countries. Furthermore, the comparison of any financial ratios affected by inventory-costing methods could mislead users. Refer to Chapter 6 for a complete discussion of ratios affected by inventory-costing choices.

Business Combinations. Another interpretational problem can result when companies combine. When business combinations occur in the United States, two accounting methods are acceptable; namely, the purchase method or the pooling of interests method. In order to use the pooling of interests method, a set of restrictive criteria must be met. In the United Kingdom, the pooling of interests rules are less restrictive. In South Korea, unaudited financial statements are attached to the parent company as supplemental information. In Italy, consolidated financial statements are rarely published. In Japan, the pooling of interests rules are less restrictive than in the United States, but acquisitions and mergers are quite rare in Japan.

As discussed in Chapter 6, the method used to account for business combinations can result in significant differences in reported asset values. Recall that the pooling of interests method results in greater reported earnings and lower assets than the purchase method.

Goodwill. When the purchase method is used and the purchase price exceeds the book value of the purchased company, an intangible asset emerges upon purchase. This asset is commonly called goodwill, and in the United States, goodwill is generally amortized over a 40-year period. However, in Switzerland and the United Kingdom, goodwill is traditionally written off immediately. In West Germany, goodwill is recorded as an asset but is amortized over a short period of time. In Italy, goodwill can be capitalized as an asset, or it can be written off immediately.

Since the amount of recorded goodwill is often material, it can have a significant impact on total recorded assets and on net income. The accounting treatment of goodwill affects any financial ratios that use recorded asset values or net income in their calculation.

The GAAP differences discussed in this section are presented as examples of the potential for interpretational problems that are encountered in international financial reporting. The differences discussed are not a comprehensive set of differences. Previous research has identified 32 situations where alternative GAAP can have a material impact on financial statements.[8]

---

[8]F. D. S. Choi, and V. B. Bavishi, "Diversity in Multinational Accounting," *Financial Executive* (August 1982), 45 – 49.

Currency Exchange Rates

Contractual agreements that require the exchange of goods or services reflect an exchange price in monetary units. The monetary unit utilized to record the transaction is the local currency. For example, a subsidiary in Germany of a U.S. corporation will record transactions in terms of *marks*, the German monetary unit, because of the convenience of using the local currency. This presents reporting difficulties when the subsidiary's financial statements are combined with those of the parent company in the United States to produce consolidated financial statements in U.S. dollars. These difficulties stem from the use of the dollar in the United States and the mark in Germany because the exchange rate between the dollar and the mark is not constant.[9]

Two separate problems emanated from exchange rate fluctuations: accounting for *translation* gains and losses and accounting for *transaction* gains and losses.

Translation Gains and Losses. To demonstrate the problem, assume the following facts:

> The German subsidiary of an American corporation builds a manufacturing plant at a cost of 10 million marks at a time when the exchange rate is 1 mark = $1.00 United States. The plant is not financed by a loan. At the end of the first year of operations, the subsidiary owes German suppliers 1 million marks for raw materials. The raw materials were purchased when the exchange rate was 1 mark = $1.45 United States. The exchange rate at the balance sheet date is 1 mark = $1.50.

The cost of the plant translates to $10 million at the time of purchase. However, at the balance sheet date, the cost translates to $15 million (10 million marks X $1.50 at the current exchange rate). In other words, it would now require $15 million to build the plant that had originally cost $10 million, which is a $5 million "paper" gain. On the other hand, the amounts owed to suppliers at the time the transaction was initiated translated to $1.45 million (1 million marks X $1.45). It will now require $1.5 million (1 million marks X $1.50) to pay the suppliers, a $50,000 "paper" loss.

The reporting difficulties revolve around which rate to use in the translation process to U.S. dollars when the subsidiary's financial

---

[9]Currency exchange rates fluctuate because of a variety of economic and political differences between countries. The primary causes for exchange rate fluctuations concern differences in trade balances, rates of interest and inflation, and political stability.

statements are combined with the U.S. parent company's. *SFAS 8* required the temporal method for translation, which uses the exchange rate, in effect, at the time of acquisition of assets and liabilities. The resulting paper gains or losses were recorded on the consolidated income statement, causing volatility in reported earnings.

Because of this volatility in earnings, *SFAS 52* rescinded *SFAS 8*. *SFAS 52* classifies subsidiaries as either autonomous units or integral units of the parent company. *SFAS 8* rules still apply to integral subsidiaries. However, most subsidiaries qualify as autonomous units. Based on *SFAS 52* rules, balance sheet items of autonomous units are translated at year-end rates, while income statement items are translated at average-for-the-year rates. Consequently, translation for autonomous subsidiaries does not affect consolidated net income, but it does affect total equity.[10]

The translation problem by itself can cause interpretational problems to an analyst. The problem is compounded because it is also one of differences in GAAP. That is, *SFAS 52* applies to U.S. companies. Other countries do not necessarily follow *SFAS 52* rules.

Transaction Gains and Losses. Another problem concerns translating foreign currency into home-country currency for transactions between unrelated corporations.[11] For example, assume that an American company contracts with a British company to import automobiles and that it agrees to purchase each auto for 10,000 *pounds*, the British monetary unit. The American company will record the transaction in dollars, but the British company wants payment in pounds. Assume the exchange rate is 1 pound equals $1 at the time the contract is signed. Further, assume that payment is to be made at the time of delivery of the autos, which is 120 days from the contract date.

The American company is exposed to a risk that the pound may increase in value relative to the dollar, which would require payment of more than $10,000. On the other hand, if the dollar appreciates against the pound, the U. S. company will have to pay less dollars than it originally contracted for. Most companies do not wish to remain exposed to this risk because of the possible disruption of future plans, which are based on a fixed acquisition cost. That is, most companies do

---

[10]See the last paragraph of Footnote 3 in Chapter 4.

[11]Transactions between related entities involve a consideration of transfer pricing and elimination of profit and other financial statement effects in order to prevent "double counting" when consolidated financial statements are prepared. See an advanced accounting text for additional information.

not speculate on changes in currency values and prefer to plan on costs pegged at known levels.

Therefore, *forward-exchange contracts* are generally obtained. A forward-exchange contract obligates the parties to the contract to exchange specific amounts of currency at set exchange rates at a given date in the future. In this case, the U. S. company will contract for 10,000 pounds in the future at the current exchange rate of 1 pound equal $1. The U. S. company will incur a nominal fee in acquiring the contract so that the actual cost will be slightly greater than $10,000. Nevertheless, the forward-exchange contract eliminates the risk that the pound will appreciate and fixes the cost of each auto at $10,000, plus the cost of the forward-exchange contract.[12]

Cultural Differences

Interpretational differences can also arise due to cultural differences between countries. This type of difference can be present irrespective of differences in GAAP.

For example, previous research has shown that ratio analysis applied after adjustment of foreign financial statements to a common GAAP can still be misleading.[13] A sample of Japanese and Korean companies' financial statements was grouped by industry and adjusted to U.S. GAAP. This sample was compared to U.S. companies' financial statements in the same industries. The researchers discovered that the debt ratios of the Japanese and Korean companies were, on average, 58 percent and 48 percent, respectively, higher than that of their U.S. counterparts.

Recall from Chapter 4 that, generally, the lower the debt ratio, the more attractive the investment. This is because, as debt increases relative to total assets, risk of investment also increases. At least, this is true from a U.S. perspective.

But earlier in this chapter, it was noted that the primary resource providers in Japan were a few large banks and that ownership in Japanese corporations was concentrated rather than diverse, as in the

---

[12]Note that the other party in the forward-exchange contract is most likely not the British auto manufacturer. The other party could be another British company wishing to eliminate its foreign-exchange risk due to a contract that requires the British company to pay a third party in dollars. Or, the other party to the forward-exchange contract may be a currency speculator.

[13]F. D. S. Choi, et al., "Analyzing Foreign Financial Statements: The Use and Misuse of International Ratio Analysis", *Journal of International Business Studies* (Spring/Summer 1983), 113 – 131.

United States. The same is true for Korea. Accordingly, a low debt ratio of a corporation in Japan or Korea is indicative of low confidence in the corporation by banks. Therefore, a low debt ratio of a Japanese or Korean corporation can indicate a high degree of risk associated with that company; quite the opposite is true in the United States.

In summary, there are many factors that can cause interpretational problems when comparing financial statements of corporations from different countries. The use of different GAAP and different currencies are obvious causes. However, due to cultural differences, more subtle interpretational problems can arise. Accordingly, financial statements should be analyzed with the understanding

> ...that accounting measurements reflected in corporate financial reports represent, in one sense, merely "numbers" that have limited meaning and significance in and of themselves. Meaning and significance come from and depend upon an understanding of the environmental context from which the numbers are drawn as well as the relationship between the numbers and the underlying economic phenomena that are the real items of interest.[14]

HOW MULTINATIONAL CORPORATIONS OVERCOME INTERPRETATIONAL PROBLEMS IN INTERNATIONAL FINANCIAL REPORTING

The form and content of financial reporting differs between countries due to several reasons, that have been previously discussed. Since accounting is a social science, the primary set of factors influencing financial reporting is endemic to a particular country. These endemic factors affect financial statements through the mode of preparation and disclosure. Accounting theory affects financial statements through the formulation of GAAP, which is the basis for recording transactions that are summarized in the financial statements. Endemic factors also influence accounting theory. (See Figure 10.1.)

The purpose of financial reporting is to communicate information to financial statement users who require the information for decision-making purposes. When a corporation seeks capital from foreign investors or creditors, it recognizes that it must meet the needs of those investors. Otherwise, a gap in the usefulness of financial statements

---

[14]Ibid. 126.

FIGURE 10-1

FACTORS INFLUENCING FINANCIAL REPORTING

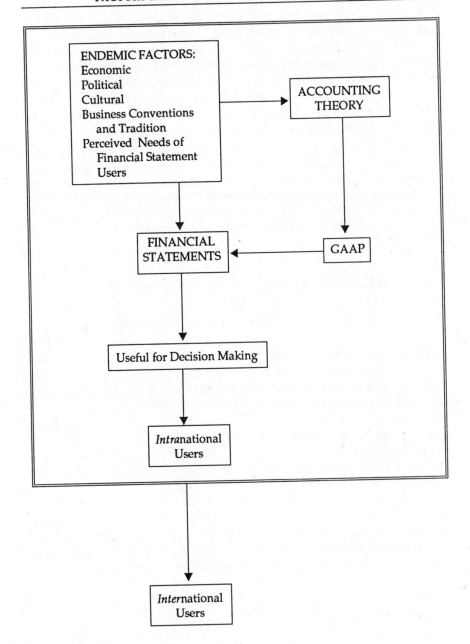

for international users is likely to exist. How do multinational companies close this gap in utility? There are several alternatives.

Convenience Translations

Financial statements are prepared in the home country's language. Unless a foreign investor understands the native language of the corporation's home country, the financial statements are meaningless.

Therefore, multinational corporations can make their financial statements more useful to foreign investors by translating the language into the foreign user's language. However, home-country GAAP remains unadjusted, and the home-country monetary unit is used in *convenience translations*.

Convenience Financial Statements

One method to further reduce the gap in usefulness is to provide *convenience financial statements*. This approach not only translates the language, but it also converts the home country's monetary unit into the currency of the foreign user.

While convenience financial statements look very similar to the financial statements of the foreign user's home country, they are not. This is because the home country's GAAP are used in preparing the convenience statements. Therefore, convenience statements are not directly comparable to financial statements that are prepared in the foreign user's home country.

Restated Financial Statements

Preparing *restated financial statements* is the most costly approach to the reporting entity, which continues to prepare financial statements for the home country using home-country GAAP. Therefore, at least two sets of financial statements are prepared. The language, the currency, and the accounting principles of the foreign country in which the financial statements are distributed are used in the restated financial statements. This approach reduces the utility gap for international users and enables a direct comparison to companies within the foreign user's home country. Of course, restated financial statements are subject to the same limitations discussed in the first nine chapters of this book.

In summary, financial statements are devices designed to communicate useful information to resource providers. Moreover, financial statements are a product of the environment in which they are created. Therefore, financial statements prepared in one country can lack the utility desired by resource providers in a different country. Due to the increased demand for capital, multinational corporations are devising methods to communicate more useful information to foreign users.

One important approach used to resolve many of the interpretational problems faced by international users is to harmonize financial reporting through a global standard-setting organization. The attempt to harmonize global accounting standards is discussed in the following section.

INTERNATIONAL STANDARD SETTING

Recognizing the need for reducing the diversity in international financial reporting, professional accounting organizations in ten countries formed the International Accounting Standards Committee (IASC) in 1973. Membership is now composed of accounting organizations from approximately 80 countries. The IASC is a private organization; governments cannot be members.

The IASC issues pronouncements that suggest preferred accounting principles and/or financial reporting practices. To date, the IASC has issued approximately 30 *International Accounting Standards* (*IASs*). Before issuing an IAS, the IASC follows a due process approach similar to that of the FASB.

However, unlike FASB *SFASs*, compliance with IASs is entirely voluntary in the international arena. Nevertheless, the IASC is gaining acceptance. The International Organization of Securities Commissions believes that "conformity with *IASs* could become the only additional requirement to compliance with standards (including the law) of the home country in financial statements used in multinational [securities] offerings."[15]

The SEC is also considering accepting IASC IASs in lieu of compliance with U.S. GAAP.[16]

---

[15]D. Cairns, "Calling All National Standard Setters," *Accountancy* (February 1988), 13.

[16]J. B. Hoyle, *Advanced Accounting* , 614.

The future of the IASC can perhaps be best described as follows:

...The fact is IASC does have a window of opportunity in which substantial progress seems possible. The convergence of several powerful forces opens that window and provides real encouragement to those who believe sound and credible (true and fair) financial information is essential to achieving the benefits of a world economy characterized by relative freedom from national constraints on trade.

Those forces include: increased cross-border financing; emergence of true multinational companies; a heightened willingness to cooperate across borders (e.g., the European Communities) to enhance national, regional and even global economic strength; an awareness by securities regulators around the world of the necessity for comparable and credible data; and a vehicle, IASC, to articulate standards that can move us closer to the level of comparable and credible data that a free world economy requires.[17]

Auditing standards also differ from country to country. In an effort to harmonize auditing standards, the International Auditing Practices Committee (IAPC) has issued 26 *International Auditing Guidelines* (*IAGs*). However, as with *IASs*, *IAGs* do not override local auditing standards. Compliance with *IAGs* is, therefore, voluntary.

SUMMARY

As international commerce increases, there is a concomitant increase in the demand for capital. Capital is provided by investors and creditors that seek the highest return on investment at any given level of risk. Investment decisions are made from financial information. A primary source of financial information is provided by financial statements.

The first nine chapters of this book discussed financial reporting within the United States borders. The limitations of financial reporting become magnified when financial reporting takes place across national boundaries because of differences in cultural and political values, and business conventions. Multinational corporations attempt to overcome these limitations in various ways. Three methods discussed in this chapter are convenience translations, convenience statements, and restated financial statements. Convenience translations are the least costly of the three methods discussed, and restated financial statements are the most costly.

---

[17]A. Wyatt, "International Accounting Standards: A New Perspective," *Accounting Horizons* (September 1989), 107 – 108.

International resource providers are unlikely to invest in foreign companies if they are unable to understand the financial statements published by foreign companies. Therefore, multinational corporations make decisions concerning the trade-off between costs incurred in the approach to international financial reporting and the expected benefits obtained through the potential for acquiring capital from foreign sources.

An international standard-setting body, the IASC, has been formed to harmonize international accounting standards and financial reporting. While the IASC has met some resistance to harmonization, it is gaining international acceptance.

However, even if a set of global accounting standards and financial reporting conventions is promulgated and universally accepted, there are still important limitations to interpreting financial statements of multinational corporations. Limitations will remain because accounting is a social science and a product of endemic factors that are often unique to a specific country. These endemic factors of the home country produce the potential for foreign users to misunderstand the economic implications of events reported through financial statements.

Because of the uncertainties present in business and because any set of financial statements is only a model that represents an abstraction of reality, limitations of financial reporting will always exist. This does not render financial statements meaningless; it only means that financial statement users should conduct an analysis with a heightened sense of awareness in regard to the limitations of financial reporting.

READING LIST

Beresford, D. R. "Accounting for International Operations." *The CPA Journal* (October 1988): 79–80.

Choi, F.D. S., Min, S. K., Nam, S. O., Hino, H., Ujiie, J., and Stonehill, A. I. "Analyzing Foreign Financial Statements: The Use and Misuse of International Ratio Analysis." *Journal of International Business Studies* (Spring/Summer 1983): 113–31.

Coburn, D. L., Ellis, J. K.,and Milano, D. R. "Dilemmas in MNC Transfer Pricing." *Management Accounting* (November 1981): 53–58, 69.

Collins, S. H. "The Move to Globalization." *Journal of Accountancy* (March 1989): 82.

Gray, S. J. "Toward a Theory of Cultural Influence on the Development of Accounting Systems Internationally." *Abacus* (March 1988): 1–15.

McKinnon, J. L. "Application of Anglo-American Principles of Consolidation to Corporate Financial Disclosures in Japan." *Abacus* (June 1984): 16–33.

McKinnon, J. L., and Harrison., G. L. "Cultural Influence on Corporate and Governmental Involvement in Accounting Policy Determination in Japan." *Journal of Accounting and Public Policy_* (Fall 1985): 201–23.

Meek, G. K. "Competition Spurs Worldwide Harmonization." *Management Accounting* (August 1984): 47– 49.

Mueller, G. G., Gernon, H. and Meek, G. K. *Accounting: An International Perspective* 2nd ed. (Irwin 1991).

Moulin, D. J., and Solomon, M. B. "Practical Means of Promoting Common International Standards." *The CPA Journal* (December 1989): 38–48.

Pratt, J., and Behr, G. "Environmental Factors, Transaction Costs, and External Reporting: A Cross-National Comparison." *The International Journal of Accounting* (Spring 1987): 1–24.

Revsine, L. "The Rationale Underlying the Functional Currency Choice," *The Accounting Review* (July 1984): 504–14.

Slipkowsky, J. W. "An Appraisal of the International Accounting Standards Committee." *The CPA Journal* (May 1986): 84.

Slipkowsky, J. N., "The Volvo Way of Financial Reporting." *Management Accounting* (October 1988): 22–26.

Taylor, S. L. "International Accounting Standards: An Alternative Rationale." *Abacus* (September 1987): 157–71.

Tremblay, T. "Toward Accounting Without National Boundaries." *CA Magazine* (October 1986): 54–59.

Wyatt, A. "International Accounting Standards: A New Horizon." *Accounting Horizons* (September 1989): 105–8.

Index